DELIBERATE PRACTICE IN

CHILD AND ADOLESCENT PSYCHOTHERAPY

Essentials of Deliberate Practice Series

Tony Rousmaniere and Alexandre Vaz, Series Editors

ESSENTIALS OF DELIBERATE PRACTICE SERIES

TONY ROUSMANIERE AND ALEXANDRE VAZ, SERIES EDITORS

DELIBERATE PRACTICE IN

CHILD AND ADOLESCENT PSYCHOTHERAPY

JORDAN BATE

TRACY A. PROUT

TONY ROUSMANIERE

ALEXANDRE VAZ

AMERICAN PSYCHOLOGICAL ASSOCIATION

Published by
American Psychological Association
750 First Street, NE
Washington, DC 20002
https://www.apa.org

Order Department
https://www.apa.org/pubs/books
order@apa.org

In the U.K., Europe, Africa, and the Middle East, copies may be ordered from Eurospan
https://www.eurospanbookstore.com/apa
info@eurospangroup.com

Typeset in Cera Pro by Circle Graphics, Inc., Reisterstown, MD

Printer: Gasch Printing, Odenton, MD
Cover Designer: Naylor Design, Washington, DC

Library of Congress Cataloging-in-Publication Data

Names: Bate, Jordan, author. | Prout, Tracy A., author. | Rousmaniere, Tony, author. |
   Vaz, Alexandre, author.
Title: Deliberate practice in child and adolescent psychotherapy /
   by Jordan Bate, Tracy A. Prout, Tony Rousmaniere, and Alexandre Vaz.
Description: Washington, DC : American Psychological Association, [2022] |
   Series: Essentials of deliberate practice | Includes bibliographical
   references and index.
Identifiers: LCCN 2021049625 (print) | LCCN 2021049626 (ebook) |
   ISBN 9781433837487 (paperback) | ISBN 9781433837494 (ebook)
Subjects: LCSH: Child psychotherapy. | Adolescent psychotherapy.
Classification: LCC RJ504 .B398 2022 (print) | LCC RJ504 (ebook) |
0 DDC 618.92/8914--dc23/eng/20211117
LC record available at https://lccn.loc.gov/2021049625
LC ebook record available at https://lccn.loc.gov/2021049626

https://doi.org/10.1037/0000288-000

Printed in the United States of America

10 9 8 7 6 5 4 3 2 1

Contents

Series Preface

Tony Rousmaniere and Alexandre Vaz

We are pleased to introduce the Essentials of Deliberate Practice series of training books. We are developing this book series to address a specific need that we see in many psychology training programs. The issue can be illustrated by the training experiences of Mary, a hypothetical second-year graduate school trainee. Mary has learned a lot about mental health theory, research, and psychotherapy techniques. Mary is a dedicated student; she has read dozens of textbooks, written excellent papers about psychotherapy, and receives near-perfect scores on her course exams. However, when Mary sits with her clients at her practicum site, she often has trouble performing the therapy skills that she can write and talk about so clearly. Furthermore, Mary has noticed herself getting anxious when her clients express strong reactions, such as getting very emotional, hopeless, or skeptical about therapy. Sometimes this anxiety is strong enough to make Mary freeze at key moments, limiting her ability to help those clients.

During her weekly individual and group supervision, Mary's supervisor gives her advice informed by empirically supported therapies and common factor methods. The supervisor often supplements that advice by leading Mary through role-plays, recommending additional reading, or providing examples from her own work with clients. Mary, a dedicated supervisee who shares tapes of her sessions with her supervisor, is open about her challenges, carefully writes down her supervisor's advice, and reads the suggested readings. However, when Mary sits back down with her clients, she often finds that her new knowledge seems to have flown out of her head, and she is unable to enact her supervisor's advice. Mary finds this problem to be particularly acute with the clients who are emotionally evocative.

Mary's supervisor, who has received formal training in supervision, uses supervisory best practices, including the use of video to review supervisees' work. She would rate Mary's overall competence level as consistent with expectations for a trainee at Mary's developmental level. But even though Mary's overall progress is positive, she experiences some recurring problems in her work. This is true even though the supervisor is confident that she and Mary have identified the changes that Mary should make in her work.

The problem with which Mary and her supervisor are wrestling—the disconnect between her knowledge about psychotherapy and her ability to reliably perform psychotherapy—is the focus of this book series. We started this series because most therapists experience this disconnect, to one degree or another, whether they are beginning trainees or highly experienced clinicians. In truth, we are all Mary.

To address this problem, we are focusing this series on the use of deliberate practice, a method of training specifically designed for improving reliable performance of complex skills in challenging work environments (Rousmaniere, 2016, 2019; Rousmaniere et al., 2017). Deliberate practice entails experiential, repeated training with a particular skill until it becomes automatic. In the context of psychotherapy, this involves two trainees role-playing as a client and a therapist, switching roles every so often, under the guidance of a supervisor. The trainee playing the therapist reacts to client statements, ranging in difficulty from beginner to intermediate to advanced, with improvised responses that reflect fundamental therapeutic skills.

To create these books, we approached leading trainers and researchers of major therapy models with these simple instructions: Identify 12 essential skills for your therapy model where trainees often experience a disconnect between cognitive knowledge and performance ability—in other words, skills that trainees could write a good paper about but often have challenges performing, especially with challenging clients. We then collaborated with the authors to create deliberate practice exercises specifically designed to improve reliable performance of these skills and overall responsive treatment (Hatcher, 2015; Stiles et al., 1998; Stiles & Horvath, 2017). Finally, we rigorously tested these exercises with trainees and trainers at multiple sites around the world and refined them based on extensive feedback.

Each book in this series focuses on a specific therapy model, but readers will notice that most exercises in these books touch on common factor variables and facilitative interpersonal skills that researchers have identified as having the most impact on client outcome, such as empathy, verbal fluency, emotional expression, persuasiveness, and problem focus (e.g., Anderson et al., 2009; Norcross et al., 2019). Thus, the exercises in every book should help with a broad range of clients. Despite the specific theoretical model(s) from which therapists work, most therapists place a strong emphasis on pantheoretical elements of the therapeutic relationship, many of which have robust empirical support as correlates or mechanisms of client improvement (e.g., Norcross et al., 2019). We also recognize that therapy models have already-established training programs with rich histories, so we present deliberate practice not as a replacement but as an adaptable, transtheoretical training method that can be integrated into these existing programs to improve skill retention and help ensure basic competency.

About This Book

This book in the series is on child therapy, a broad umbrella term for a diverse set of treatments that draw from a developmental perspective that privileges the unique needs of children and adolescents in psychotherapy. Despite the diversity of child therapy approaches, a common maxim is the importance of "meeting the child where they are." A broad and deep familiarity with the theoretical and empirical literature on child development and specific psychotherapy approaches with young people is important, yet this knowledge can never replace direct, hands-on experiences with child clients and the training and supervision process. The importance of experiential learning in the training and supervision process is magnified by the reality that, especially for novice trainees who are just beginning to work with children, there are relatively few opportunities to practice the wide range of clinical skills that are theoretically at one's disposal.

In this book, we adopt deliberate practice methods to support experiential—learn by doing—training opportunities. The methods and stimuli described can facilitate practicing a range of important child therapy skills. In addition, the book supports fine-tuning the "how" of intervention delivery, including in a flexible manner across diverse clinical scenarios. Importantly, this book is not intended to replace core coursework and exposure to foundational child therapy theory and principles of practice. Rather, it is intended to augment other common training components. This book is about providing opportunities for trainees to practice not only what they would say to a child or adolescent client but also how they would say it. In essence, this book aims to help trainees (at all professional levels) learn how to responsively and fluidly apply foundational "tried-and-true" child therapy concepts and strategies, which will add to their overall repertoire of clinical skills and principles. With such an expanded repertoire, therapists can maximize their ability to foster a strong therapeutic alliance, ensure safety of their young clients, and implement whichever type of child therapy treatment they are learning.

Acknowledgments

This book would not have been possible without our students. Several years before we began writing, we started using deliberate practice with our psychotherapy practicum students at the Ferkauf Graduate School of Psychology. We knew very little at the time and did our best to use this innovative training method (fumbling often!); our students were resourceful, creative, and resilient throughout. As practicing therapists, we continually learn so much from our students as they raise important questions and challenge our thinking in thoughtful and incisive ways. Practicum students also generously participate in ongoing research about deliberate practice as a training method—for this, we are extraordinarily grateful. Later, Jordan developed many of the exercises included in this book for her course "Beginning Work With Children and Families." That was our initial "lab" for testing out these exercises. The feedback we received from students in that course was invaluable for shaping the introductory text and prompts in each exercise. Once we finalized the exercises for this book, they were sent to students and supervisors around the globe. The feedback from these volunteers helped us tailor the exercises to a wider audience, beyond our classrooms. We also extend our gratitude to Lauren Smith for her assistance with citations and references for this book.

Finally, the writing of any book takes time—namely, time away from family, friends, and other endeavors. To our partners, pets, and children, we are grateful for all of your support and encouragement along the way.

We'd like to acknowledge Rodney Goodyear for his significant contribution to starting and organizing this book series. We are grateful to Susan Reynolds, David Becker, and Emily Ekle at American Psychological Association Books for providing expert guidance and insightful editing that has significantly improved the quality and accessibility of this book. We are deeply grateful to K. Anders Ericsson, the inventor of the concept of deliberate practice.

The exercises in this book underwent extensive testing at training programs around the world. We are deeply grateful to the following supervisors and trainees who tested exercises and provided invaluable feedback:

- Layla Inés Davis, Eva Watts, and Carla Cañedo-Villa, Southwestern Community College, San Diego, CA, United States
- Caitlyn Francis, University of Arizona, Tucson, AZ, United States
- Sibel Halfon, Hazal Çelik, and Dilara Güvenç, İstanbul Bilgi University, İstanbul, Turkey

- Kelsey Hill, Eastern Michigan University, Ypsilanti, MI, United States
- Lee Hughes, private practice, Gold Coast, Australia
- Kerry-Jayne Lambert and Adam Digby, University of Roehampton, London, United Kingdom
- Kiley Moore, Roosevelt University, Chicago, IL, United States
- Vera Regina Ramires, Fernanda Driemeier Schmidt, and Marina Bento Gastaud, Universidade do Vale do Rio dos Sinos, São Leopoldo, Brasil
- Austin Brown Sparks and Jasmine Dixon, Alberta Health Services, Edmonton, AB, Canada
- Kathryn D. Whistler, Yeshiva University, New York, NY, United States

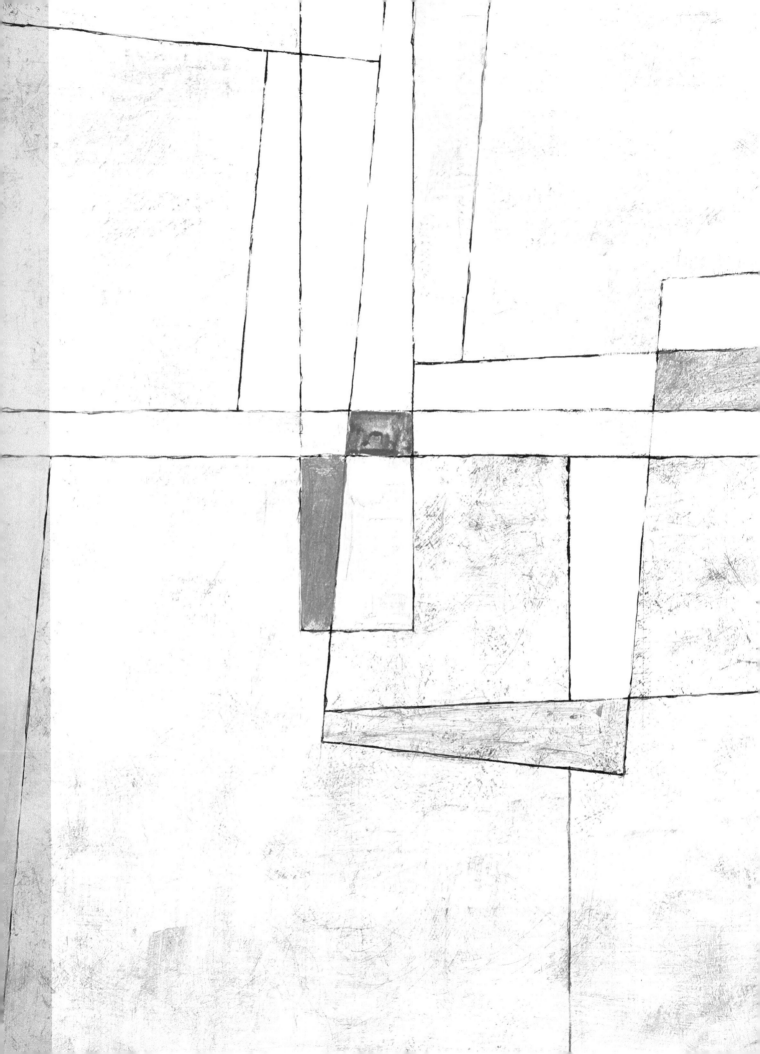

Overview and Instructions

In Part I, we provide an overview of deliberate practice, including how it can be integrated into clinical training programs for child therapy and instructions for performing the deliberate practice exercises in Part II. **We encourage both trainers and trainees to read both Chapters 1 and 2 before performing the deliberate practice exercises for the first time.**

Chapter 1 establishes a foundation for the rest of the book by introducing important concepts related to deliberate practice and its role in psychotherapy training more broadly and child therapy training more specifically. It provides a brief background on child therapy, with special attention paid to the unique needs of children. We also discuss the types of skills that are especially relevant to working with young people.

Chapter 2 lays out the basic, most essential instructions for performing the child therapy deliberate practice exercises in Part II. They are designed to be quick and simple and provide you with just enough information to get started without being overwhelmed by too much information. Chapter 3 in Part III provides more in-depth guidance, which we encourage you to read once you are comfortable with the basic instructions in Chapter 2.

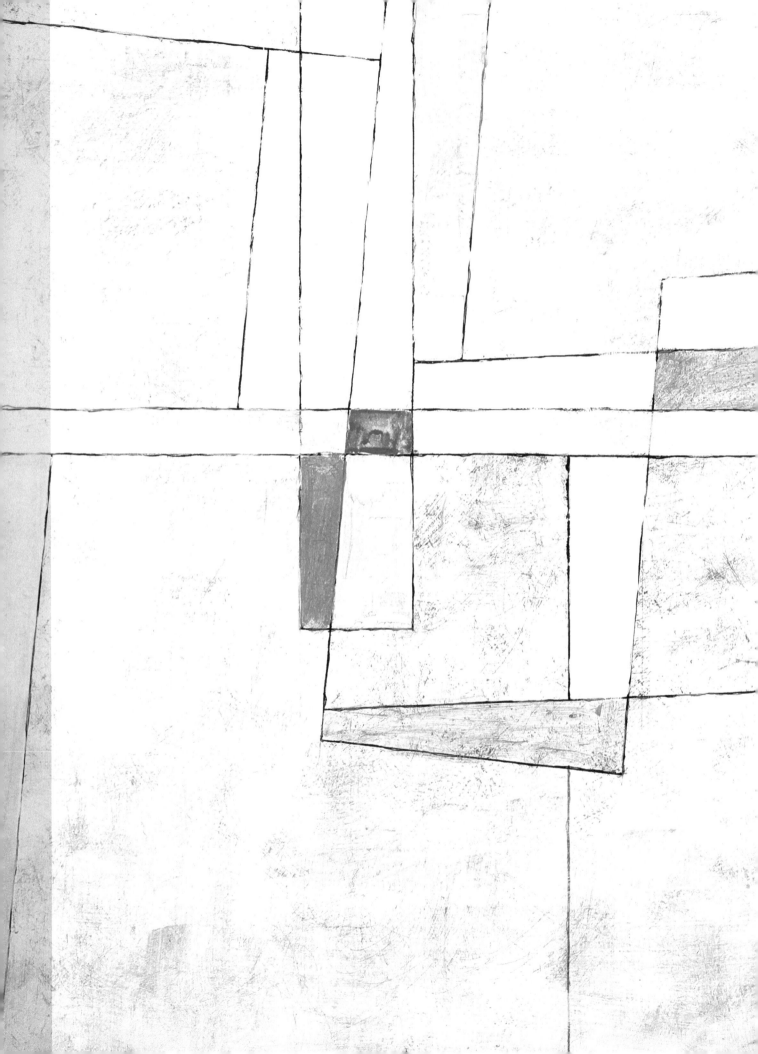

Introduction and Overview of Deliberate Practice and Child and Adolescent Psychotherapy

Welcome to *Deliberate Practice in Child and Adolescent Psychotherapy*. This is the third book in a series of deliberate practice training books, the Essentials of Deliberate Practice.

After years of doing traditional role-playing and case consultation in our training courses, we were excited to discover deliberate practice several years ago. We were impressed with the research on deliberate practice and found the method extremely helpful in our own work and in the training of future child therapists. One of the limitations we encountered was that deliberate practice stimuli were largely focused on clinical work with adults. We frequently asked colleagues who were doing this work—including Tony Rousmaniere and Alex Vaz, coauthors of this book—for child-focused stimuli and guidance on how to adapt deliberate practice to child therapy. Over time, we created our own stimuli, including videos of children and parents, for our students to use. These adapted exercises, used in our graduate courses and supervision work, incorporated play, playfulness, and the nonverbal aspects of psychotherapy with youth. We and our students have grown tremendously as we have engaged in repeated rehearsal, received and provided feedback, and explored many different formats for using deliberate practice to improve our therapy skills. We presented our work at conferences and frequently received feedback about how we ought to write this all down and disseminate it so that other trainers and students could benefit from these adaptations. Out of this feedback and our collaboration with Tony and Alex, a book was born!

Overview of The Deliberate Practice Exercises

The main focus of the book is a series of 14 exercises that have been thoroughly tested and modified based on feedback from child therapy trainers and trainees. The first 12 exercises each represent an essential child therapy skill. The last two exercises are more comprehensive, consisting of annotated child therapy transcripts and improvised mock

https://doi.org/10.1037/0000288-001
Deliberate Practice in Child and Adolescent Psychotherapy, by J. Bate, T. A. Prout, T. Rousmaniere, and A. Vaz

therapy sessions that teach practitioners how to integrate all these skills into more expansive clinical scenarios. Table 1.1 presents the 12 skills that are covered in these exercises.

Throughout all of the exercises, trainees work in pairs under the guidance of a supervisor and role-play as a client and a therapist, switching back and forth between the two roles. Each of the 12 skill-focused exercises consists of multiple client statements grouped by difficulty—beginner, intermediate, and advanced—that calls for a specific skill. For each skill, trainees are asked to read through and absorb the description of the skill, its criteria, and some examples of it. The trainee playing the client then reads the statements, which present possible content and emotional states that might arise in the context of play or talk therapy with youth from a range of ages. The trainee playing the therapist then responds in a way that demonstrates the appropriate skill. Trainee therapists will have the option of practicing a response using the one supplied in the exercise or immediately improvising and supplying their own.

After each client statement and therapist response couplet is practiced several times, the trainees will stop to receive feedback from the supervisor. Guided by the supervisor, the trainees will be instructed to try statement–response couplets several times, working their way down the list. In consultation with the supervisor, trainees will go through the exercises, starting with the least challenging and moving through to more advanced levels. The triad (supervisor–client–therapist) will have the opportunity to discuss whether exercises present too much or too little challenge and adjust up or down depending on the assessment. Some exercises provide optional modifications so that trainees role-playing as clients can improvise based on personal experience, rather than using scripted statement.

Trainees, in consultation with supervisors, can decide which skills they wish to work on and for how long. On the basis of our testing experience, we have found practice sessions last about 1 to 1.25 hours to receive maximum benefit. After this, trainees become saturated and need a break.

Ideally, child therapists will both gain confidence and achieve competence by practicing these exercises. Competence is defined here as the ability to perform a child therapy skill in a manner that is flexible and responsive to the client. The skills identified in this book are not comprehensive in the sense of representing all one needs to learn to become a competent child therapist, nor is it a comprehensive description of transtheoretical basic skills. When selecting the skills that are addressed in this book, we were guided by our perceptions of essential skills for competence in child therapy and the skills that we have observed trainees struggle with most. A short history of child therapy and a brief description of the deliberate practice methodology are provided to explain how we have arrived at the union between them.

TABLE 1.1. The 12 Child Therapy Skills Presented in the Deliberate Practice Exercises

Beginning Skills	Intermediate Skills	Advanced Skills
1. Communicating interest and curiosity 2. Naming feelings 3. Praise and encouragement 4. Observing and describing play 5. Empathic validation	6. Elaborating play 7. Exploring identity—multicultural orientation 8. Self-disclosure	9. Gathering information about safety concerns 10. Setting limits 11. Talking about sex 12. Responding to resistance and ruptures

The Goals of This Book

The primary goal of this book is to help trainees or even more experienced professionals improve and achieve competence in core child therapy skills. Therefore, the expression of that skill or competency may look somewhat different across clients or even within session with the same client.

The deliberate practice exercises are designed to achieve the following:

1. Help trainees develop the ability to apply the skills in a range of clinical situations.

2. Move the skills into procedural memory (Squire, 2004), so that trainees can access them even when they are tired, stressed, feeling overwhelmed, discouraged, or otherwise distracted.

3. Provide trainees with an opportunity to exercise the particular skill using a style and language that is congruent with who they are.

4. Provide trainees with an opportunity to use the skills in response to a broad range of client statements and affect. This will give them confidence in using the skills with a broad range of clients.

5. Provide trainees with many opportunities to fail and then correct their failed response on the basis of feedback. This should be an explicit goal of deliberate practice because it helps build trainees' confidence and persistence.

Finally, this book is in the service of helping trainees develop skills and attitudes to facilitate lifelong learning. In most performance domains, professionals use deliberate practice across the entire span of their career to achieve and maintain expertise. This book aims to help trainees discover their own personal learning style so that they can continue their professional development long after their formal training is concluded.

Who Can Benefit From This Book?

This book is designed to be used in multiple contexts, including in graduate-level courses, supervision, postgraduate training, and continuing education programs. It assumes the following:

1. The trainer is knowledgeable about and competent in child therapy.

2. The trainer is able to provide good demonstrations of how to use child therapy skills across a range of therapeutic situations via role-play or video (or both). Or the trainer has access to examples of child therapy being demonstrated through the many psychotherapy video examples available (see APA PsycTherapy videos featuring child therapy with Athena Drewes, 2017; Norka Malberg, 2018; and Eric Storch, 2020; and adolescent psychotherapy with John Curry, 2018; Trudie Rossouw, 2021; and Andrew Smiler, 2019).

3. The trainer is able to provide feedback to students regarding how to craft or improve their application of child therapy skills.

4. Trainees will have accompanying reading, such as books and articles, that explain the theory, research, and rationale of various child therapy approaches (e.g., psychodynamic, cognitive behavioral, integrative) and each particular skill. Recommended reading for each skill is provided in the sample syllabus (Appendix C).

The exercises covered in this book were piloted in 10 training sites from across four continents (North America, South America, Europe, and Oceania). Some training sites chose to translate the exercises into their native language in order to adapt them for use with their trainees. This book is designed for trainers and trainees from different cultural backgrounds worldwide.

This book is also designed for those who are training at all career stages, from beginning trainees, including those who have never worked with real clients, to seasoned therapists. All exercises feature guidance for assessing and adjusting the difficulty to precisely target the needs of each individual learner. The term *trainee* in this book is used broadly, referring to anyone in the field of professional mental health who is endeavoring to acquire child psychotherapy skills. For further guidance on how to improve multicultural deliberate practice skills, see the forthcoming book *Deliberate Practice in Multicultural Counseling* (Harris et al., 2022).

Deliberate Practice in Psychotherapy Training

How does one become an expert in their professional field? What is trainable, and what is simply beyond our reach due to innate or uncontrollable factors? Questions such as these touch on our fascination with expert performers and their development. A mixture of awe, admiration, and even confusion surround people such as Mozart, Leonardo da Vinci, and more contemporary top performers such as basketball legend Michael Jordan and chess virtuoso Garry Kasparov. What accounts for their consistently superior professional results? Evidence suggests that the amount of or time spent on a particular type of training is a key factor in developing expertise in virtually all domains. *Deliberate practice* is an evidence-based method that can improve performance in an effective and reliable manner.

The concept of deliberate practice has its origins in a classic study by K. Anders Ericsson and colleagues (1993). They found that the amount of time practicing a skill and the quality of the time spent doing so were key factors predicting mastery and acquisition. They identified five key activities in learning and mastering skills: (a) observing one's own work, (b) getting expert feedback, (c) setting small incremental learning goals just beyond the performer's ability, (d) engaging in repetitive behavioral rehearsal of specific skills, and (e) continuously assessing performance. K. A. Ericsson and his colleagues termed this process deliberate practice, a cyclical process that is illustrated in Figure 1.1.

Research has shown that lengthy engagement in deliberate practice is associated with expert performance across a variety of professional fields, such as medicine, sports, music, chess, computer programming, and mathematics (K. A. Ericsson et al., 2018). People may associate deliberate practice with the widely known "10,000-hour rule" popularized by Malcolm Gladwell in his 2008 book, *Outliers*, although the actual number of hours required for expertise varies by field and by individual (A. Ericsson & Pool, 2016). This, though, perpetuated two misunderstandings. The first is that this is the number of deliberate practice hours that everyone needs to attain expertise, no matter the domain. In fact, there can be considerable variability in how many hours are required.

The second misunderstanding is that engagement in 10,000 hours of work performance will lead one to become an expert in that domain. This misunderstanding holds considerable significance for the field of psychotherapy, where hours of work experience with clients has traditionally been used as a measure of proficiency (Rousmaniere, 2016). But, in fact, we know (Goldberg et al., 2016) that amount of experience alone

FIGURE 1.1. Cycle of Deliberate Practice

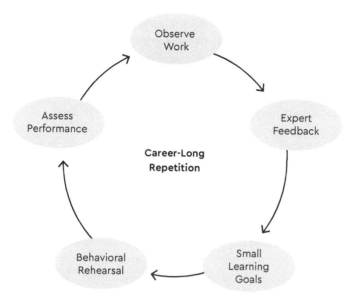

Note. From *Deliberate Practice in Emotion-Focused Therapy* (p. 7), by R. N. Goldman, A. Vaz, and T. Rousmaniere, 2021, American Psychological Association (https://doi.org/10.1037/0000227-000). Copyright 2021 by the American Psychological Association.

does not predict therapist effectiveness. It may be that the *quality* of deliberate practice is a key factor.

Psychotherapy scholars, recognizing the value of deliberate practice in other fields, have recently called for deliberate practice to be incorporated into training for mental health professionals (e.g., Bailey & Ogles, 2019; Hill et al., 2020; Rousmaniere et al., 2017; Taylor & Neimeyer, 2017; Tracey et al., 2015). There are, however, good reasons to question analogies made between psychotherapy and other professional fields, like sports or music, because by comparison psychotherapy is so complex and free form. Sports have clearly defined goals, and classical music follows a written score. In contrast, the goals of psychotherapy shift with the unique presentation of each client at each session. Therapists do not have the luxury of following a score.

Instead, good psychotherapy is more like improvisational jazz (Noa Kageyama, cited in Rousmaniere, 2016). In jazz improvisations, a complex mixture of group collaboration, creativity, and interaction are coconstructed among band members. Like psychotherapy, no two jazz improvisations are identical. However, improvisations are not a random collection of notes. They are grounded in a comprehensive theoretical understanding and technical proficiency that is only developed through continuous deliberate practice. For example, prominent jazz instructor Jerry Coker lists 18 different skill areas that students must master, each of which has multiple discrete skills, including tone quality, intervals, chord arpeggios, scales, patterns, and licks (Coker, 1990). In this sense, more creative and artful improvisations are actually a reflection of a previous commitment to repetitive skill practice and acquisition. As legendary jazz musician Miles Davis put it, "You have to play a long time to be able to play like yourself" (Cook, 2005).

The main idea that we would like to stress here is that we want deliberate practice to help child psychotherapists become themselves. The idea is to learn the skills so that you have them on hand when you want them. Practice the skills to make them your own. Incorporate those aspects that feel right for you. Ongoing and effortful deliberate practice should not be an impediment to flexibility and creativity. Ideally, it should enhance it. We recognize and celebrate that psychotherapy is an ever-shifting encounter and by no means want it to become or feel formulaic. Strong child therapists mix an eloquent integration of previously acquired skills with properly attuned flexibility. The core child therapy responses provided are meant as templates or possibilities, rather than "answers." Please interpret and apply them as you see fit, in a way that makes sense to you. We encourage flexible and improvisational play!

Simulation-Based Mastery Learning

Deliberate practice uses simulation-based mastery learning (K. A. Ericsson, 2004; McGaghie et al., 2014). That is, the stimulus material for training consists of "contrived social situations that mimic problems, events, or conditions that arise in professional encounters" (McGaghie et al., 2014, p. 375). A key component of this approach is that the stimuli being used in training are sufficiently similar to the real-world experiences, so that they provoke similar reactions. This facilitates *state-dependent learning*, in which professionals acquire skills in the same psychological environment where they will have to perform the skills (Fisher & Craik, 1977; Smith, 1979). For example, pilots train with flight simulators that present mechanical failures and dangerous weather conditions, and surgeons practice with surgical simulators that present medical complications. Training in simulations with challenging stimuli increases professionals' capacity to perform effectively under stress. For the psychotherapy training exercises in this book, the "simulators" are typical client statements that might actually be presented in the course of therapy sessions and call upon the use of the particular skill.

Declarative Versus Procedural Knowledge

Declarative knowledge is what a person can understand, write, or speak about. It often refers to factual information that can be consciously recalled through memory and often acquired relatively quickly. In contrast, *procedural learning* is implicit in memory and "usually requires *repetition of an activity*, and associated learning is demonstrated through *improved task performance*" (Koziol & Budding, 2012, pp. 2694, emphasis added). *Procedural knowledge* is what a person can perform, especially under stress (Squire, 2004). There can be a wide difference between their declarative and procedural knowledge. For example, an "armchair quarterback" is a person who understands and talks about athletics well but would have trouble performing it at a professional ability. Likewise, most dance, music, or theater critics have a high ability to write about their subjects but would be flummoxed if asked to perform them.

In child psychotherapy training, the gap between declarative and procedural knowledge appears when a trainee or therapist can recognize and perhaps even deeply appreciate, for example, involvement in a child's play that is highly attuned, picking up on relevant experiential themes that leads to an elaboration of the play narrative and complex emotions, but struggles to identify these themes and opportunities and engage their own playfulness in the moment with the child client. **The sweet spot for deliberate practice is the gap between declarative and procedural knowledge.** In other words, effortful practice should target those skills that the trainee could write a good paper about but would have trouble actually performing with a real client. We start with declarative knowledge, learning skills theoretically and observing others perform them. Once learned, with the help of deliberate practice, we work toward the development of procedural learning, with the aim of therapists having "automatic" access to each of the skills that they can pull on when necessary.

Let us turn to a little theoretical background on child psychotherapy to help contextualize the skills of the book and how they fit into the greater training model.

Child Therapy

Child therapy has its roots in movements to help support young people with learning disabilities and learning problems, including the work of Alfred Binet in France, and the child guidance movement, multidisciplinary clinics that began in Chicago in 1906 to help support children with emotional and behavioral problems and their families. Sigmund Freud and Erik Erikson both developed developmental stage theories that helped to contextualize children's unique interpersonal and intrapersonal developmental milestones. Harry Harlow, John Bowlby, and Mary Ainsworth studied children and their caregivers (Harlow with primates) to develop a comprehensive theory of attachment and its role in child development and distress. The central role of learning and social modeling in child development was highlighted by the work John Watson, B. F. Skinner, and Albert Bandura. Finally, the primary language of childhood—play—became a key component of child therapy over the course of the 20th century (see Gitlin-Weiner et al., 2000). Trailblazing therapists such as Melanie Klein, Donald Winnicott, Anna Freud, and Virginia Axline introduced the centrality of play into working with children. Whether the treatment is expressly a play therapy approach or a more traditional talk or behavioral therapy, all work with youth requires a spirit of playfulness and a kind of physicality (e.g., sitting on the floor, movement, playing games) that is atypical for adult treatments. In the past several decades, many child- and adolescent-focused treatments have been developed that integrate a century of scientific knowledge about the complex interplay of children's temperament, attachment style, family environment, intellectual abilities and learning style, trauma history, and culture.

The evidence base for child and adolescent psychotherapy has expanded dramatically over the last several decades. This includes cognitive behavioral therapy (Crowe & McKay, 2017; Weisz et al., 2017), psychodynamic psychotherapy (Abbass et al., 2013; Goodyer et al., 2017; Midgley et al., 2021; Midgley, O'Keeffe, et al., 2017), interpersonal therapy (Zhou et al., 2015), family therapy (Carr, 2009; van der Pol et al., 2017), and play therapy (Bratton et al., 2005). Although there are many types of child treatment, many with well-defined protocols and interventions, it is difficult to translate the ephemeral, in-the-moment stance of the child therapist. Increasingly, psychotherapy researchers have turned toward the importance of common factors that drive positive psychotherapy outcomes for youth and their families. These include the therapeutic alliance (with parents and children), therapist warmth and empathy, the hopes and expectations of young people and their parents with regard to the therapy process, readiness for change, treatment engagement and adherence, attachment style, interpersonal environment, and social support (Karver et al., 2005, 2006; Yasinski et al., 2018).

Child Therapy Skills in Deliberate Practice

This book is intentionally focused on enhanced child therapy skills with respect to *common factor* variables and *facilitative interpersonal skill*, such as empathy, verbal fluency, emotional expression, persuasiveness, and problem focus, that researchers have identified as important for client outcomes (e.g., Anderson et al., 2009; Karver et al., 2005, 2006). Ideally, readers will notice that these common interpersonal skills are implicit in most of the example responses throughout the book. Because it does not comprehensively cover theory or research related to the many existing child therapy modalities, it should be used in conjunction with one or more books that do, such as *Evidence-Based Psychotherapies for Children and Adolescents* (Weisz & Kazdin, 2018), *Trauma-Informed Practices With Children and Adolescents* (Steele & Malchiodi, 2012), *Psychotherapy With Infants and Young Children: Repairing the Effects of Stress and Trauma on Early Attachment* (Lieberman & Van Horn, 2011), *Mentalization-Based Treatment for Children: A Time-Limited Approach* (Midgley, Ensink, et al., 2017), *Manual of Regulation-Focused Psychotherapy for Children (RFP-C) With Externalizing Behaviors: A Psychodynamic Approach* (Hoffman et al., 2016), *Child and Adolescent Anxiety Psychodynamic Psychotherapy: A Treatment Manual* (Preter et al., 2018), or *Child-Centered Play Therapy* (VanFleet et al., 2011). For further training on general psychotherapy skills, trainers may consider using books such as Hill (2020) or, for more child-specific guidance, *Advanced Play Therapy: Essential Conditions, Knowledge, and Skills for Child Practice* (Ray, 2011). The sample syllabus provided in Appendix C of this volume also includes recommended readings for the theory and practice of child therapy. A brief review of the research on deliberate practice is provided in Chapter 2 of this book.

We view this book as focusing on both the technical and relational aspects of child and adolescent therapy. The latter includes therapists' internal capacity to tolerate and make use of internal reactions to difficult clinical scenarios (Bennett-Levy, 2019; Eubanks-Carter et al., 2015; Hayes et al., 2004). Therefore, one of the key *intrapersonal skills* in this book is helping therapists to develop self-awareness of their tendency to move away from or react to their own difficult experience. Common responses and styles of distraction are listed at the bottom of the Reaction Form in Appendix A, which is used in the exercises in this book. Some reactions are so strong that they leave therapists unable to help clients. This can be called the therapists' *psychological capacity threshold* (Rousmaniere, 2019). One of the goals of this book is to help trainees develop the psychological capacity to become aware of moments when they may be moving away from, or unhelpfully reacting to, their own internal experience so that they can stay attuned and helpful with a broader range of clients.

Therapy with children, adolescents, and their families is provided in many formats, a wide range of settings, and at a critical time in the lifespan. Child therapy includes individual talk therapy, skills-focused interventions, play therapy, dyadic (with caregiver and child), group (e.g., social skills, harm reduction, coping with divorce), parent-focused modalities (e.g., behavioral parent training, parent–child interaction therapy), school-based interventions (e.g., Cognitive Behavioral Intervention for Trauma in Schools), and integrated behavioral health in pediatric primary care. As we worked on the exercises for this book and piloted them with students in our courses, we considered how many types of child therapy could be incorporated. Child and adolescent treatment is rarely undertaken without consideration for the familial and school context within which young people are rooted. In our work, and in our training of future child and adolescent psychologists, these are critical contexts that we incorporate and collaborate with. However, we soon learned that a narrow focus on individual work with children would allow us to write a book that offered more depth and exercises with incrementally increasing difficulty. The work of child and adolescent therapy also involves challenging therapeutic moments with caregivers and other stakeholders in the child's life. We hope that you will keep these parties in mind as you work through the exercises in this book and that these child-focused prompts will help you develop skills that will generalize to your work with other important people in the child's life.

The Unique Needs of Children

In writing this book on deliberate practice for child and adolescent therapy, we aimed to focus on basic skills that are universal to a wide range of theoretical orientations in the field. Regardless of treatment approach, all child and adolescent therapies are tailored to meet the specific needs of each individual's emotional, personality, and cognitive development. Although lifespan development is also an important component of adult psychotherapy, the dramatic differences that emerge from one year and the next in the early years require child therapists to adapt rapidly to the ever-changing needs and presentation of their clients. Identity development is also a primary consideration in working with children as they move through many phases and stages in quick succession.

Working with children is distinct from psychotherapy with adults in many ways. The genesis of the therapeutic relationship itself often begins with someone other than the patient. Caregivers, teachers, pediatricians, and other adults are usually the ones who initiate therapy on behalf of the child. You are unlikely to enter the waiting room and find an adult patient lying on the floor yelling, "I don't wanna go! Take me home!" But this is a common occurrence in child psychotherapy. Children are both more resistant and more intensely engaged with the therapist than many adult patients. Young people will stomp their feet, throw things, roll their eyes, and clam up for long periods of time. But they will also animatedly act out scenes from their life, high-five the therapist, and ask intensely personal questions—all things that are less likely to occur with most adult patients. Children and adolescents require a quick-thinking, nimble, creative, flexible, patient, and adaptive therapist. This is a tall order to fill alongside learning the basics of therapy interventions. When we first began using deliberate practice ourselves, and later with our students, we were delighted to see how helpful it was in fostering these qualities. A common maxim in child therapy is to "expect the unexpected," and the repeated rehearsal of child therapy skills freed us up to be more present and comfortable in our work with children and adolescents.

In addition to a spirit of playfulness, it is important to have an in-depth understanding of child development—this includes cognitive, social-emotional, physical, and personality development. Even if you have not yet worked clinically with children, you likely know how different interacting with a 5-year-old and an 8-year-old can be. Their fine and gross motor skills, comprehension level, emotion regulation abilities, and their interests are vastly different. I (Tracy) can remember a day, early in my clinical training, where I saw two children in back-to-back sessions. It just so happened that both of them—one a teenager and the other just 4 years old—reported the recent death of a family pet. I was struck by how different these sessions were and was very thankful for my child development courses, which helped me anticipate how each child's understanding of death, ability to talk directly about their feelings, and the ways in which they chose to process this loss would differ dramatically. The words and tone of voice we use, the degree of playfulness, the type of interventions, and the therapist's willingness to tolerate developmentally appropriate child and adolescent behaviors (e.g., eye-rolling, oppositional/disruptive behavior, cheating in game play) are informed by the unique developmental stage of each child.

Children are uniquely vulnerable. They are at the mercy of the adults who are entrusted with their care. Child therapists are responsible for assessing and monitoring children's safety; this includes looking out for domestic violence; neglect; physical, sexual, verbal, and emotional abuse; and self-inflicted harmful behaviors. As child therapists, we have a duty to protect young people, and our roles as "mandated reporters" are dictated by legislative and ethical guidelines. In our experience, this is one of the most difficult aspects of being a child therapist. When we guide our students through the process of doing a full risk assessment, making a report to child protective services, or informing parents about their child's nonsuicidal self-injury or suicidal ideation, we are reminded of how activating these incidents are, especially in the beginning of one's career as a therapist. We have included three exercises—Exercise 9: Gathering Information About Safety Concerns, Exercise 10: Setting Limits, and Exercise 11: Talking About Sex—to help you practice both how to respond and how to self-regulate during these challenging moments in child therapy. It is important to find the right balance between concern and calm when faced with these risk factors; becoming too alarmed may make it difficult for you to obtain critical information you will need to assess potential risk, and avoiding or downplaying the potential risk may have dire consequences for the child and your own ethical responsibilities. For any report of suspected abuse or self-harm, we encourage you to consult closely with your supervisor and to follow all of your local laws and ethical guidelines of your clinical discipline.

Being a child therapist requires a great deal of flexibility and creativity. Children have intense and ever-changing interests. As a result, we continue to learn about new cartoon characters, the latest online gaming and social media platforms, Japanese anime, and the many other things that capture their interest. We do our best to keep up. Young people have no qualms about pointing out our errors, and often, they do so good-naturedly. After I (Tracy) mixed up some social media terms while trying to gather more information about online bullying (news flash: you don't friend someone on Snapchat), my adolescent patient told me, "That was an epic fail!" I laughed heartily in the moment and upon reflection because it highlighted so many key aspects of deliberate practice for child therapy that are covered in this book. I was trying to gather more information about safety concerns (Exercise 9) that also involved some sexual content (Exercise 11). I was also trying to demonstrate interest and curiosity (Exercise 1) and empathy (Exercise 5). My reaction to this teenager's critique was also, I hope, nondefensive and responsive, in keeping with the skill criteria in Exercise 12. I made a mistake, which is really what deliberate practice is all about. The purpose of these exercises is to work through the many possible mistakes we can make as child therapists and to do so in the safety of a training environment with immediate feedback and repeated rehearsal.

Deliberate practice for child therapy offers opportunities to build skills that will help you effectively harness these common factors in the service of your patients and their families. For example, when a young person is resistant to change, has poor engagement in the therapy process, and minimal hope for the future, how will you build a therapeutic alliance? Many treatment manuals offer "troubleshooting" sections for addressing some of these challenges. But practicing these skills in a regimented manner is the best way to develop the skills you will need for everyday clinical practice—in those moments when you are actually sitting with a young person and you feel taken aback, frustrated, and unsure of what to do next. It is challenging to use the right language for each developmental stage, maintain the appropriate amount of warmth and neutrality in your voice, and the wherewithal to know when to proceed with your treatment goals/agenda and when to pivot and follow the child's lead. The aim of this book is to give you the opportunity to practice your responses—repeatedly— so that you can gain confidence in your child therapy skills while also recognizing the lifelong learning process that lies ahead.

Categorizing Child Therapy Skills

The exercises in this book are laid out in a sequential order so that they build on each other. Students in my (Jordan's) class have noted their surprise that what seemed like very challenging later exercises were actually easier than they thought because they were able to draw on the skills they had already practiced and grown more comfortable with.

The Child Therapy Skills Presented in Exercises 1 Through 12

The exercises begin with the skills necessary from the first session onward (Exercises 1–5)— these are skills we expect to use in every session. We start with communicating interest and curiosity, a key to alliance building, gathering information, and furthering exploration. We then move into other basic therapy skills, including naming feelings, praise and encouragement, observing and describing play, and empathy.

Exercises 6 through 8 are more challenging but necessary to deepening the work as therapy progresses. The skills in these exercises include elaborating play, exploring identity using a multicultural orientation, and implementing self-disclosure.

Finally, Exercises 9 through 12 offer an opportunity to practice skills that we have found tend to make trainees and even more experienced therapists anxious but are needed in the therapy process and often represent critical moments. Such skills are gathering information about safety concerns, setting limits, talking about sex, and responding to resistance and ruptures.

A Note About Vocal Tone, Facial Expression, and Body Posture

The meaning that is understood from the messages that we transmit varies greatly, depending on the nonverbal and paraverbal cues that support the verbal language. Imagine if someone tells you, "I'm leaving now, and I'll be back later" (this phrase is used in research on nonverbal communication). You would get a very different feeling and understanding of what they mean and intend to communicate depending on their vocal quality (whether their voice sounds friendly and upbeat, threatening and loud, or grumbling to themselves), their facial expression (if they are smiling or if they are red in the face), and their actions and posture (if they are making eye contact and waving goodbye, if they slam the door, or if their head is hung). Depending on the combination of cues, you may feel worried, angry, sad, confused, concerned, relieved, relaxed, happy, or any number of other emotions. And your response would likely vary accordingly.

It is increasingly clear what a central role nonverbal and paraverbal communication plays in the therapeutic process, both in terms of how clients communicate with us and how we as therapists communicate and are understood and perceived by our clients. Developmentally, we learn about ourselves and the world through other people. We take in not only what they say but also how they say it. This nonverbal and paraverbal information aids in establishing epistemic trust—that is, trust in the information that is communicated to us from other people (Fonagy & Allison, 2014). Furthermore, how vocal quality is matched to interventions can affect their effectiveness (Greenberg et al., 1996).

We would argue that vocal tone, facial expression, and body posture are perhaps even more crucial to be aware of and practice using in child therapy, in part because the therapy is often more physically active. Although sometimes we might be sitting across from each other, face to face, more often we are seated on the floor or at a lower table, move around the room, play with toys, draw, or write, among many other things. Even in teletherapy, there is often more going on than the visual content. Children may move around their room or their home, they show us what is in their space, we share our screens and play games together, or they may be playing popular games like Minecraft or Roblox, and we are talking and engaging around those activities. Thus, how we sound and how we use our faces and bodies become more relevant—and often more challenging as well and requiring more practice.

The Role of Deliberate Practice in Child Therapy Training

As we described earlier, this book applies a transtheoretical lens to the deliberate practice of child therapy skills. In training and beyond, therapists are exposed to a range of treatment models for working with children and adolescents, which are described in treatment manuals, supported by empirical research published in peer-reviewed journals, and even demonstrated in videos with master clinicians. Common elements of child and adolescent therapy models include specific approaches to assessment and case formulation; structures for the beginning, middle, and end of treatment; therapeutic tasks and intervention techniques for targeting problems; ways of tracking outcomes; and styles of supervision.

Although these resources guide the therapist about what to do and how to do it, they have traditionally offered few opportunities for therapists to practice being with a client and using certain techniques in the moment. Consequently, until trainees actually deliver the treatment, they are likely to feel unsure of themselves, perhaps stiff, and maybe even confused. As trainers and supervisors, we admittedly find ourselves saying, "It will make more sense when you're in the room," "Do what feels right to you," and "Don't worry too much, focus on being present."

The purpose of this book is to give trainees—and therapists in general—what they are asking for: an opportunity to practice being with child and adolescent clients when it is not the "real thing." Through the exercises, trainees will get to practice responding to a range of "children" and "adolescents" in vignettes that are intended to reflect a diversity of ages, genders, cultural backgrounds, personalities, and situations. Deliberate practice allows trainees to get comfortable listening to children and adolescents, adjusting their language to match the developmental level of children, and managing the emotional reactions that arise within them, as they formulate and provide a response. Because this book does not focus on a specific treatment model, the techniques that trainees might use in their responses can vary, as long as they are appropriate for the skill being practiced and the trainee can meet the skill criteria.

Training in Play and Playfulness

Through play, children express themselves; explore internal experiences; make links between thoughts, feelings, and behaviors; and practice interpersonal relationships. The use of play may vary depending on the orientation of the therapy. In a psychodynamic approach, play is likely to be unstructured and child-led. In cognitive and behavioral therapies, more structured games explicitly addressing skills might be employed. All therapists we know have their own personal arsenal of toys and games that they find helpful in various therapeutic situations. Furthermore, regardless of orientation, skilled child therapists know that playfulness is often the best way to engage and building a relationship with children where they will feel safe and comfortable opening up and working on the things that trouble them. But many adults have not played in a long time! Furthermore, playing can bring up our own childhood memories, both good and bad. Therefore, this book gives therapists an opportunity to practice playing and playfulness and to build comfort, flexibility, and creativity that can later be brought into the therapy room.

Overview of the Book's Structure

This book is organized into three parts. Part I contains this chapter and Chapter 2, which provides basic instructions on how to perform these exercises. We found through testing that providing too many instructions upfront overwhelmed trainers and trainees, and they ended up skipping past them as a result. Therefore, we kept these instructions as brief and simple as possible to focus only on the most essential information that trainers and trainees will need to get started with the exercises. Further guidelines for getting the most about deliberate practice are provided in Chapter 3, and additional instructions for monitoring and adjusting the difficulty of the exercises are provided in Appendix A. **Do not skip the instructions in Chapter 2, and be sure to read the additional guidelines and instructions in Chapter 3 and Appendix A once you are comfortable with the basic instructions.**

Part II contains the 12 skill-focused exercises, which are ordered based on their difficulty: beginner, intermediate, and advanced (see Table 1.1). They each contain a brief overview of the exercise, example client–therapist interactions to help guide trainees, step-by-step instructions for conducting that exercise, and a list of criteria for mastering the relevant skill. The client statements and sample therapist responses are then presented, also organized by difficulty (beginner, intermediate, and advanced). The statements and responses are presented separately so that the trainee playing the therapist has more freedom to improvise responses without being influenced by the sample responses, which should only be turned to if the trainee has difficulty improvising their own responses. The advanced exercises specify the client's age, which the earlier exercises do not, which is intended to challenge trainees to tailor their responses to the developmental level of the client. The last two exercises in Part II provide opportunities to practice the 12 skills within simulated psychotherapy sessions. Exercise 13 provides a sample psychotherapy session transcript in which the child therapy skills are used and clearly labeled, thereby demonstrating how they might flow together in an actual therapy session. Child therapy trainees are invited to run through the sample transcript with one playing the therapist and the other playing the client to get a feel for how a session might unfold. Exercise 14 provides suggestions for undertaking actual mock sessions, as well as client profiles ordered by difficulty (beginner, intermediate, and advanced) that trainees can use for improvised role-plays.

Part III contains Chapter 3, which provides additional guidance for trainers and trainees. While Chapter 2 is more procedural, Chapter 3 covers big-picture issues. It highlights six key points for getting the most out of deliberate practice and describes the importance of appropriate responsiveness, attending to trainee well-being and respecting their privacy, and trainer self-evaluation, among other topics.

Three appendixes conclude this book. Appendix A provides instructions for monitoring and adjusting the difficulty of each exercise as needed. It provides a Deliberate Practice Reaction Form for the trainee playing the therapist to complete to indicate whether the exercise is too easy or too difficult. Appendix B includes a Deliberate Practice Diary Form that can be used during a training session's final evaluation to process the trainees' experiences, but its primary purpose is to provide trainees a format to explore and record their experiences while engaging in additional, between-session deliberate practice activities without the supervisor. Appendix C presents a sample syllabus demonstrating how the 12 deliberate practice exercises and other support material can be integrated into a wider child psychotherapy training course. Instructors may choose to modify the syllabus or pick elements of it to integrate into their own courses.

Downloadable versions of this book's appendixes, including a color version of the Deliberate Practice Reaction Form, can be found in the "Clinician and Practitioner Resources" tab at https://www.apa.org/pubs/books/deliberate-practice-child-adolescent-psychotherapy.

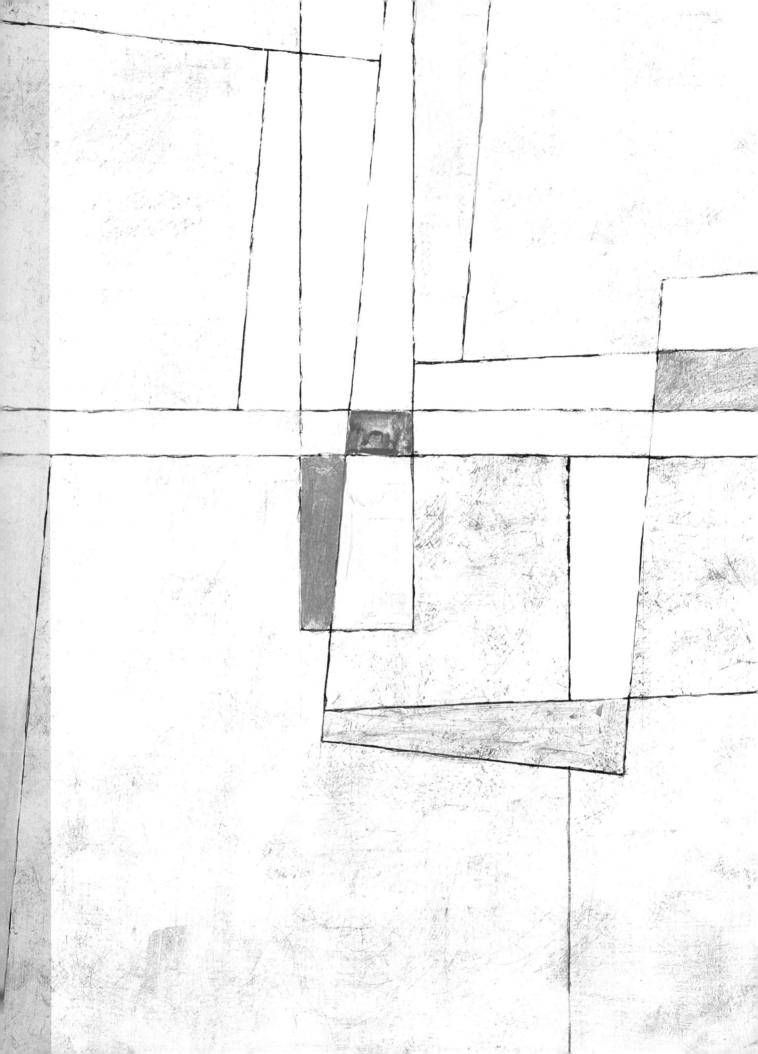

Instructions for the Child and Adolescent Psychotherapy Deliberate Practice Exercises

This chapter provides basic instructions that are common to all the exercises in this book. More specific instructions are included in each exercise. Chapter 3 also provides important guidance for trainees and trainers that will help them get the most out of deliberate practice. Appendix A offers additional instructions for monitoring and adjusting the difficulty of the exercises as needed after getting through all the client statements in a single difficulty level, including a Deliberate Practice Reaction Form that the trainee playing the therapist can complete to indicate whether they found the statements too easy or too difficult. **Difficulty assessment is an important part of the deliberate practice process and should not be skipped.**

Overview

The deliberate practice exercises in this book involve role-plays of hypothetical situations in child therapy. The role-play involves three people: one trainee role-plays the therapist, another trainee role-plays the client, and a trainer (professor/supervisor) observes and provides feedback. Alternatively, a peer can observe and provide feedback.

This book provides a script for each role-play, each with a client statement and also with an example therapist response. The client statements are graded in difficulty from beginning to advanced, although these difficulty grades are only estimates. The actual perceived difficulty of client statements is very subjective and varies widely by trainee. For example, some trainees may experience a stimulus of a client being angry as being easy to respond to, whereas another trainee may experience it as very difficult. Thus, it is important for trainees to provide difficulty assessments and adjustments to ensure that they are practicing at the right difficulty level—neither too easy nor too hard.

https://doi.org/10.1037/0000288-002

Deliberate Practice in Child and Adolescent Psychotherapy, by J. Bate, T. A. Prout, T. Rousmaniere, and A. Vaz
Copyright © 2022 by the American Psychological Association. All rights reserved.

Time Frame

We recommend a 90-minute time block for every exercise, structured roughly as follows:

- First 20 minutes: Orientation. The trainer explains the child therapy skill and demonstrates the exercise procedure with a volunteer trainee.

- Middle 50 minutes: Trainees perform the exercise in pairs. The trainer or a peer provides feedback throughout this process and monitors the exercise, adjusting the difficulty as needed after each set of statements (see Appendix A for more information about difficulty assessment).

- Final 20 minutes: Review, feedback, and discussion.

Preparation

1. Every trainee will need their own copy of this book.

2. Each exercise requires the trainer to fill out a Deliberate Practice Reaction Form after completing all the statements from a single difficulty level. The trainees should also complete a Deliberate Practice Diary Form during a training session's final evaluation and/or between sessions, particularly during additional deliberate practice activities. These forms are available at https://www.apa.org/pubs/books/deliberate-practice-child-adolescent-psychotherapy (see the "Clinician and Practitioner Resources" tab) and in Appendixes A and B, respectively.

3. Trainees are grouped into pairs. One volunteers to role-play the therapist and one to role-play the client (they will switch roles after 15 minutes of practice). As noted previously, an observer who might be either the trainer or a fellow trainee will work with each pair.

The Role of the Trainer

The primary responsibilities of the trainer are as follows:

1. Provide corrective feedback, which includes both information about how well the trainee's response met expected criteria and any necessary guidance about how to improve the response.

2. Remind the trainee to do difficulty assessments and adjustments after each level of client statements is completed (beginning, intermediate, and advanced).

How to Practice

Each exercise includes its own step-by-step instructions. Trainees should follow these instructions carefully, as every step is important.

Skill Criteria

Each of the first 12 exercises focuses on one essential child therapy skill with two to four skill criteria that describe the important components or principles for that skill.

The goal of the role-play is for trainees to practice improvising responses to the client statement in a manner that (a) is attuned to the client, (b) meets skill criteria as much as possible, and (c) feels authentic for the trainee. Trainees are provided scripts with example therapist responses to give them a sense of how to incorporate the skill criteria into a response. **It is important, however, that trainees do not read the example responses verbatim in the role-plays!** Therapy is highly personal and improvisational; the goal of deliberate practice is to develop trainees' ability to improvise within a consistent framework. Memorizing scripted responses would be counterproductive for helping trainees learn to perform therapy that is responsive, authentic, and attuned to each individual client.

Jordan Bate and Tracy A. Prout wrote the scripted example responses. However, a trainee's personal style of therapy may differ slightly or greatly from that in the example scripts. It is essential that, over time, trainees develop their own style and voice, while simultaneously being able to intervene according to the model's principles and strategies. To facilitate this, the exercises in this book were designed to maximize opportunities for improvisational responses informed by the skill criteria and ongoing feedback. Trainees will note that some of the scripted responses do not meet all the skill criteria: These responses are provided as examples of flexible application of child therapy skills in a manner that prioritizes attunement with the child or adolescent client.

The goal for the role-plays is for trainees to practice improvising responses to the client statements in a manner that

- is attuned to the client,
- meets as many of the skill criteria as possible, and
- feels authentic for the trainee.

Review, Feedback, and Discussion

The review and feedback sequence after each role-play has these two elements:

- First, the trainee who played the client **briefly** shares how it felt to be on the receiving end of the therapist's response. This can help assess how well trainees are attuning with the client.

- Second, the trainer provides **brief** feedback (less than 1 minute) based on the skill criteria for each exercise. Keep feedback specific, behavioral, and brief to preserve time for skill rehearsal. If one trainer is teaching multiple pairs of trainees, the trainer walks around the room, observing the pairs and offering brief feedback. When the trainer is not available, the trainee playing the client gives peer feedback to the therapist, based on the skill criteria and how it felt to be on the receiving end of the intervention. Alternatively, a third trainee can observe and provide feedback.

Trainers (or peers) should remember to keep all feedback specific and brief and not to veer into discussions of theory. There are many other settings for extended discussion of child therapy theory and research. In deliberate practice, it is of utmost importance to maximize time for continuous behavioral rehearsal via role-plays.

Final Evaluation

After both trainees have role-played the client and the therapist, the trainer provides an evaluation. Participants should engage in a short group discussion based on this evaluation. This discussion can provide ideas for where to focus homework and future deliberate practice sessions. To this end, Appendix B presents a Deliberate Practice Diary Form, which can also be downloaded from https://www.apa.org/pubs/books/ deliberate-practice-child-adolescent-psychotherapy (see the "Clinician and Practitioner Resources" tab). This form can be used as part of the final evaluation to help trainees process their experiences from that session with the supervisor. However, it is designed primarily to be used by trainees as a template for exploring and recording their thoughts and experiences between sessions, particularly when pursuing additional deliberate practice activities without the supervisor, such as rehearsing responses alone or if two trainees want practice the exercises together—perhaps with a third trainee filling the supervisor's role. Then, if they want, the trainees can discuss these experiences with the supervisor at the beginning of the next training session.

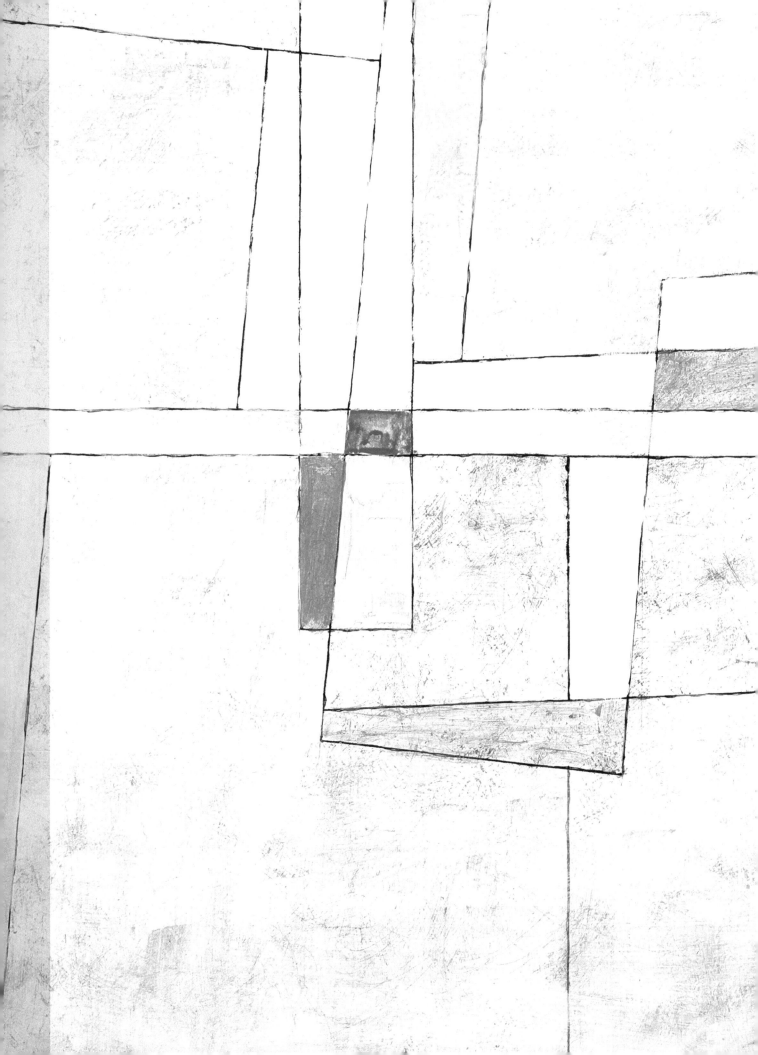

Deliberate Practice Exercises for Child and Adolescent Psychotherapy Skills

This section of the book includes 12 deliberate practice exercises for essential child therapy skills. These exercises are organized in a developmental sequence, from those that are more appropriate to someone just beginning child therapy training to those that are suitable for someone at a more advanced level. Although we anticipate that most trainers would use these exercises in the order we have suggested, some trainers may find it more appropriate to their training circumstances to use a different order. Exercises for advanced child and adolescent therapy skills include specific information about the client's age. This additional information is intended to challenge trainees to tailor their responses to the developmental level of the client. Finally, we also provide two comprehensive exercises that bring together the child therapy skills using an annotated child therapy session transcript and mock child therapy sessions.

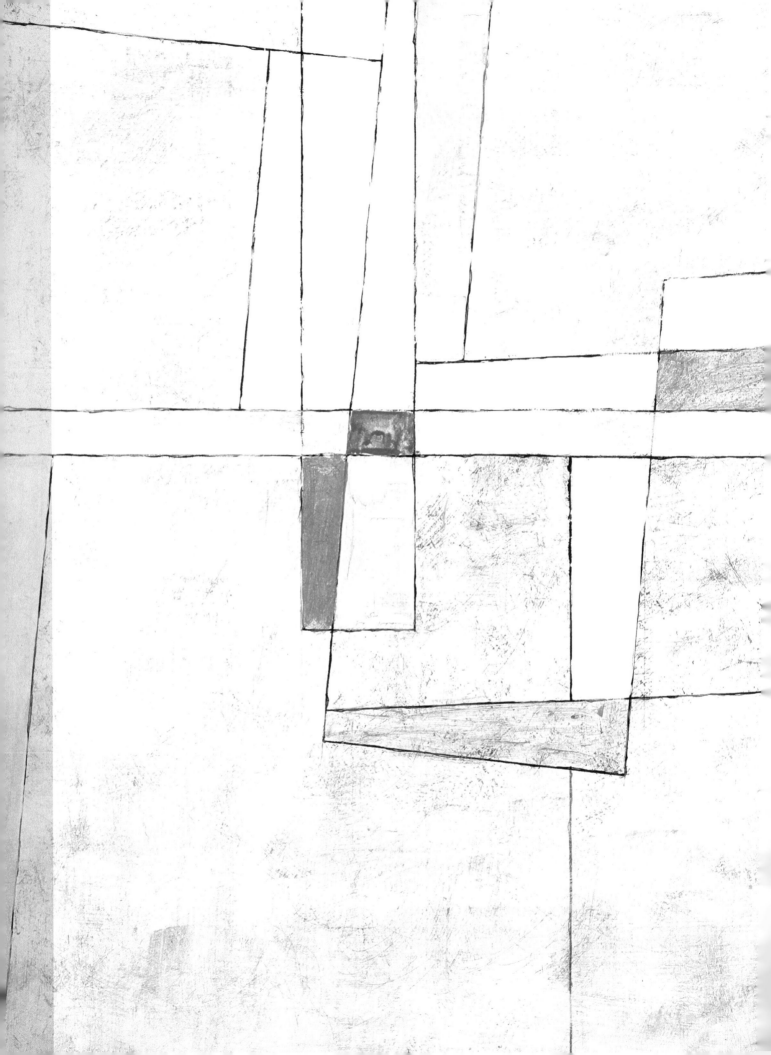

Communicating Interest and Curiosity

Preparations for Exercise 1

1. Read the instructions in Chapter 2.

2. Download the Deliberate Practice Reaction Form and the Deliberate Practice Diary Form at https://www.apa.org/pubs/books/deliberate-practice-child-adolescent-psychotherapy (see the "Clinician and Practitioner Resources" tab; also available in Appendixes A and B, respectively).

Skill Description

Skill Difficulty Level: Beginner

This skill is the most basic stance the therapist uses throughout therapy with children. The therapist displays a genuine interest and curiosity in getting to know the child—what they enjoy, what they think and feel, and the difficult things they have experienced. The goals are to convey that you value the child's experiences and perspectives and to show that you want to be working with them and want to know more about what they think and feel. The therapist verbally communicates that they want to hear more or get to know the child by making observations about what might be important or of interest to them, asking questions, and inviting them to join in playing or talking. Responses target something the child has already said or done and encourage further exploration or elaboration (through talking or play). Interest and curiosity are also communicated to patients through nonverbal cues such as focusing one's eyes on or orienting one's body posture toward the patient. Tone of voice may be enthusiastic, wondering, warm, or focused. Although therapists may label an affect or emotion, the focus of interest and curiosity is on encouraging the child to say more and to find out what is on their mind.

https://doi.org/10.1037/0000288-003
Deliberate Practice in Child and Adolescent Psychotherapy, by J. Bate, T. A. Prout, T. Rousmaniere, and A. Vaz

SKILL CRITERIA FOR EXERCISE 1
1. Communicate that you want to hear more or get to know the child (for example, by making observations about what might be important or of interest to them, asking questions, inviting them to join in playing or talking, or encouraging further exploration or elaboration).
2. Use a curious tone of voice and not-knowing stance (avoid interpretations, drawing conclusions, or offering solutions).

Definition of Terms

Joint Attention: Refers to the situation when you and the child are paying attention to the same thing. It might involve looking at something together (e.g., looking out a window at the airplane in the sky) or playing a game together or being engaged in a conversation.

Examples of Therapists Using The Skill of Communicating Interest and Curiosity

Note: Underlined text in brackets should be read aloud to provide context.

Example 1

CHILD CLIENT: [*Angry*] My mom is the worst.

THERAPIST: You sound pretty angry, what happened?

Example 2

CHILD CLIENT: [*Anxious*] I don't really know what to talk about today. Everything is fine.

THERAPIST: Well, I'm curious to know what things are on your mind or what's going on in your life, not just when things are difficult but also when they're fine. Could you tell me, were there any really good moments or difficult ones this week?

Example 3

CHILD CLIENT: [*Anxious, playing with toy animals*] And then all the animals went to the party at the farm, but they told the elephant he couldn't come.

THERAPIST: Oh no, they told the elephant he couldn't come! How come they're excluding him?

INSTRUCTIONS FOR EXERCISE 1

Step 1: Role-Play and Feedback

- The client says the first beginner client statement, also reading aloud any <u>underlined text</u> in brackets to provide context. The therapist improvises a response based on the skill criteria.

- The trainer (or, if not available, the client) provides brief feedback based on the skill criteria.

- The client then repeats the same statement, and the therapist again improvises a response. The trainer (or client) again provides brief feedback.

Step 2: Repeat

- Repeat Step 1 for all the statements in the current difficulty level (beginner, intermediate, or advanced).

Step 3: Assess and Adjust Difficulty

- The therapist completes the Deliberate Practice Reaction Form (see Appendix A) and decides whether to make the exercise easier or harder or to repeat the same difficulty level.

Step 4: Repeat for Approximately 15 Minutes

- Repeat Steps 1 to 3 for at least 15 minutes.
- The trainees then switch therapist and client roles and start over.

Now it's your turn! Follow Steps 1 and 2 from the instructions.

Remember: The goal of the role-play is for trainees to practice improvising responses to the client statements in a manner that (a) uses the skill criteria and (b) feels authentic for the trainee. **Example therapist responses for each client statement are provided at the end of this exercise. Trainees should attempt to improvise their own responses before reading the example responses.**

BEGINNER-LEVEL CLIENT STATEMENTS FOR EXERCISE 1
Beginner Client Statement 1
[**Sad**] My sister never lets me play with her when she has friends over even when I ask really nicely.
Beginner Client Statement 2
[**Optimistic, building tower with blocks**] It's easy to build! Don't worry, I got this.
Beginner Client Statement 3
[**Stressed/frustrated, playing with superhero toys**] Superman keeps flying but then crashing into the ground!
Beginner Client Statement 4
[**Frustrated**] My mom is the worst.

🛑 **Assess and adjust the difficulty before moving to the next difficulty level (see Step 3 in the exercise instructions).**

INTERMEDIATE-LEVEL CLIENT STATEMENTS FOR EXERCISE 1
Intermediate Client Statement 1
[**Hopeless**] My parents force me to come here every week. I already told you that therapy won't work for me.
Intermediate Client Statement 2
[**Worried**] Yeah, I just don't like texting my friends first because what if they don't respond? Then I'll know for sure they don't like me anymore.
Intermediate Client Statement 3
[**Dismissive, <u>falls while attempting to show you high kick</u>**] Sometimes I fall at karate practice, too, but it's no big deal.
Intermediate Client Statement 4
[**Stressed, <u>playing with dolls in a dollhouse</u>**] Mommy has to make dinner, feed the doggies, her other babies, and clean the house before she can talk to you, baby.
Intermediate Client Statement 5
[**Angry**] You don't understand. My parents are actually the worst. They track my location 24/7 and never let me stay out with my friends.
Intermediate Client Statement 6
[**Anxious**] I don't really know what to talk about today. Everything is fine.
Intermediate Client Statement 7
[**Angry**] No! I don't want to stop playing yet; please can we just have 5 more minutes?
Intermediate Client Statement 8
[**Confused, <u>while moving quickly from playing with one toy to another</u>**] Umm, nope, I don't know why I'm here. My mom said if I come then I get to eat ice cream after dinner tonight.

 Assess and adjust the difficulty before moving to the next difficulty level (see Step 3 in the exercise instructions).

ADVANCED-LEVEL CLIENT STATEMENTS FOR EXERCISE 1
Advanced Client Statement 1
[**Worried**] Sometimes I get scared that my daddy will hurt my mommy. But please don't tell my daddy I said that! I'm nervous he will yell at me if he finds out I told someone.
Advanced Client Statement 2
[**Embarrassed, <u>throws slime into the garbage</u>**] This slime is way too sticky! I told you we needed to use different clay. This always happens. Let's just play a different game, okay?!
Advanced Client Statement 3
[**Anxious, <u>playing with toy animals</u>**] And then all the animals went to the party at the farm, but they told the elephant he couldn't come.
Advanced Client Statement 4
[**Anxious/irritable**] I just hate the sound of other people chewing their food, so that's why I sit in my room during dinner and other meals. It freaks me out because it's so disgusting. I can't see why that's such a big deal to everyone.

🛑 **Assess and adjust the difficulty here (see Step 3 in the exercise instructions). If appropriate, follow the instructions to make the exercise even more challenging (see Appendix A).**

Example Therapist Responses: Interest and Curiosity

Remember: Trainees should attempt to improvise their own responses before reading the example responses. **Do not read the following responses verbatim unless you are having trouble coming up with your own responses!**

EXAMPLE RESPONSES TO BEGINNER-LEVEL CLIENT STATEMENTS FOR EXERCISE 1
Example Response to Beginner Client Statement 1
Even when you ask nicely? What kinds of things do she and her friends play that you want to play too?
Example Response to Beginner Client Statement 2
Ooh, look at you, a strong builder. What is it that you're building?
Example Response to Beginner Client Statement 3
Oh no! Superman! [Talking to the figurine] Are you ok? What keeps making you crash?
Example Response to Beginner Client Statement 4
Tell me, what happened?

EXAMPLE RESPONSES TO INTERMEDIATE-LEVEL
CLIENT STATEMENTS FOR EXERCISE 1

Example Response to Intermediate Client Statement 1

I hear you, and you must have your reasons for being pretty sure it won't work. What makes you think that?

Example Response to Intermediate Client Statement 2

What makes you think they don't like you now?

Example Response to Intermediate Client Statement 3

Oh, man. You kind of brush it off and just get right back at it, even though it might hurt or be kind of frustrating. Can you teach me some of the moves you're learning these days?

Example Response to Intermediate Client Statement 4

Mommy has a lot of things to do. What is Baby wanting from Mommy?

Example Response to Intermediate Client Statement 5

What's that like for you then when you are with your friends?

Example Response to Intermediate Client Statement 6

Well, I'm curious to know what things are on your mind or what's going on in your life—not just when things are difficult but also when they're fine. Could you tell me, what were the good moments this week?

Example Response to Intermediate Client Statement 7

I know, it's tough to stop playing when we are in the middle. We can't keep playing today, but where should we store these toys so we can play with them again next week?

Example Response to Intermediate Client Statement 8

Ooh, ice cream, delicious. Are you curious about why they wanted you to come here? Or does it not matter so much and you are just happy you will get ice cream?

EXAMPLE RESPONSES TO ADVANCED-LEVEL CLIENT STATEMENTS FOR EXERCISE 1
Example Response to Advanced Client Statement 1
Has Daddy hurt Mommy before?
Example Response to Advanced Client Statement 2
This has happened to you before with the slime, huh? What happened that time?
Example Response to Advanced Client Statement 3
They're excluding the elephant? How come they won't let him come?
Example Response to Advanced Client Statement 4
Of course I won't ever be able to hear what you hear, but what is it about their chewing that freaks you out? or What's it like for you to eat your meals in your room?

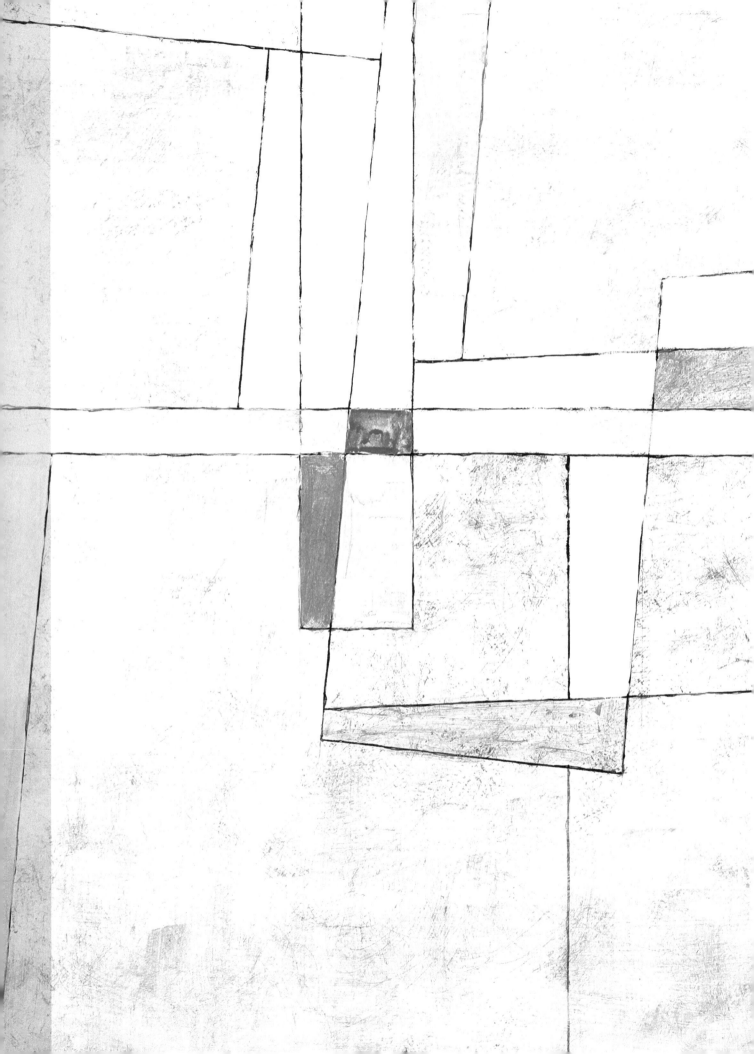

Naming Feelings

Preparations for Exercise 2

1. Read the instructions in Chapter 2.

2. Download the Deliberate Practice Reaction Form and the Deliberate Practice Diary Form at https://www.apa.org/pubs/books/deliberate-practice-child-adolescent-psychotherapy (see the "Clinician and Practitioner Resources" tab; also available in Appendixes A and B, respectively).

Skill Description

Skill Difficulty Level: Beginner

This skill might sound simple, but naming feelings requires the ability to observe how the patient looks and sounds, attune to their emotions, and then to name the feelings as accurately as possible. With children or parents, the therapist may name a variety of feelings:

-   the feelings the child is experiencing right now in therapy
-   the feelings the child experienced in a situation outside the therapy room
-   the feelings other people experienced in a situation outside the therapy room
-   the feelings characters in the play might be experiencing

Naming feelings plays an important role in emotion regulation. When someone puts words to what we are feeling, we often feel less alone, and this helps us to calm down. To name feelings, the therapist pays attention to the content of what the child is saying and also notes the feelings on the child's face, in their body, or in their voice as they speak. Do they seem anxious, sad, or angry?

When naming feelings with children, it is important to mark them as being your perception of the feelings they or someone else had. You are not telling them what

https://doi.org/10.1037/0000288-004

Deliberate Practice in Child and Adolescent Psychotherapy, by J. Bate, T. A. Prout, T. Rousmaniere, and A. Vaz

they feel as if you know for certain, because one aspect of mental states is that we can never know for certain what someone else is thinking or feeling; we need to check it out with them to see if we are right.

The goal is to get as close as possible to describing the feelings involved so that the child feels understood. Choosing your words might require thinking outside the box to find words that are specific to the child or the moment, rather than feelings that are more common and general, like *frustrated* or *hard*. In many cases, there might be mixed emotions, and it could be helpful to name those. For example, "It sounds like you feel a mix of relief that it's over, and also sadness that it's over."

You do not need to worry too much about being wrong in the emotions you name. If you have shown interest and curiosity, then the child will likely appreciate that you are trying to understand them and be able to correct you about what they are feeling. Some kinds of therapy focus on naming feelings that are visible and already being expressed by the patient either verbally or in their behavior. Other ways of working focus on naming feelings that the child might not be aware of, or the feelings that might be "underneath" other feelings. For example, a child might look angry on the outside after her mother leaves the room, but underneath her anger is sadness or a feeling of loss. For this exercise, there is not a right or wrong feeling to name, as long as it is plausible.

SKILL CRITERIA FOR EXERCISE 2

1. Tentatively identify an emotion that the child or character in the play or story may be feeling, using a specific, descriptive emotion word.
2. Use emotional expression in your face and voice as you name the feeling.

Examples of Therapists Using Skill of Naming Feelings

Note: Underlined text in brackets should be read aloud to provide context.

Example 1

CHILD CLIENT: [*Quickly, playing with toy figurines*] Blast, the bombs are exploding everywhere! The cars have to drive fast to get away!

THERAPIST: Oh no! Bombs exploding! I wonder if the people in the cars feel scared?!

Example 2

CHILD CLIENT: [*Concerned, talking to baby doll*] Oh no, baby is crying.

THERAPIST: Oh no, baby is crying. Is she sad? [*Talking to baby doll*] What's wrong, baby?

Example 3

CHILD CLIENT: [*Withdrawn*] I don't want to talk about it.

THERAPIST: Hmm, it sounds like it's something that hurts to think about.

INSTRUCTIONS FOR EXERCISE 2

Step 1: Role-Play and Feedback

- The client says the first beginner client statement, also reading aloud any <u>underlined text</u> in brackets to provide context. The therapist improvises a response based on the skill criteria.

- The trainer (or if not available, the client) provides brief feedback based on the skill criteria.

- The client then repeats the same statement, and the therapist again improvises a response. The trainer (or client) again provides brief feedback.

Step 2: Repeat

- Repeat Step 1 for all the statements in the current difficulty level (beginner, intermediate, or advanced).

Step 3: Assess and Adjust Difficulty

- The therapist completes the Deliberate Practice Reaction Form (see Appendix A) and decides whether to make the exercise easier or harder or to repeat the same difficulty level.

Step 4: Repeat for Approximately 15 Minutes

- Repeat Steps 1 to 3 for at least 15 minutes.
- The trainees then switch therapist and client roles and start over.

Now it's your turn! Follow Steps 1 and 2 from the instructions.

Remember: The goal of the role-play is for trainees to practice improvising responses to the client statements in a manner that (a) uses the skill criteria and (b) feels authentic for the trainee. **Example therapist responses for each client statement are provided at the end of this exercise. Trainees should attempt to improvise their own responses before reading the example responses.**

BEGINNER-LEVEL CLIENT STATEMENTS FOR EXERCISE 2
Beginner Client Statement 1
[**Hurt, <u>playing with action figures</u>**] Ouch, ouch! Spider-Man keeps getting pushed off the building!
Beginner Client Statement 2
[**Optimistic, <u>drawing</u>**] I'm drawing a really pretty flower and a sun now; do you like it?
Beginner Client Statement 3
[**Frustrated, <u>playing a board game</u>**] Ummm, I told you this game is too hard! I want to play something else instead.
Beginner Client Statement 4
[**Sad**] I don't want to play Uno since my sister always wins when we play together.
Beginner Client Statement 5
[**Quickly, <u>playing with toy figurines</u>**] Blast, the bombs are exploding everywhere! The cars have to drive fast to get away!

Assess and adjust the difficulty before moving to the next difficulty level (see Step 3 in the exercise instructions).

INTERMEDIATE-LEVEL CLIENT STATEMENTS FOR EXERCISE 2
Intermediate Client Statement 1
[**Anxious**] Yeah, I *could* sleep in my own bed by myself with the lights off, I just don't want to right now . . . mommy's bed is just comfier . . . that's all.
Intermediate Client Statement 2
[**Worried, <u>pretending to play with toys</u>**] Quick!! The bad guy is chasing us! We have to run away as fast as we can before he catches up!!!
Intermediate Client Statement 3
[**Stressed**] Ugh, I never get anything right! I have this really big test tomorrow in social studies, and I keep failing the practice tests. Can we, like, end early today or something?
Intermediate Client Statement 4
[**Angry**] My mom took away my new Nintendo Switch for no reason. She just hates me. Like I didn't even do anything wrong!!! I have no clue when I can have it back either.
Intermediate Client Statement 5
[**Sad, <u>talking to the baby doll</u>**] Oh no, baby is crying.
Intermediate Client Statement 6
[**Angry**] You were 5 minutes late today when we always start on time. I don't understand . . . are you going to go over 5 minutes too to make up the time?
Intermediate Client Statement 7
[**Confused**] Just so you know, I'm technically way too old to be playing with dolls and toys. Now that I'm in fourth grade, none of my friends play with Barbies anymore.

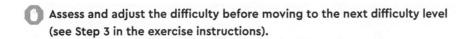 **Assess and adjust the difficulty before moving to the next difficulty level (see Step 3 in the exercise instructions).**

ADVANCED-LEVEL CLIENT STATEMENTS FOR EXERCISE 2
Advanced Client Statement 1
[**Worried**] I'm super happy that I get to stay in my house for school so that I don't get sick. It stinks not seeing my friends, but basically everyone is getting sick from being outside so I think we should do online school forever.
Advanced Client Statement 2
[**Withdrawn**] I don't want to talk about it.
Advanced Client Statement 3
[**Embarrassed**] You have to promise not to tell my parents but . . . one time I got in a really bad fight with another girl at my school and she's really tall, so I called her a giraffe in front of all the boys—but only because she was mean to me first!
Advanced Client Statement 4
[**Confused**] Well, since my dad never lived with us, I have a lot of cousins that I don't know. But then also cousins that I do know—so yeah, I guess I have kind of a big family. Which makes holidays better?
Advanced Client Statement 5
[**Irritable**] My dad said he won't force me to come to therapy, so I quit. All we do is talk about things that have already happened. It's pointless. I'm totally fine . . . plus I just don't have the time anymore to sit here and talk, talk, talk.
Advanced Client Statement 6
[**Anxious, irritable**] I just hate the sound of other people chewing their food, so that's why I sit in my room during dinner and other meals. It freaks me out because it's so disgusting. I can't see why that's such a big deal to everyone.

> **Assess and adjust the difficulty here (see Step 3 in the exercise instructions). If appropriate, follow the instructions to make the exercise even more challenging (see Appendix A).**

Example Therapist Responses: Naming Feelings

Remember: Trainees should attempt to improvise their own responses before reading the example responses. **Do not read the following responses verbatim unless you are having trouble coming up with your own responses!**

EXAMPLE RESPONSES TO BEGINNER-LEVEL CLIENT STATEMENTS FOR EXERCISE 2
Example Response to Beginner Client Statement 1
[Talking to Spider-Man] You keep getting hurt over and over. You must feel so frustrated!
Example Response to Beginner Client Statement 2
Wow, that's beautiful. It seems like you feel proud of what you created.
Example Response to Beginner Client Statement 3
This is really frustrating for you. Maybe you feel ignored because I didn't respond to you when you said it was hard earlier.
Example Response to Beginner Client Statement 4
I can sense a real sadness in what you just said.
Example Response to Beginner Client Statement 5
[Speaking to the cars] This is really scary! There are bombs going off all over. We need to get to safety!

EXAMPLE RESPONSES TO INTERMEDIATE-LEVEL CLIENT STATEMENTS FOR EXERCISE 2
Example Response to Intermediate Client Statement 1
I hear you . . . you *could* sleep on your own, but it doesn't feel as comfortable in your own bed. Sounds like you feel safer there.
Example Response to Intermediate Client Statement 2
Oh, man! I'm worried something bad will happen! Are you worried too?
Example Response to Intermediate Client Statement 3
Sounds like things feel really stressful right now. Can we talk more about that before we decide what to do about ending today?
Example Response to Intermediate Client Statement 4
That's super frustrating! It sounds like you're angry and confused about why the Switch got taken away.
Example Response to Intermediate Client Statement 5
[Talking directly to the baby doll] Sweet baby. You're crying and maybe feeling really sad about something . . .
Example Response to Intermediate Client Statement 6
I did start late today. Maybe you are feeling angry about that and wondering if you're going to get the full amount of time?
Example Response to Intermediate Client Statement 7
Hmm . . . so no one else plays with Barbies, but you still like them. Maybe that feels a little confusing to have different interests than other fourth-graders?

EXAMPLE RESPONSES TO ADVANCED-LEVEL CLIENT STATEMENTS FOR EXERCISE 2

Example Response to Advanced Client Statement 1

Doing online school forever has its drawbacks, but it sure helps you feel safe. It sounds like you're a little worried about the risks out in the world right now.

Example Response to Advanced Client Statement 2

You're letting me know what you need right now. I wonder if you don't want to talk about it because you're worried about how I'll react or how it will feel to say it out loud?

Example Response to Advanced Client Statement 3

I want to hear more about how she was mean to you and what happened. But before that, I want to understand how you're feeling. Maybe you feel a bit embarrassed about calling this girl a giraffe and worried that I'll tell your parents what happened?

Example Response to Advanced Client Statement 4

So, in some ways you have a big family, but you don't really know them. That might feel a little confusing. Sounds like you're not so sure it makes holidays better . . .

Example Response to Advanced Client Statement 5

So far, it seems like therapy has been a big waste of time and you're feeling irritated about even having to come to these sessions.

Example Response to Advanced Client Statement 6

Listening to other people chew their food really gets under your skin. From what you said, it sounds super uncomfortable. And you seem annoyed about everyone trying to get you to eat with them.

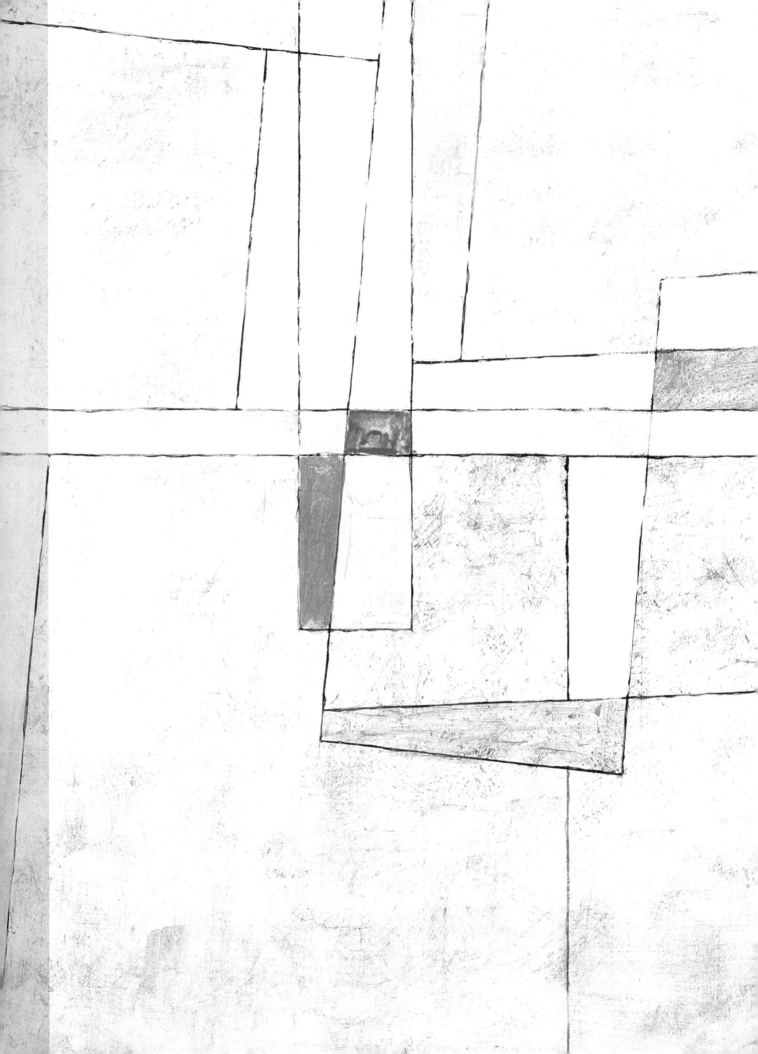

Praise and Encouragement

Preparations for Exercise 3

1. Read the instructions in Chapter 2.

2. Download the Deliberate Practice Reaction Form and the Deliberate Practice Diary Form at https://www.apa.org/pubs/books/deliberate-practice-child-adolescent-psychotherapy (see the "Clinician and Practitioner Resources" tab; also available in Appendixes A and B, respectively).

Skill Description

Skill Difficulty Level: Beginner

Praise is a skill that is highlighted in nearly every book or training for parents because it is important for children's development that they feel they are approved of and loved. Praise brings attention to desired behavior and is a positive reinforcer. With parents, this is sometimes called "catching the child being good." Although therapists and parents are different in many ways, it is important that children feel like they have their therapist's positive regard or approval too, especially because children often feel like they are coming to therapy because they are "bad" or something is wrong with them. Barish (2018) wrote that children in therapy often feel discouraged. Therefore, it is important that as therapists we find opportunities to use praise and encouragement with children in therapy. But for praise and encouragement to be therapeutic, it is important that they be done in specific ways. Praise and encouragement should help build the child's motivation and self-esteem. Thus, it is important to give attention to efforts and not (only) achievements. Therapeutic praise is not saying "Good job!" to everything. It is noticing "That was hard, but you did it!" or even "This is hard, but I think we'll get it eventually!"

https://doi.org/10.1037/0000288-005

Deliberate Practice in Child and Adolescent Psychotherapy, by J. Bate, T. A. Prout, T. Rousmaniere, and A. Vaz

Encouragement is important—specifically for building hope and positive expectations about therapy, which have been shown to relate to better outcomes. The therapist essentially communicates to the child or the parent, "I believe in you." Encouragement often begins with acknowledging discouragement, which is an important first step to avoid offering empty praise. Encouragement also addresses hope by promoting the child's sense of agency and the pathways to achieve their goals. In other words, helping the child hardness their sense of power (realistically) and scaffolding their process for achieving their goals. An optimistic tone for encouragement and praise strengthens these interventions.

SKILL CRITERIA FOR EXERCISE 3

1. Acknowledge the child's feelings (e.g., discouragement, anxiety). Or if the feelings are unclear, inquire about what they are.
2. Clearly identify the child's strengths or sense of agency, avoiding good–bad comments and praising efforts, not achievements.

Examples of Therapists Using the Skill Praise and Encouragement

Note: Underlined text in brackets should be read aloud to provide context.

Example 1

CHILD CLIENT: [*Frustrated, _building a tower_*] Ugh, it keeps falling.

THERAPIST: I know, it's frustrating, you've been really patient and you're working really hard. I wonder if we might try again, putting bigger blocks on the bottom?

Example 2

CHILD CLIENT: [*Anxious*] I suck at chemistry. I am basically failing.

THERAPIST: It's tough in school, there are so many subjects, and some come more easily to us than others. I know from what you've told me, you've been giving it your all. What's been hard for you in chemistry? Maybe if we talk about it, we can help you feel a bit better.

Example 3

CHILD CLIENT: [*Sad*] Danielle said she doesn't want to be friends anymore.

THERAPIST: It hurts when people don't want to be our friends anymore. Especially when you've put a lot of effort into the friendship. Did you get a chance to ask her why?

INSTRUCTIONS FOR EXERCISE 3

Step 1: Role-Play and Feedback

- The client says the first beginner client statement, also reading aloud any <u>underlined text</u> in brackets to provide context. The therapist improvises a response based on the skill criteria.

- The trainer (or if not available, the client) provides brief feedback based on the skill criteria.

- The client then repeats the same statement, and the therapist again improvises a response. The trainer (or client) again provides brief feedback.

Step 2: Repeat

- Repeat Step 1 for all the statements in the current difficulty level (beginner, intermediate, or advanced).

Step 3: Assess and Adjust Difficulty

- The therapist completes the Deliberate Practice Reaction Form (see Appendix A) and decides whether to make the exercise easier or harder or to repeat the same difficulty level.

Step 4: Repeat for Approximately 15 Minutes

- Repeat Steps 1 to 3 for at least 15 minutes.
- The trainees then switch therapist and client roles and start over.

Now it's your turn! Follow Steps 1 and 2 from the instructions.

Remember: The goal of the role-play is for trainees to practice improvising responses to the client statements in a manner that (a) uses the skill criteria and (b) feels authentic for the trainee. **Example therapist responses for each client statement are provided at the end of this exercise. Trainees should attempt to improvise their own responses before reading the example responses.**

BEGINNER-LEVEL CLIENT STATEMENTS FOR EXERCISE 3
Beginner Client Statement 1
[**Frustrated, <u>building a tower</u>**] Ugh, it keeps falling.
Beginner Client Statement 2
[**Anxious**] I suck at chemistry. I am basically failing.
Beginner Client Statement 3
[**Sad**] Danielle said she doesn't want to be friends anymore.
Beginner Client Statement 4
[**Frustrated**] My sister is so annoying sometimes.
Beginner Client Statement 5
[**Worried**] I think my friends purposefully made a separate text group without me in it. I can just tell they're making plans without me.
Beginner Client Statement 6
[**Stressed, <u>playing with dolls in a dollhouse</u>**] Mommy has to make dinner, feed the doggies, her other babies, and clean the house before she can talk to you, baby.

Assess and adjust the difficulty before moving to the next difficulty level (see Step 3 in the exercise instructions).

INTERMEDIATE-LEVEL CLIENT STATEMENTS FOR EXERCISE 3
Intermediate Client Statement 1
[**Hopeless**] Nobody understands me, not even my parents. Why can't they just leave me alone instead of making me come talk to you?
Intermediate Client Statement 2
[**Dismissive**] Umm, yeah, so I didn't practice the deep breathing since it seemed like a waste of time and I don't know . . . I just forgot, I guess.
Intermediate Client Statement 3
[**Angry, <u>playing with toys</u>**] Ugh, no more questions! My mommy said I didn't have to talk to you today if I didn't want to. I'm so tired and I just want to play with my animals.
Intermediate Client Statement 4
[**Angry**] No! I don't want to stop playing yet. Please can we just have 5 more minutes?
Intermediate Client Statement 5
[**Confused**] Wait—so do you play with other kids in this playroom too? Because I didn't draw that elephant on the whiteboard so someone else must have.

🛑 **Assess and adjust the difficulty before moving to the next difficulty level (see Step 3 in the exercise instructions).**

ADVANCED-LEVEL CLIENT STATEMENTS FOR EXERCISE 3
Advanced Client Statement 1
[**Frustrated, <u>playing with action figure</u>**] Ugh! Superman's cape keeps falling off. And now he's crashing into buildings . . . he can't stop flying and spinning out of control!
Advanced Client Statement 2
[**Embarrassed, <u>throws slime into the garbage</u>**] This slime is way too sticky! I told you we needed to use different clay. This always happens. Let's just play a different game, okay!?
Advanced Client Statement 3
[**Anxious, irritable**] Yeah, I guess I want to have friends, but I also don't really care. I don't know I'm just really different from everyone at my school, like they just don't get me.
Advanced Client Statement 4
[**Anxious, <u>responding to camera recording session</u>**] I don't like it when you watch me play. Can you sit over there farther away and move the video camera over there too?

Assess and adjust the difficulty here (see Step 3 in the exercise instructions). If appropriate, follow the instructions to make the exercise even more challenging (see Appendix A).

Example Therapist Responses: Praise and Encouragement

Remember: Trainees should attempt to improvise their own responses before reading the example responses. **Do not read the following responses verbatim unless you are having trouble coming up with your own responses!**

EXAMPLE RESPONSES TO BEGINNER-LEVEL CLIENT STATEMENTS FOR EXERCISE 3
Example Response to Beginner Client Statement 1
You are working so hard to make it stand tall (Criterion 2)—how frustrating that it isn't working. (Criterion 1)
Example Response to Beginner Client Statement 2
Chemistry has been such a challenge this year. (Criterion 1) Despite your best efforts, you're struggling. (Criterion 2) What are some of the ways it is hard for you?
Example Response to Beginner Client Statement 3
What a disappointment. (Criterion 1) You've poured a lot into this friendship. (Criterion 2) Can you tell me more about what happened?
Example Response to Beginner Client Statement 4
Sisters can be super annoying! (Criterion 1) Even when you work hard to be kind and supportive of them. (Criterion 2) What's been going on lately?
Example Response to Beginner Client Statement 5
It's really painful to be left out like that. (Criterion 1) It's clear how much you value your friendships and you put your whole heart into them. (Criterion 2) What have you noticed that makes you think they're excluding you?
Example Response to Beginner Client Statement 6
[Talking directly to the last baby mentioned] Hi, baby. You're sitting over here watching Mommy rush around, and she doesn't have time to talk to you. You're being so patient and understanding (Criterion 2), but I bet it's hard to wait. (Criterion 1)

EXAMPLE RESPONSES TO INTERMEDIATE-LEVEL CLIENT STATEMENTS FOR EXERCISE 3
Example Response to Intermediate Client Statement 1
It sounds like you want to find someone who can understand and also want to be left alone. That's a hard place to be. (Criterion 1) Is there a way our time together could be helpful and not feel like another thing you're being forced to do?
Example Response to Intermediate Client Statement 2
I'm glad you're telling me and appreciate your honesty. (Criterion 2) Can you say more about what makes it feel like a waste of time? (Criterion 1)
Example Response to Intermediate Client Statement 3
I am asking a lot of questions today! And you've done a lot of hard work answering them. (Criterion 2) I can understand why you're tired of talking. (Criterion 1) Maybe playing for a bit is a good idea.
Example Response to Intermediate Client Statement 4
It's really hard to have to end the fun we've been having. I can totally understand your wanting to stay longer. (Criterion 1) I appreciate your ability to put that into words. (Criterion 2)
Example Response to Intermediate Client Statement 5
Oh, that must feel confusing to think about other kids being in this space too. (Criterion 1) I appreciate you asking about this and letting me know what you're wondering about. (Criterion 2)

EXAMPLE RESPONSES TO ADVANCED-LEVEL CLIENT STATEMENTS FOR EXERCISE 3
Example Response to Advanced Client Statement 1
Superman, you're usually so strong and put together (Criterion 2), but right now it's so hard to keep it together! (Criterion 1) How can we help you feel more in control?
Example Response to Advanced Client Statement 2
Ugh! This is really frustrating, and it's happened to us a few times now. (Criterion 1) Good idea to do something different (Criterion 2)—maybe that will feel better.
Example Response to Advanced Client Statement 3
Sounds like you feel a bit like an outsider. (Criterion 1) On the one hand you don't really care, but it must be hard, in some ways, to feel like all the other kids don't understand you. You've been trying really hard to figure out how you fit into the whole group. (Criterion 2) What would you want them to know about you?
Example Response to Advanced Client Statement 4
You're needing some space from me and the video camera. (Criterion 1) I'm glad you told me that. (Criterion 2)

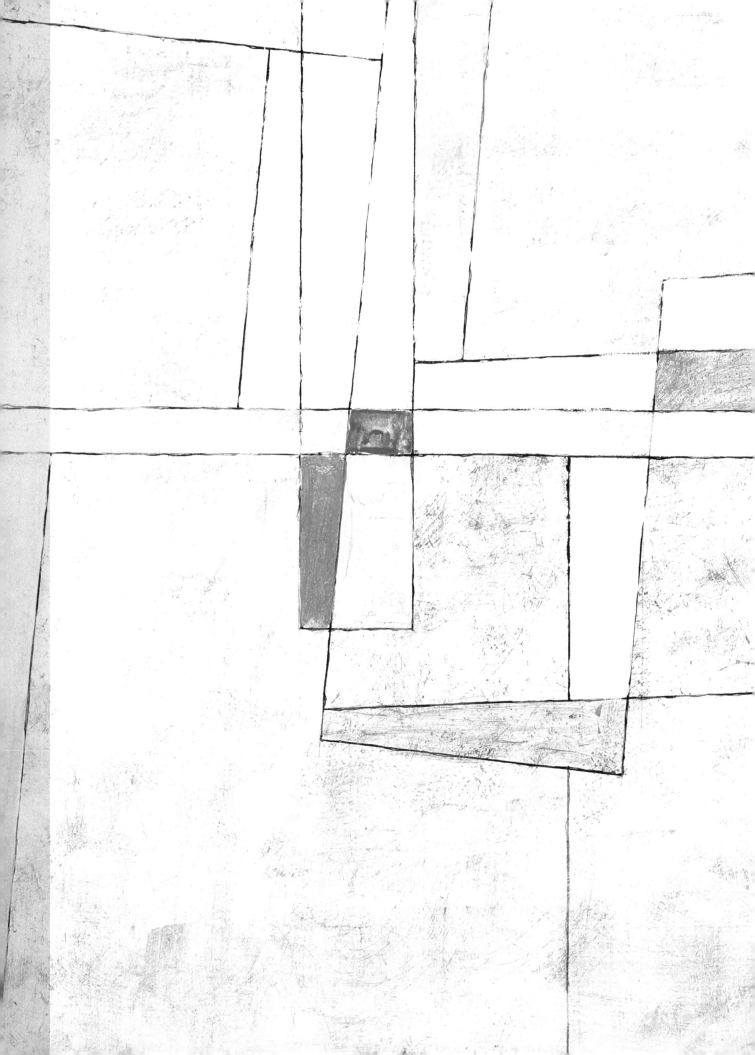

Observing and Describing Play

Preparations for Exercise 4

1. Read the instructions in Chapter 2.

2. Download the Deliberate Practice Reaction Form and the Deliberate Practice Diary Form at https://www.apa.org/pubs/books/deliberate-practice-child-adolescent-psychotherapy (see the "Clinician and Practitioner Resources" tab; also available in Appendixes A and B, respectively).

Skill Description

Skill Difficulty Level: Beginner

In therapy, adults communicate their thoughts and feelings by talking about them. In contrast, children communicate their thoughts and feelings through play. Children may play with dolls and dollhouses, action figures, stuffed animals, or puppets. They may play dress up or make believe. They may create stories in their play, or they may build with blocks and LEGOs or make creations with sand or Play-Doh. They may draw, paint, or play board games or cards.

Observing and describing play allows us to step into the child's inner world, just as we step into an adult patient's inner world by talking with them about it. Some interventions refer to observing and describing play as "sportscasting" because, like the sportscaster of a game like football or baseball, the therapist takes the position of onlooker and puts words to what they see happening in the play or the game. As with the earlier skills you have already practiced, observing is an element of this skill that is nonverbal. The therapist aims to be present and engaged with the child but is non-intrusive. Using the sportscaster analogy, you are positioned watching intently from the sidelines and putting words to what you see, showing great interest in it, but you are not running onto the field and getting in the middle of it.

https://doi.org/10.1037/0000288-006

Deliberate Practice in Child and Adolescent Psychotherapy, by J. Bate, T. A. Prout, T. Rousmaniere, and A. Vaz

There are many elements of play that can be described, and what you choose to describe may depend on the theoretical orientation or approach that you are using and also where in the therapy process you are (e.g., how long you have been working with the patient, what the goals are). At the most basic level, you can reflect on what you see happening, how the child is moving the pieces, or where they are moving them. For example, "You are flipping the cards very fast" (in a game of War), or "Ooh, it looks like the baby has decided to go upstairs" (in dollhouse play). You might describe something you see clearly to show the child that you are paying attention, or you might use the description as an opportunity to clarify what is happening, with a more curious tone. If the child has clearly invited you into their play, you may describe it "from the inside," for example, narrating your own moves.

SKILL CRITERIA FOR EXERCISE 4

1. Listen with attention and interest.
2. Describe one or two elements of the play, keeping the language simple.
3. Do not interrupt play.

Examples of Therapists Using Skill of Observing and Describing Play

Note: Underlined text in brackets should be read aloud to provide context.

Example 1

CHILD CLIENT: [*Playing, pretending to shoot a gun at a LEGO tower*] Pow! Pow! Pow! Quick, we gotta move around to the other side in case they try to escape from the other exit!

THERAPIST: First they shot at them in the front, and now they're moving around back to make sure they can't escape.

Example 2

CHILD CLIENT: [*Sweetly, setting up the stuffed animals and a tea set*] Okay, Annabella, you sit here. Oh, Roger, he keeps falling over. Mr. Pigsy sits here next to Mrs. Pigsy.

THERAPIST: They're all finding their places around the table, getting ready for tea, it looks like.

Example 3

CHILD CLIENT: [*Anxious, playing Connect Four, going slowly, and trying to figure out where they are going to put their piece*] Mmm, I dunno what to do.

THERAPIST: You're looking very carefully at all of the angles to make your move.

INSTRUCTIONS FOR EXERCISE 4
Step 1: Role-Play and Feedback
• The client says the first beginner client statement, also reading aloud any <u>underlined text</u> in brackets to provide context. The therapist improvises a response based on the skill criteria. • The trainer (or, if not available, the client) provides brief feedback based on the skill criteria. • The client then repeats the same statement, and the therapist again improvises a response. The trainer (or client) again provides brief feedback.
Step 2: Repeat
• Repeat Step 1 for all the statements in the current difficulty level (beginner, intermediate, or advanced).
Step 3: Assess and Adjust Difficulty
• The therapist completes the Deliberate Practice Reaction Form (see Appendix A) and decides whether to make the exercise easier or harder or to repeat the same difficulty level.
Step 4: Repeat for Approximately 15 Minutes
• Repeat Steps 1 to 3 for at least 15 minutes. • The trainees then switch therapist and client roles and start over.

Now it's your turn! Follow Steps 1 and 2 from the instructions.

Remember: The goal of the role-play is for trainees to practice improvising responses to the client statements in a manner that (a) uses the skill criteria and (b) feels authentic for the trainee. **Example therapist responses for each client statement are provided at the end of this exercise. Trainees should attempt to improvise their own responses before reading the example responses.**

BEGINNER-LEVEL CLIENT STATEMENTS FOR EXERCISE 4
Beginner Client Statement 1
[Playing, <u>pretending to shoot a gun at a LEGO tower</u>] Pow! Pow! Pow! Quick, we gotta move around to the other side in case they try to escape from the other exit!
Beginner Client Statement 2
[Sweetly, <u>setting up the stuffed animals and a tea set</u>] Okay, Annabella, you sit here. Oh, Roger, he keeps falling over. Mr. Pigsy sits here next to Mrs. Pigsy.
Beginner Client Statement 3
[Anxious, <u>playing Connect Four, going slowly, and trying to figure out where they are going to put their piece</u>] Mmm, I dunno what to do.
Beginner Client Statement 4
[Angry, <u>setting up a dollhouse</u>] Ugh, no! The dining room table goes here, not there! Never mind, I'll do it myself.
Beginner Client Statement 5
[Hopeless, <u>playing with animals</u>] Well, now we're on a farm, but the horsey doesn't have any food to eat since his friend ate all the hay.

🛑 **Assess and adjust the difficulty before moving to the next difficulty level (see Step 3 in the exercise instructions).**

INTERMEDIATE-LEVEL CLIENT STATEMENTS FOR EXERCISE 4

Intermediate Client Statement 1

[**Worried, <u>playing with dolls</u>**] So I'm your backup singer at a concert and you're the really famous one, so you get to sign all the autographs, which is pretty cool.

Intermediate Client Statement 2

[**Dismissive, <u>falls while attempting to show you high kicks</u>**] You weren't supposed to see that one. Just pretend you didn't. Ha! Okay, did you see that one!? I'm the best in my karate class.

Intermediate Client Statement 3

[**Stressed, <u>playing with dolls in a dollhouse</u>**] Mommy has to make dinner, feed the doggies, her other babies, and clean the house before she can talk to you, baby.

Intermediate Client Statement 4

[**Angry, <u>playing with toy animals</u>**] Ugh this always happens! Doggie is trying to lick the kitty, but doggie knows she's allergic!

Intermediate Client Statement 5

[**Anxious, <u>playing with stuffed animals</u>**] No! The bunny has to sit all by herself. She hurt herself when she fell from the tree so now she needs to rest while the other animals play.

Intermediate Client Statement 6

[**Confused, <u>moving quickly from playing with one toy to another</u>**] Umm . . . there are so many toys here, and I don't really know where to start.

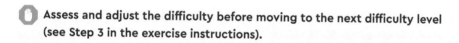 **Assess and adjust the difficulty before moving to the next difficulty level (see Step 3 in the exercise instructions).**

ADVANCED-LEVEL CLIENT STATEMENTS FOR EXERCISE 4
Advanced Client Statement 1
[**Worried, <u>playing with dolls</u>**] When Big Girl was a baby, she got to sit on her mommy's lap and eat sweet candy and chocolate . . . but now she's too big for that and little brother took her place.
Advanced Client Statement 2
[**Embarrassed, <u>playing with slime, throws slime into the garbage</u>**] This slime is way too sticky! I told you we needed to use different clay. This always happens. Let's just play a different game, okay!?
Advanced Client Statement 3
[**<u>Playing with animal figures</u>**] And then all the animals went to the party at the farm, but they told the elephant he couldn't come.
Advanced Client Statement 4
[**Frustrated, <u>playing with dolls</u>**] Ya know, when I was little, my real clothes fit on my baby stuffed animal. It was pretty cool. But oh my gosh, none of these small clothes fit on this big doll!
Advanced Client Statement 5
[**Anxious/irritable, <u>playing with princess figure and toy car</u>**] Oh no! The princess's dress got caught in the car door—we have to help her get out before it's too late! What if her dress rips or she falls out . . . or gets really hurt?!

🛑 **Assess and adjust the difficulty here (see Step 3 in the exercise instructions). If appropriate, follow the instructions to make the exercise even more challenging (see Appendix A).**

Example Therapist Responses: Observing and Describing Play

Remember: Trainees should attempt to improvise their own responses before reading the example responses. **Do not read the following responses verbatim unless you are having trouble coming up with your own responses!**

EXAMPLE RESPONSES TO BEGINNER-LEVEL CLIENT STATEMENTS FOR EXERCISE 4
Example Response to Beginner Client Statement 1
There's shooting! We've got to move quickly so we can stop them.
Example Response to Beginner Client Statement 2
Everyone is getting set up for the tea party—all in their places. Roger's having a hard time staying in his seat.
Example Response to Beginner Client Statement 3
You're taking your time, trying to figure out what's the next best move.
Example Response to Beginner Client Statement 4
Jeez! If you want the job done right, you have to do it yourself it seems.
Example Response to Beginner Client Statement 5
That horsey looks so hungry. I can't believe his friend didn't offer him any of the hay.

EXAMPLE RESPONSES TO INTERMEDIATE-LEVEL CLIENT STATEMENTS FOR EXERCISE 4
Example Response to Intermediate Client Statement 1
Well, I do love signing autographs for our fans but . . . you're left out of that somehow?
Example Response to Intermediate Client Statement 2
You want to make sure I focus on the good stuff. I *saw* that last kick! Wow!
Example Response to Intermediate Client Statement 3
So, the Mommy is so busy and has so many things to do. You're letting that baby know she has to wait. I see.
Example Response to Intermediate Client Statement 4
That doggie keeps doing the same thing even though she *knows* kitty might have an allergic reaction.
Example Response to Intermediate Client Statement 5
Ooooh, that little bunny got hurt and now she's all by herself? And she has to watch all those other animals who get to keep having fun?
Example Response to Intermediate Client Statement 6
You're trying out one thing after another and nothing feels quite right.

EXAMPLE RESPONSES TO ADVANCED-LEVEL CLIENT STATEMENTS FOR EXERCISE 4
Example Response to Advanced Client Statement 1
So, Big Girl is remembering all of those sweet memories and maybe also a little sad that she can't have those things now. She feels like she's been replaced by her little brother?
Example Response to Advanced Client Statement 2
It really doesn't feel good to have all that stickiness. It's so sticky you had to throw it out and we need to totally switch gears.
Example Response to Advanced Client Statement 3
Wow—those animals must be having fun at their party. And what about elephant?
Example Response to Advanced Client Statement 4
This big doll is too big for her clothes—it's like she's grown too big for those little kid things, huh?
Example Response to Advanced Client Statement 5
Oh no! Something really bad could happen if we don't act fast. How can we save her?

Empathic Validation

Preparations for Exercise 5

1. Read the instructions in Chapter 2.

2. Download the Deliberate Practice Reaction Form and the Deliberate Practice Diary Form at https://www.apa.org/pubs/books/deliberate-practice-child-adolescent-psychotherapy (see the "Clinician and Practitioner Resources" tab; also available in Appendixes A and B, respectively).

Skill Description

Skill Difficulty Level: Intermediate

Empathic validation is closely related to the earlier skill of naming feelings. It is an important therapist skill—not only to facilitate children's empathy but also because it enhances the therapeutic alliance and thus is associated with positive change in various ways. Carl Rogers (1980) defined *empathy* as "the therapist's sensitive ability and willingness to understand the client's thoughts, feelings, and struggles from the client's point of view" (p. 85). We can empathize with a patient's feelings, as well as their thoughts, fears, needs, and wishes or wants. Empathic validation is not approval; it is communicating that, good or bad, we can see how the child or parent would end up feeling a certain way and how those feelings or thoughts would underlie their actions. Empathic validation begins with finding something in what the child says that we can genuinely empathize with and sharing our understanding with them in a way that indicates "we get it"—while also not being taken over by it. The therapist recognizes and feels for a moment the patient's emotional state but is not overwhelmed or afraid of it. The second part of empathy is identifying the effect the feeling (or thought, need, or wish) has on the patient. An empathic statement puts the two of these together. To summarize, your goal is to find an aspect of the child's thoughts, feelings, or experience

https://doi.org/10.1037/0000288-007

that you can understand and identify the effect these have on them. The way you communicate empathy is also important and it takes practice to find the right tone—consider how to communicate with feeling, without being overly neutral or unemotional.

SKILL CRITERIA FOR EXERCISE 5
1. Identify an aspect of the child's thoughts, feelings, or experience you can understand.
2. Identify the (possible) impact of that thought, feeling, or experience on the child.
3. Communicate with compassion, care, and tenderness.

Examples of Therapists Using Empathic Validation

Note: Underlined text in brackets should be read aloud to provide context.

Example 1

CHILD CLIENT: [*Worried*] I wish I could talk to my friends in a big group, but it's just impossible—it's too scary to even think about.

THERAPIST: It must be really hard to feel silenced because of the fear you have. I can imagine that it gets a little lonely sometimes, wishing you felt more comfortable talking in the big group.

Example 2

CHILD CLIENT: [*Upset*] I wanted to play mom in House, but Julia said she was the mom. And she's always the mom! I never get to be the mom.

THERAPIST: It sounds like it doesn't feel fair, that you haven't gotten to be the mom yet. It's really frustrating when things are not fair, it can feel like we are powerless. Is that how you were feeling?

Example 3

CHILD CLIENT: [*Sad, <u>male client playing with doll</u>*] My dad doesn't let me play with this kind of stuff.

THERAPIST: So, there are rules about what you're allowed to play with when you're with your dad. It might feel kind of freeing to be able to play with dolls here, but maybe you're also a little unsure about whether it's okay?

INSTRUCTIONS FOR EXERCISE 5

Step 1: Role-Play and Feedback

- The client says the first beginner client statement, also reading aloud any <u>underlined text</u> in brackets to provide context. The therapist improvises a response based on the skill criteria.

- The trainer (or if not available, the client) provides brief feedback based on the skill criteria.

- The client then repeats the same statement, and the therapist again improvises a response. The trainer (or client) again provides brief feedback.

Step 2: Repeat

- Repeat Step 1 for all the statements in the current difficulty level (beginner, intermediate, or advanced).

Step 3: Assess and Adjust Difficulty

- The therapist completes the Deliberate Practice Reaction Form (see Appendix A) and decides whether to make the exercise easier or harder or to repeat the same difficulty level.

Step 4: Repeat for Approximately 15 Minutes

- Repeat Steps 1 to 3 for at least 15 minutes.
- The trainees then switch therapist and client roles and start over.

Now it's your turn! Follow Steps 1 and 2 from the instructions.

Remember: The goal of the role-play is for trainees to practice improvising responses to the client statements in a manner that (a) uses the skill criteria and (b) feels authentic for the trainee. **Example therapist responses for each client statement are provided at the end of this exercise. Trainees should attempt to improvise their own responses before reading the example responses.**

BEGINNER-LEVEL CLIENT STATEMENTS FOR EXERCISE 5
Beginner Client Statement 1
[**Worried**] I wish I could talk to my friends in a big group, but it's just impossible—it's too scary to even think about.
Beginner Client Statement 2
[**Upset, related to friend in school**] I wanted to play mom in House, but Julia said she was the mom. And she's always the mom! I never get to be the mom.
Beginner Client Statement 3
[**Sad, <u>male client playing with doll</u>**] My dad doesn't let me play with this kind of stuff.
Beginner Client Statement 4
[**Frustrated**] It's so annoying. My mom basically ignores everything I say unless it relates to schoolwork, since that's all she cares about.
Beginner Client Statement 5
[**Forceful, <u>male client playing with animals</u>**] Your pig isn't invited to the party, sorry not sorry! Only girl animals are allowed.

 **Assess and adjust the difficulty before moving to the next difficulty level (see Step 3 in the exercise instructions).**

INTERMEDIATE-LEVEL CLIENT STATEMENTS FOR EXERCISE 5
Intermediate Client Statement 1
[**Worried**] Yeah, I just don't like texting my friends first because what if they don't respond? Then I'll know for sure they don't like me anymore.
Intermediate Client Statement 2
[**Stressed, <u>playing with dolls in a dollhouse</u>**] Mommy has to make dinner, feed the doggies, her other babies, and clean the house before she can talk to you, baby.
Intermediate Client Statement 3
[**Anxious, irritable**] I just hate the sound of other people chewing their food, so that's why I sit in my room during dinner and other meals. It freaks me out because it's so disgusting. I can't see why that's such a big deal to everyone.
Intermediate Client Statement 4
[**Angry**] No! This is my playroom, so the rule is that other kids aren't allowed to draw on the whiteboard unless they ask me first.
Intermediate Client Statement 5
[**Confused, <u>while moving quickly from playing with one toy to another</u>**] Umm nope, I don't know why I'm here. My mom said if I come then I get to eat ice cream after dinner tonight.

🛑 **Assess and adjust the difficulty before moving to the next difficulty level (see Step 3 in the exercise instructions).**

ADVANCED-LEVEL CLIENT STATEMENTS FOR EXERCISE 5
Advanced Client Statement 1
[**Embarrassed**] I don't want to tell you this since it's really awkward, so you can't ask me any questions after, okay? But . . . last night I had an accident in my bed after a really bad dream.
Advanced Client Statement 2
[**Anger, directed at parents**] You don't understand. My parents are actually the worst. They track my location 24/7 and never let me stay out with my friends.
Advanced Client Statement 3
[**Angry, the client's <u>father did not show up</u>**] The asshole, he didn't show up. As usual. He doesn't give a shit.
Advanced Client Statement 4
[**Anxious**] I don't really know what to talk about today. Everything is fine.
Advanced Client Statement 5
[**Hopeless**] I don't want to be here. I already told you that therapy won't work for me.
Advanced Client Statement 6
[**Anxious, tearful**] Every time you talk to me about practicing deep breathing, I can't stop thinking about the boy who died over the summer when the police held him in a choke hold. He lived in my neighborhood.

⬛ **Assess and adjust the difficulty here (see Step 3 in the exercise instructions). If appropriate, follow the instructions to make the exercise even more challenging (see Appendix A).**

Example Therapist Responses: Empathic Validation

Remember: Trainees should attempt to improvise their own responses before reading the example responses. **Do not read the following responses verbatim unless you are having trouble coming up with your own responses!**

EXAMPLE RESPONSES TO BEGINNER-LEVEL CLIENT STATEMENTS FOR EXERCISE 5
Example Response to Beginner Client Statement 1
I can understand how that would feel really scary and overwhelming. (Criterion 1) You probably have things you want to share but it feels like you can't. (Criterion 2)
Example Response to Beginner Client Statement 2
It sounds like it doesn't feel fair, that you haven't gotten to be the mom yet. It's really frustrating when things are not fair (Criteria 1 and 3), it can feel like we are powerless. (Criterion 2) Is that how you were feeling?
Example Response to Beginner Client Statement 3
That's hard to feel like you're limited in what you can play with at home. (Criteria 1 and 3) How does it feel to be able to play with dolls here? (Criterion 2)
Example Response to Beginner Client Statement 4
There's so much pressure on you to do well in school and it sounds like you have a lot of other things you'd like your mom to understand and know about you. (Criteria 1 and 3) I wonder if it makes you feel a little unseen or not fully known by your mom. (Criterion 2)
Example Response to Beginner Client Statement 5
So it's really important that the party be just for girls. Boy animals can't come in. (Criterion 1) Maybe they would mess it up? (Criteria 2 and 3)

EXAMPLE RESPONSES TO INTERMEDIATE-LEVEL CLIENT STATEMENTS FOR EXERCISE 5
Example Response to Intermediate Client Statement 1
It's really like taking a risk for you to reach out to them first. (Criterion 1) You feel so unsure about whether they'll respond, but then you wind up kind of isolated anyway. (Criteria 2 and 3)
Example Response to Intermediate Client Statement 2
[**Speaking to the baby doll**] Mommy is so busy! It's like she doesn't even have time for you baby. (Criterion 1) I might feel kind of lonely and impatient having to wait all this time. (Criteria 2 and 3)
Example Response to Intermediate Client Statement 3
It feels like everyone is trying to force you to do something that makes you really freaked out. (Criterion 1) And it's hard to understand why they would want you to come eat with them, especially since it's so disgusting to you. (Criteria 2 and 3)
Example Response to Intermediate Client Statement 4
These other kids are not following your rules. (Criterion 1) You really want to be the boss of this space, and it doesn't feel good to think about other people coming in here and messing things up. (Criteria 2 and 3)
Example Response to Intermediate Client Statement 5
Well, that ice cream sounds excellent. But it must feel strange to be coming here and not know why. (Criteria 2 and 3)

EXAMPLE RESPONSES TO ADVANCED-LEVEL CLIENT STATEMENTS FOR EXERCISE 5
Example Response to Advanced Client Statement 1
It took some courage to share this with me. (Criterion 1) It sounds like you want me to know about it, but we should go at your pace, especially if you're feeling uneasy about talking about it. (Criteria 2 and 3)
Example Response to Advanced Client Statement 2
It's so hard to feel like you have no freedom or independence. (Criterion 1) I can imagine that having your location tracked feels kind of oppressive. (Criteria 2 and 3)
Example Response to Advanced Client Statement 3
I imagine waiting for him caused a lot of anger to build (Criterion 1), and I can see how him not showing would lead you to feel like he doesn't care about you. (Criteria 2 and 3)
Example Response to Advanced Client Statement 4
Everything is fine. I'm wondering what I hear in your voice—it sounds like you're a little unsure? Or maybe there is something wrong but you're not sure you want to talk about it? (Criterion 1) Sometimes when everything feels a bit confusing or complicated, it can be hard to even put it into words. Maybe it feels safer to just keep it inside. (Criteria 2 and 3)
Example Response to Advanced Client Statement 5
Things have been really rough for you lately. (Criterion 1) It must be hard to have any hope that they could improve or that us talking together here could help. (Criteria 2 and 3)
Example Response to Advanced Client Statement 6
Wow—okay. That makes a lot of sense. (Criterion 3) So when I'm talking about something that's supposed to be relaxing, it's actually really upsetting. (Criteria 2 and 3)

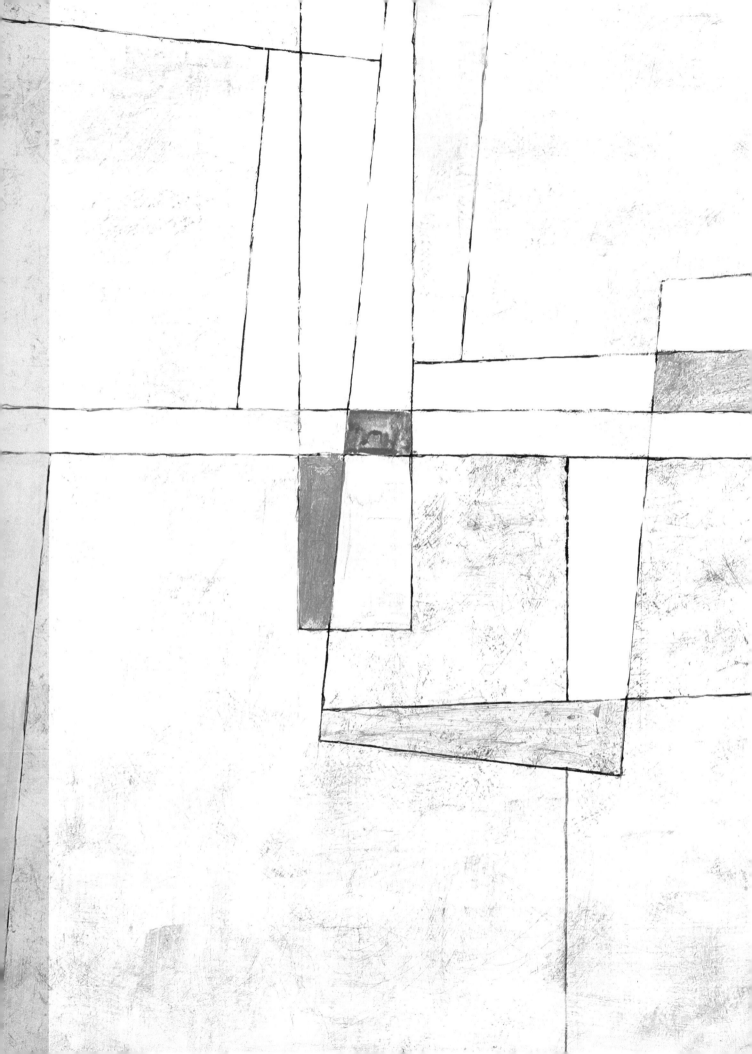

Elaborating Play

Preparations for Exercise 6

1. Read the instructions in Chapter 2.

2. Download the Deliberate Practice Reaction Form and the Deliberate Practice Diary Form at https://www.apa.org/pubs/books/deliberate-practice-child-adolescent-psychotherapy (see the "Clinician and Practitioner Resources" tab; also available in Appendixes A and B, respectively).

Skill Description

Skill Difficulty Level: Intermediate

In Exercise 4, you worked on describing play, which is an entry point into play that is useful for therapists and parents. The next step in child therapy is to help children to make use of play by facilitating elaboration of play and play narratives. For example, research shows that the ability to complete the narratives in play predicts children's internalizing and externalizing symptoms 3 years later in both children who have experienced sexual abuse and those who have not (Normandin et al., 2021).

Therapists elaborate children's play by integrating the skills of interest and curiosity and naming feelings into the arena of play. Importantly, this skill is distinct from simply observing and describing play, which is its own important skill. When therapists elaborate on play, they are bringing themselves into the play. Therapists can elaborate play in a number of ways: They can introduce new characters or a plot twist in the play, they can expand on the emotions in the play, or they can pick up on a specific aspect of the emotions, themes, or representations of relationships and inquire about them. How the therapist elaborates play will depend on how they conceptualize the child's problems or difficulties.

https://doi.org/10.1037/0000288-008

SKILL CRITERIA FOR EXERCISE 6

1. Identifies a core emotional or relational theme.
2. Introduces a character, emotion, plot twist, or question that would likely prompt the child to think and expand the narrative in the play.
3. Does not step outside of the play.

Examples of Therapists Using Skill of Elaborating Play

Note: Underlined text in brackets should be read aloud to provide context.

Example 1

CHILD CLIENT: [*Calm, playing with doll figures—child of cisgender, heterosexual parents*] They have to go to the hospital—the mommy is about to have the baby. Here, she is in the hospital now, and the doctor is with her.

THERAPIST: Is she all alone in the hospital? Where is daddy?

Example 2

CHILD CLIENT: [*Anxious, playing basketball*] Okay, I am going to see if I can make it from here. [*Shoots and misses, appears to be getting frustrated*] It's your turn.

THERAPIST: [*Playfully makes worst shot*] Okay, hmm, I think maybe instead of trying to make a perfect shot, I am going to try to do my worst shot possible. Wanna try making your worst shot possible?

Example 3

CHILD CLIENT: [*Focused, pretending to be Bloxburg in Roblox, an online computer game where you build your own house*] Okay, I have a lot of work to do building my house, so you can get started on yours.

THERAPIST: Hmm, so I have to figure out how to build my house all by myself. I wonder if I am going to be able to figure it out all alone.

INSTRUCTIONS FOR EXERCISE 6

Step 1: Role-Play and Feedback

- The client says the first beginner client statement, also reading aloud any <u>underlined text</u> in brackets to provide context. The therapist improvises a response based on the skill criteria.

- The trainer (or if not available, the client) provides brief feedback based on the skill criteria.

- The client then repeats the same statement, and the therapist again improvises a response. The trainer (or client) again provides brief feedback.

Step 2: Repeat

- Repeat Step 1 for all the statements in the current difficulty level (beginner, intermediate, or advanced).

Step 3: Assess and Adjust Difficulty

- The therapist completes the Deliberate Practice Reaction Form (see Appendix A) and decides whether to make the exercise easier or harder or to repeat the same difficulty level.

Step 4: Repeat for Approximately 15 Minutes

- Repeat Steps 1 to 3 for at least 15 minutes.
- The trainees then switch therapist and client roles and start over.

Now it's your turn! Follow Steps 1 and 2 from the instructions.

Remember: The goal of the role-play is for trainees to practice improvising responses to the client statements in a manner that (a) uses the skill criteria and (b) feels authentic for the trainee. **Example therapist responses for each client statement are provided at the end of this exercise. Trainees should attempt to improvise their own responses before reading the example responses.**

BEGINNER-LEVEL CLIENT STATEMENTS FOR EXERCISE 6
Beginner Client Statement 1
[Calm, <u>playing with doll figures—child of cisgender, heterosexual parents</u>] They have to go to the hospital—the mommy is about to have the baby. Here she is in the hospital now, and the doctor is with her.
Beginner Client Statement 2
[Anxious, <u>playing basketball</u>] Okay, I am going to see if I can make it from here. [<u>Shoots and misses, appears to be getting frustrated</u>] It's your turn.
Beginner Client Statement 3
[Focused, <u>pretending to b e Bloxburg in Roblox, an online computer game where you build your own house</u>] Okay, I have a lot of work to do building my house, so you can get started on yours.
Beginner Client Statement 4
[Optimistic, <u>building a tower with blocks</u>] It's easy to build! Don't worry, I got this.
Beginner Client Statement 5
[Sad, <u>playing with toy animals</u>] Where did my horse's shirt thingy go? I think your pig took it by accident.
Beginner Client Statement 6
[Stressed/frustrated, <u>playing with superhero toys</u>] Superman keeps flying but then crashes into the ground!

 **Assess and adjust the difficulty before moving to the next difficulty level (see Step 3 in the exercise instructions).**

INTERMEDIATE-LEVEL CLIENT STATEMENTS FOR EXERCISE 6
Intermediate Client Statement 1
[**Hopeless, playing with a dollhouse**] We'll never be able to fit all of this stuff inside this tiny, tiny house. There's just too much furniture. It will never work.
Intermediate Client Statement 2
[**Worried, in a play kitchen**] My boss is going to be so mad at me if I don't flip the pancake exactly right! It needs to be perfectly golden brown.
Intermediate Client Statement 3
[**Dismissive, falls while attempting to show you high kicks**] Sometimes I fall at karate practice too, but it's no big deal.
Intermediate Client Statement 4
[**Stressed, speaking on behalf of a doll**] Oh no! I left the stove on and now everything is burnt! I can't do anything right at this restaurant.
Intermediate Client Statement 5
[**Angry, throwing toys against the wall**] The bad guy broke Superman's heels and now he can't walk! The bad guy has to pay for what he did.
Intermediate Client Statement 6
[**Anxious**] Shhh!! You have to be quiet since Superman is sleeping and he'll get attacked if we wake him up.
Intermediate Client Statement 7
[**Confused, while moving quickly from playing with one toy to another**] Look how hard I can smash the ducky on the floor! Oh yay, I just found Iron Man under the firetruck.

Assess and adjust the difficulty before moving to the next difficulty level (see Step 3 in the exercise instructions).

ADVANCED-LEVEL CLIENT STATEMENTS FOR EXERCISE 6
Advanced Client Statement 1
[**Worried, <u>playing with superhero toys</u>**] Spider-Man, you're being so bad!
Advanced Client Statement 2
[**Angry, <u>throws a toy at the ground</u>**] Now you have to give away your powers to Ducky because you're being a bad guy.
Advanced Client Statement 3
[**Frustrated, <u>playing with cars</u>**] Vroom, vroom, vroom here comes the ultra-fast yellow car—watch out! Ugh! Oh no, the engine is broken again—why does this happen every single time?!
Advanced Client Statement 4
[**Embarrassed**] My mommy said that if I work really hard at being good then I get to bring my own doll into session next time. So please, please don't tell mommy that I accidentally drew on the walls today, I promise I'll be good starting right now.
Advanced Client Statement 5
[**Anxious, <u>playing with toys while addressing a video camera in playroom</u>**] Umm, I'm going to lock away the animals and hide them so that no one else can find them using the video camera over there. We just have to remember the hiding place, okay?
Advanced Client Statement 6
[**Anxious, <u>cleaning up toys</u>**] We have to make it to 1,000 points! I'll put away the cars, and you put away all the other toys, okay!? C'mon go faster or else we can't play cars ever again!
Advanced Client Statement 7
[**Angry, <u>speaking for an action figure</u>**] No! We don't want to stop playing yet! [**Then sweetly**] Please . . . can we just have 5 more minutes?

🛑 **Assess and adjust the difficulty here (see Step 3 in the exercise instructions). If appropriate, follow the instructions to make the exercise even more challenging (see Appendix A).**

Example Therapist Responses: Elaborating Play

Remember: Trainees should attempt to improvise their own responses before reading the example responses. **Do not read the following responses verbatim unless you are having trouble coming up with your own responses!**

EXAMPLE RESPONSES TO BEGINNER-LEVEL CLIENT STATEMENTS FOR EXERCISE 6
Example Response to Beginner Client Statement 1
Oh, wow. This is such a big day! I wonder how the big sister at home is feeling right now.
Example Response to Beginner Client Statement 2
That was a rough one! I'm going to try and shoot for the spot you hit. Not sure I'll make it.
Example Response to Beginner Client Statement 3
You're so busy and also really good at this. If I need some help, can I ask you?
Example Response to Beginner Client Statement 4
You're the boss of those blocks. That's for sure. What's the tower going to be used for?
Example Response to Beginner Client Statement 5
This pig is always up to something! Your poor horse. How is your horse feeling without his shirt thing?
Example Response to Beginner Client Statement 6
He can't seem to stay in flight. What's happened to his superhero powers today?

EXAMPLE RESPONSES TO INTERMEDIATE-LEVEL CLIENT STATEMENTS FOR EXERCISE 6
Example Response to Intermediate Client Statement 1
Everything is so crowded. Such a tiny house somehow wound up with so much furniture. How does that even happen?
Example Response to Intermediate Client Statement 2
What a tough boss you have! It must be hard to cook well under all that pressure. What happens when your boss gets mad at you?
Example Response to Intermediate Client Statement 3
And you just took a tumble here too. I don't know anything about karate. I'd love to learn some moves.
Example Response to Intermediate Client Statement 4
[**Speaking to doll**] What a day you're having! You're not alone here today. Can we work together to clean this up and make something really yummy?
Example Response to Intermediate Client Statement 5
[**Picks up bad guy character, speaking for bad guy**] I keep hurting you and now I have to pay! I do feel a little bad for breaking your heels. I've got this healing potion in my cape—you want it?
Example Response to Intermediate Client Statement 6
[**Whispering**] We have to be super careful. It sounds so dangerous for him to wake up. Who is going to come attack him and why?
Example Response to Intermediate Client Statement 7
There's so much going on here. You found Iron Man, and even before that, you were really showing your strength.

EXAMPLE RESPONSES TO ADVANCED-LEVEL CLIENT STATEMENTS FOR EXERCISE 6
Example Response to Advanced Client Statement 1
[**Voicing Spider-Man's response**] I am feeling kind of bad about myself actually. What did I do that was so bad?
Example Response to Advanced Client Statement 2
Man, being the bad guy really stinks! I don't want to give up my powers, but I guess I have to. Ducky, what are you going to do with all these superpowers?
Example Response to Advanced Client Statement 3
Every time! Even with the ultra-fast one. What's going on with these engines? Should we get some pit bosses in here to figure out what's going wrong?
Example Response to Advanced Client Statement 4
You're right that it was an accident when you made that mark on the wall. And I can see how nervous you're feeling about getting in trouble with Mom. What if you were the mommy and someone told you your doll had drawn on the wall by accident? Would your doll get in trouble?
Example Response to Advanced Client Statement 5
Yeah, we can work together to remember where we put them. Who are we hiding them from?
Example Response to Advanced Client Statement 6
Gosh—there's so much pressure! I don't know if I'm going to make it. What if I fall behind? I'd feel so sad to never, ever be able to play cars again.
Example Response to Advanced Client Statement 7
[**Picking up another action figure, speaking in character's voice**] You really want to stay in this playroom. Maybe it feels hard to say goodbye.

Exploring Identity— Multicultural Orientation

Preparations for Exercise 7

1. Read the instructions in Chapter 2.

2. Download the Deliberate Practice Reaction Form and the Deliberate Practice Diary Form at https://www.apa.org/pubs/books/deliberate-practice-child-adolescent-psychotherapy (see the "Clinician and Practitioner Resources" tab; also available in Appendixes A and B, respectively).

Skill Description

Skill Difficulty Level: Intermediate

Exploring identity is central to work with children and adolescents, as they are in the process of developing their sense of self and making meaning of their social environments. There are numerous aspects of identity, including age, disability status, religion, race, ethnicity, socioeconomic status, sexual orientation, gender, indigenous heritage, national origin, and other aspects of the self. We have found the multicultural orientation framework helpful in our approach to working with clients. *Multicultural orientation* (Davis et al., 2018) refers to a way of understanding and relating to clients' cultural identities. It is a lifelong process that includes three central components: (a) cultural humility, remaining other-oriented and maintaining a lifelong stance of learning and self-reflection; (b) cultural opportunities, inquiring and initiating conversations that facilitate exploration of the client's identity; and (c) cultural comfort, feeling at ease, calm, and relaxed with clients whose backgrounds are different from the therapist's. These elements of a multicultural orientation represent the three essential skill criteria that therapist responses should exhibit.

Exploring identity with young people goes beyond asking them about their identities. As therapists, it is important to listen for what aspects of identity are most salient

https://doi.org/10.1037/0000288-009

Deliberate Practice in Child and Adolescent Psychotherapy, by J. Bate, T. A. Prout, T. Rousmaniere, and A. Vaz

for the child at any given moment. Instead of labeling or making assumptions about identities, we help children and adolescents put words to how they experience their identities—that is, what it is like for them to hold certain identities or what aspects of their identity mean to them. Exploration of identity can include inquiries about what how their identities intersect, and how they have been impacted by current events. A developmental lens is also crucial, recognizing that how children see themselves is likely to change over time. Therapists can help children reflect on how their identities have developed.

There is no one way to explore identities with young people. The most important skill as a therapist is to show that you are comfortable talking about various forms of identity and that you want to understand their experiences. While it is impossible to avoid stereotypes and biases, therapists must be aware of the assumptions they may be inclined to make and make a concerted effort to be open and curious. At times, therapists may find it helpful to tell children and adolescents that they ask questions because they do not want to make any assumptions about their experience.

Finally, therapists must be aware of their own identities, both those that may be visible to a patient (e.g., skin color) and those that are less or not visible (e.g., religion, socio-economic status). The use of self-disclosure around one's own identities as a therapist is approached differently depending on the orientation of the therapy and characteristics of the patient. All therapists, though, should be mindful of how their patients may perceive them and how the therapeutic relationship may be shaped by their identity in relation to the patient's identity (e.g., a trans patient with a cisgender therapist or an Indigenous patient with a White therapist). Being able to invite discussion (without forcing it) is the foundation of exploring identity in the therapeutic relationship.

SKILL CRITERIA FOR EXERCISE 7

1. Communicate genuine interest and openness to client's perspective (cultural humility).
2. Inquire about cultural implications of incident using a tentative/hypothesizing tone (cultural opportunities).
3. Nonverbal: Appear grounded and comfortable (cultural comfort).

Examples of Exploring Identity—Multicultural Orientation

Note: <u>Underlined text</u> in brackets should be read aloud to provide context.

Example 1

CHILD CLIENT: [*Anxious*] I don't love school. I don't really fit in, you know? I'm not like everyone else.

THERAPIST: I'd like to hear more about that. What do you feel sets you apart from the other kids in your school?

Example 2

CHILD CLIENT: [*Anxious, <u>playing basketball, no eye contact</u>*] People always ask me if I play basketball . . . I guess they just assume since I'm really tall that I'm athletic.

THERAPIST: Hmmm . . . that's a pretty big assumption. It must be hard to have people make snap judgments about who you are based on a simple external characteristic. I'd like to know more about what you think are your most important characteristics. What do you wish people would know and understand about you?

Example 3

CHILD CLIENT: [*Confident*] Look, I'm a cis, straight, White dude. I've got no right to complain about my issues.

THERAPIST: Those are important parts of your identity. I'm curious about how being cis, straight, and White become things that silence you or don't allow you to share what you're struggling with.

INSTRUCTIONS FOR EXERCISE 7

Step 1: Role-Play and Feedback

- The client says the first beginner client statement, also reading aloud any <u>underlined text</u> in brackets to provide context. The therapist improvises a response based on the skill criteria.

- The trainer (or, if not available, the client) provides brief feedback based on the skill criteria.

- The client then repeats the same statement, and the therapist again improvises a response. The trainer (or client) again provides brief feedback.

Step 2: Repeat

- Repeat Step 1 for all the statements in the current difficulty level (beginner, intermediate, or advanced).

Step 3: Assess and Adjust Difficulty

- The therapist completes the Deliberate Practice Reaction Form (see Appendix A) and decides whether to make the exercise easier or harder or to repeat the same difficulty level.

Step 4: Repeat for Approximately 15 Minutes

- Repeat Steps 1 to 3 for at least 15 minutes.
- The trainees then switch therapist and client roles and start over.

Now it's your turn! Follow Steps 1 and 2 from the instructions.

Remember: The goal of the role-play is for trainees to practice improvising responses to the client statements in a manner that (a) uses the skill criteria and (b) feels authentic for the trainee. **Example therapist responses for each client statement are provided at the end of this exercise. Trainees should attempt to improvise their own responses before reading the example responses.**

BEGINNER-LEVEL CLIENT STATEMENTS FOR EXERCISE 7
Beginner Client Statement 1
[**Anxious**] I don't love school. I don't really fit in, you know? I'm not like everyone else.
Beginner Client Statement 2
[**Anxious, <u>playing basketball, no eye contact</u>**] People always ask me if I play basketball . . . I guess they just assume since I'm really tall that I'm athletic.
Beginner Client Statement 3
[**Confident**] Look, I'm a cis, straight, White dude. I've got no right to complain about my issues.
Beginner Client Statement 4
[**Excited, <u>playing with Star Wars toys</u>**] Darth Vader! Bam! He's Black like my daddy.
Beginner Client Statement 5
[**Matter-of-factly**] My parents are, like, typical Asian parents, I think. Education is really important to them.
Beginner Client Statement 6
[**Uncertain**] I don't know how to describe my sexual identity. Not straight? I guess I'd say bisexual. But I really don't want my parents to know that.
Beginner Client Statement 7
[**Sad**] There's a word in my language that could perfectly express what I'm feeling. I don't know how to say it in English.
Beginner Client Statement 8
[**Cheerfully**] I don't even need to wear glasses. I started wearing these after a kid on my block kept making fun of me for my small eyes. The glasses make my eyes look bigger, which makes my life easier.
Beginner Client Statement 9
[**Anxious**] There are things I can't talk about with you because of my parents' undocumented status in this country. We're not even allowed to be here.

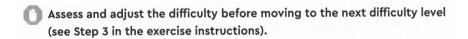 **Assess and adjust the difficulty before moving to the next difficulty level (see Step 3 in the exercise instructions).**

INTERMEDIATE-LEVEL CLIENT STATEMENTS FOR EXERCISE 7
Intermediate Client Statement 1
[**Optimistic**] I always hear my brother using derogatory slurs with his friends . . . but it's whatever—no big deal!
Intermediate Client Statement 2
[**Hopeless**] Why can't people just leave me alone about this? I'm tired of coming out to new therapists every year.
Intermediate Client Statement 3
[**Sad**] I heard some kids after school making fun of my dad's accent.
Intermediate Client Statement 4
[**Worried**] You can't tell my parents that I'm bisexual. They're already really strict, and I just don't want to give them another reason to punish me.
Intermediate Client Statement 5
[**Stressed**] I mean my friends are okay. It's just annoying that because I'm Hispanic they always ask me if a word or phrase is offensive or not . . . like, I don't know!
Intermediate Client Statement 6
[**Dismissive**] Yeah, I'm a guy who's into girls, with my ears pierced, and occasionally like to wear eye shadow sometimes . . . what's the big deal?
Intermediate Client Statement 7
[**Cheerful, laughing**] A poor kid like me—everyone knows I'm not going to make it.
Intermediate Client Statement 8
[**Anxious**] When I feel anxious, I just realize I don't have to worry because the world is nothingness. I'm an atheist. You're not religious, are you?

🛑 **Assess and adjust the difficulty before moving to the next difficulty level (see Step 3 in the exercise instructions).**

ADVANCED-LEVEL CLIENT STATEMENTS FOR EXERCISE 7
Advanced Client Statement 1
[**Excited**] I saved my allowance for weeks and finally got this awesome skin-whitening cream a few weeks ago. Can you tell a difference?
Advanced Client Statement 2
[**Sad**] I'm so hungry. I've been throwing my lunch out so I don't have to listen to kids complaining about how it smells.
Advanced Client Statement 3
[**Angry**] I really don't want to come here. There's no way you can understand what it's like to be me.
Advanced Client Statement 4
[**Worried, <u>playing with superhero toys</u>**] Spider-Man is a boy! That means he *has* to like cars and trains and superheroes; he can't be playing with your girl dolly.
Advanced Client Statement 5
[**Frustrated**] OMG. How hard is it to use correct pronouns for people?! I even have they/them in my Zoom name! I'm never speaking to my teacher again, she's the worst.
Advanced Client Statement 6
[**Annoyed**] I don't get why people say "Black Lives Matter" when all lives matter.
Advanced Client Statement 7
[**Embarrassed**] Well I got a tattoo that's super meaningful to me, but I can't tell you where or what it means. I'm scared you'll have to tell my parents and they would totally ground me for this.
Advanced Client Statement 8
[**Anxious**] Umm, I'm not sure how to respond to these questions about gender and stuff. I mean I'm attracted to the individual, not the gender or label of the person. It's hard to explain. But yeah, you can really use any pronouns with me. I don't really care.
Advanced Client Statement 9
[**Dismissive**] I don't think it matters what race you are. Like the teachers always want to talk about race and I'm like, colorblind. It just doesn't matter to me.

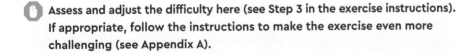 **Assess and adjust the difficulty here (see Step 3 in the exercise instructions). If appropriate, follow the instructions to make the exercise even more challenging (see Appendix A).**

Example Therapist Responses: Exploring Identity—Multicultural Orientation

Remember: Trainees should attempt to improvise their own responses before reading the example responses. **Do not read the following responses verbatim unless you are having trouble coming up with your own responses!**

EXAMPLE RESPONSES TO BEGINNER-LEVEL CLIENT STATEMENTS FOR EXERCISE 7
Example Response to Beginner Client Statement 1
I'd like to hear more about that. (Criterion 1) What do you feel like sets you apart from the other kids in your school? (Criterion 2)
Example Response to Beginner Client Statement 2
Hmmm . . . that's a pretty big assumption. It must be hard to have people make snap judgments about who you are based on a simple external characteristic. I'd like to know more about what you think are your most important characteristics. (Criterion 1) What do you wish people would know and understand about you? (Criterion 2)
Example Response to Beginner Client Statement 3
Those are important parts of your identity. (Criterion 1) I'm curious about how being cis, straight, and White become things that silence you or don't allow you to share what you're struggling with. (Criterion 2)
Example Response to Beginner Client Statement 4
He *is* Black just like your daddy. And also like you? (Criteria 1 and 2)
Example Response to Beginner Client Statement 5
Yeah, people do say that about Asian parents. I'm interested in knowing what yours are like specifically, and what your relationship with them is like. (Criterion 1) How do you understand the emphasis they put on education, like, where do you think that comes from or what does it mean in your family? (Criterion 2)
Example Response to Beginner Client Statement 6
I can't quite tell if your uncertainty is because you are still figuring it out or whether you are feeling hesitant to share that with me because you aren't sure how I'll react. (Criterion 1) How do you imagine your parents would react? (Criterion 2)
Example Response to Beginner Client Statement 7
I can imagine it's hard to fully communicate your experience to me in a language that is not the one you grew up with. (Criterion 1) What would it be like to tell me the word in your native language? (Criterion 2)
Alternative:
I can imagine it's hard to fully communicate your experience to me in a language that is not the one you grew up with. (Criterion 1) What is it like for you to shift back and forth between languages? (Criterion 2)
Example Response to Beginner Client Statement 8
So you found a way to protect yourself from being made fun of. (Criterion 1) Can you tell me more about what kids on your block were saying and how you felt about it? (Criterion 2)
Example Response to Beginner Client Statement 9
I can hear how worried you are. (Criterion 1) Being undocumented makes the stakes really high for you and your parents. I'd like to know more about what that's been like for you (Criterion 2), but first, maybe I can tell you a little about confidentiality here, so you can feel a bit safer?

EXAMPLE RESPONSES TO INTERMEDIATE-LEVEL CLIENT STATEMENTS FOR EXERCISE 7

Example Response to Intermediate Client Statement 1

So, on the one hand it's no big deal. But it's on your mind . . . you're mentioning it. (Criterion 1) What is it like for you when he says those things? (Criterion 2)

Example Response to Intermediate Client Statement 2

There's a kind of burden with having to talk about this over and over again. (Criterion 1) Like other people—maybe even me—are implying this is the main characteristic that defines you? (Criterion 2)

Example Response to Intermediate Client Statement 3

Wow. That must have been really painful to hear. (Criterion 1) Can you tell me more? (Criterion 2)

Example Response to Intermediate Client Statement 4

I'm glad you shared this with me and that you feel safe enough to do so. I definitely will not tell your parents this—that is for whenever you are ready, even if that is years from now. It must be really hard to have to hide parts of yourself away. (Criterion 1) Can you tell me more about the process of coming out to yourself? (Criterion 2)

Example Response to Intermediate Client Statement 5

Yeah, so they're looking to you to be the voice of all people of color? (Criterion 1) How do you feel when they turn to you with these questions? (Criterion 2)

Example Response to Intermediate Client Statement 6

What *is* the big deal? I'd like to hear more about the people in your life who do see it as a big deal. (Criterion 1) What is that like for you? (Criterion 2)

Example Response to Intermediate Client Statement 7

I can't help but notice you're laughing as you say that. (Criterion 1) There's something very sad in what you said—it's like you feel your story has already been written. What led you to feel that way? (Criterion 2)

Example Response to Intermediate Client Statement 8

I'd like to pause first before answering that question. It sounds like atheism is something that is helpful and meaningful to you, and I'd like to understand it more. (Criterion 1) I'm also curious about how my sharing my own religious and spiritual identity might impact our work and your sense of being understood here. (Criterion 2)

EXAMPLE RESPONSES TO ADVANCED-LEVEL CLIENT STATEMENTS FOR EXERCISE 7
Example Response to Advanced Client Statement 1
I'm not sure I can. But I am very curious about this. It sounds like you worked really hard to be able to buy this cream. (Criterion 1) What prompted you to want to lighten your skin? (Criterion 2)
Example Response to Advanced Client Statement 2
The pressures at school must be really intense. You're going hungry just to avoid their complaining. That must be so hard. (Criterion 1) What have the kids been saying? (Criterion 2)
Example Response to Advanced Client Statement 3
You know, in many ways you're right. I can't fully understand what it's like being you. But I would like to try and also help empower you to understand yourself. (Criterion 1) Can we talk about the things that you think might get in the way of me being able to understand? (Criterion 2)
Example Response to Advanced Client Statement 4
Wow! There are some serious rules for Spider-Man. (Criterion 1) What would happen if he *did* play with the girl dolly? What would his superhero buddies think? (Criterion 2)
Example Response to Advanced Client Statement 5
Your teacher keeps screwing up your pronouns. That must be so frustrating. (Criterion 1) Can you tell me more about what it feels like for you when she misgenders you? (Criterion 2)
Example Response to Advanced Client Statement 6
Well, there are some reasons I can try to explain, if that would be helpful. (Criterion 1) But first, I wonder what it feels like to you when people say Black Lives Matter? It sounds like maybe you feel they are saying that you don't matter? (Criterion 2)
Example Response to Advanced Client Statement 7
I have to admit, now I'm super curious, especially because you said it's so meaningful to you. (Criterion 1) To be clear, tattoos are not something I would tell your parents about. If you feel comfortable telling me about it, I'd love to hear more. (Criterion 2)
Example Response to Advanced Client Statement 8
It seems like there's a lot of flexibility for you, around who you're attracted to. I want to be sensitive to your needs and your identity. (Criterion 1) I'm not sure if you really don't care about pronouns or maybe you're not sure if it's okay to ask me to use the ones you feel most comfortable with. (Criterion 2)
Example Response to Advanced Client Statement 9
It seems teachers and lots of other people are talking more about race and how it is an important part of identity. But, for you, it feels less central. (Criterion 1) Can you tell me more about that? (Criterion 2)

Self-Disclosure

Preparations for Exercise 8

1. Read the instructions in Chapter 2.

2. Download the Deliberate Practice Reaction Form and the Deliberate Practice Diary Form at https://www.apa.org/pubs/books/deliberate-practice-child-adolescent-psychotherapy (see the "Clinician and Practitioner Resources" tab; also available in Appendixes A and B, respectively).

Skill Description

Skill Difficulty Level: Intermediate

When therapists think about self-disclosure, they often imagine the patient asking them a personal question about themselves and how they would answer. There are, however, multiple forms of self-disclosure. Disclosing personal information about yourself and/or your background is one type of self-disclosure. Some personal disclosures are overt (e.g., responding to a question, informing the patient of an upcoming leave or vacation) and others are more subtle or indirect (e.g., your appearance, office decor, noise from a family member in the background during a virtual session). Children's questions provide helpful information about what is important to them and what is going through their minds. It is usually helpful to validate the child's interest and curiosity, while inviting them to elaborate on the thoughts and feelings that were underlying the question. Sometimes therapists will not answer personal questions because even if the patient is curious and wants to know, knowing about the therapist may limit opportunities for exploration and also make the patient more vulnerable to feeling judged in the future. For example, if a child asks, "Were you ever afraid of the dark?" it may not be advisable to simply respond, "No, I was never afraid of the dark." Instead, you might consider ways to help the client open up about their fears (e.g., "The dark can be really

https://doi.org/10.1037/0000288-010

scary, especially when you're a kid. How do you feel when you're in the dark?" or "I think I was when I was younger. What's it like for you when the lights are out?") In some cases, personal disclosures can facilitate the therapeutic process. For example, in the case of LGBTQIA+ children and adolescents, therapist self-disclosure about their own queer identity or allyship may be particularly beneficial.

Disclosing your experience, thoughts, or feelings in the moment is another form of self-disclosure. This type of disclosure might include (a) saying how you feel during a particular interaction (e.g., feeling like it is impossible for you to win at the game), (b) describing how you experience the client (e.g., they seem to be protecting you), or (c) being transparent about your own mind during the therapy process (e.g., why you asked a certain question). Each of these is also a form of self-disclosure. Disclosing your own feelings and experiences in the moment is often a way of showing empathy (e.g., "I feel a bit sad watching your doll searching for her mommy"). This type of self-disclosure can also be a way of modeling mentalization—that is, understanding of how thoughts and feelings underlie behavior in the self and others. For example, when a child is playing roughly, the therapist can model what effect this has and what they think and feel, as follows: "When you start to play so rough, I worry that one of us might get hurt. Can we try to slow down and take a breath, to make sure we both stay safe?"

Self-disclosures should be made judiciously, intentionally, and thoughtfully. Therapists must be mindful of how they think the disclosure will help the patient and the therapeutic process. It is also crucial that therapists not disclose anything that they are not comfortable sharing with the patient. The decision of whether to disclose or not depends on your personal comfort level, the specific clinical situation, and the nuances of your client. We cannot tell you exactly whether, when, or how to use self-disclosure; rather, we provide these exercises to give you an opportunity to try out different ways of responding so you will feel more confident when these opportunities arise. (For some examples of inappropriate self-disclosure, see Appendix E8.1 at the end of this exercise.) The exercises in this chapter will help you identify your own comfort level and to consider what you think is appropriate for different types of clients. Additionally, we encourage you to consult with your supervisor or a colleague for guidance about specific situations.

SKILL CRITERIA FOR EXERCISE 8

1. Validate the child's curiosity or experience, and the tone is nondefensive.
2. Disclose information or something about yourself, including your own thoughts and feelings.
3. Inquire about the reasons and motivations behind the child's statement and/or invite the child to elaborate.

Examples of Self-Disclosure

Note: <u>Underlined text</u> in brackets should be read aloud to provide context.

Example 1

CHILD CLIENT: [*Curious*] Where are you from?

THERAPIST: Knowing where a person is from can say a lot about them. I'm thinking about whether it would be helpful for you to know the answer. Does something make you think I might not be from New York City?

Example 2

CHILD CLIENT: [*Excited*] Have you seen *Harry Potter*?

THERAPIST: Great question! I have seen *Harry Potter*. I'm curious, what made you wonder about that today? What was on your mind?

Example 3

CHILD CLIENT: [*Irritated*] I don't want to talk to you anymore. You know so much about me, and I don't know anything about you. It's not fair.

THERAPIST: I get that, and I'm feeling torn right now. I'd like to make it feel more fair and comfortable for you, but I am not sure what I could share about myself that would help with that. In fact, I am concerned it could backfire, and you might find it disappointing and wish you didn't know something I shared. What do you think?

INSTRUCTIONS FOR EXERCISE 8

Step 1: Role-Play and Feedback

- The client says the first beginner client statement, also reading aloud any <u>underlined text</u> in brackets to provide context. The therapist improvises a response based on the skill criteria.

- The trainer (or if not available, the client) provides brief feedback based on the skill criteria.

- The client then repeats the same statement, and the therapist again improvises a response. The trainer (or client) again provides brief feedback.

Step 2: Repeat

- Repeat Step 1 for all the statements in the current difficulty level (beginner, intermediate, or advanced).

Step 3: Assess and Adjust Difficulty

- The therapist completes the Deliberate Practice Reaction Form (see Appendix A) and decides whether to make the exercise easier or harder or to repeat the same difficulty level.

Step 4: Repeat for Approximately 15 Minutes

- Repeat Steps 1 to 3 for at least 15 minutes.
- The trainees then switch therapist/client roles and start over.

Now it's your turn! Follow Steps 1 and 2 from the instructions.

Remember: The goal of the role-play is for trainees to practice improvising responses to the client statements in a manner that (a) uses the skill criteria and (b) feels authentic for the trainee. **Example therapist responses for each client statement are provided at the end of this exercise. Trainees should attempt to improvise their own responses before reading the example responses.**

BEGINNER-LEVEL CLIENT STATEMENTS FOR EXERCISE 8
Beginner Client Statement 1
[**Curious**] Where are you from?
Beginner Client Statement 2
[**Excited**] Have you seen *Harry Potter*?
Beginner Client Statement 3
[**Curious**] How old are you?
Beginner Client Statement 4
[**Anxious, <u>playing basketball</u>**] Okay, I am going to see if I can make it from here. [**<u>Shoots and misses,</u> frustrated**] Did *you* play basketball when you were my age?
Beginner Client Statement 5
[**Curious**] Where do all these toys come from? Are they *your* kids' toys?
Beginner Client Statement 6
[**Curious**] How long have you been a feelings doctor?

Assess and adjust the difficulty before moving to the next difficulty level (see Step 3 in the exercise instructions).

INTERMEDIATE-LEVEL CLIENT STATEMENTS FOR EXERCISE 8
Intermediate Client Statement 1
[**Confrontational**] Have *you* ever been in therapy?
Intermediate Client Statement 2
[**Irritated**] I don't want to talk to you anymore. You know so much about me, and I don't know anything about you. It's not fair.
Intermediate Client Statement 3
[**Worried, <u>playing in a toy kitchen</u>**] My boss is going to be so mad at me if I don't flip the pancake exactly right! Does your boss get mad at you too?
Intermediate Client Statement 4
[**Anxious**] My mommy told me you're still in college. Is that true?
Intermediate Client Statement 5
[**Curious**] Do you have a husband yet? My daddy said that your shiny ring means you're married.
Intermediate Client Statement 6
[**Curious**] Do you have kids?
Intermediate Client Statement 7
[**Quiet, withdrawn**] My dog is my best friend in the world. Do you have any pets?
Intermediate Client Statement 8
[**Angry**] No! I don't want to stop playing yet. You choose the game this time. What's your favorite game to play with me?
Intermediate Client Statement 9
[**Confused**] So, you're in school just like me? I'm in second grade, what grade are you in?

🛑 **Assess and adjust the difficulty before moving to the next difficulty level (see Step 3 in the exercise instructions).**

ADVANCED-LEVEL CLIENT STATEMENTS FOR EXERCISE 8
Advanced Client Statement 1
[**Annoyed**] How many other kids come into your playroom? I just saw another kid walk by the waiting room.
Advanced Client Statement 2
[**Sad**] Yeah, sometimes I get spanked. But I understand why. I mean if your kid stole something from the store like I did, wouldn't you have spanked them too?
Advanced Client Statement 3
[**Confused**] Wait, so are you Korean or Vietnamese? My daddy is Korean and you kind of look like him.
Advanced Client Statement 4
[**Anxious, <u>playing with toys, but looking at the video camera in the playroom</u>**] Umm, I'm going to lock away these animals and hide them so that no one else can find them using the video camera over there. Do my parents spy on us playing together?
Advanced Client Statement 5
[**Plaintive**] Why do we have to end in June? I don't want to meet with a different therapist. Why do you need to take a summer vacation?

✋ **Assess and adjust the difficulty here (see Step 3 in the exercise instructions). If appropriate, follow the instructions to make the exercise even more challenging (see Appendix A).**

Example Therapist Responses: Self-Disclosure

Remember: Trainees should attempt to improvise their own responses before reading the example responses. **Do not read the following responses verbatim unless you are having trouble coming up with your own responses!**

EXAMPLE RESPONSES TO BEGINNER-LEVEL CLIENT STATEMENTS FOR EXERCISE 8
Example Response to Beginner Client Statement 1
Knowing where a person is from can say a lot about them. (Criterion 1) I'm thinking about whether it would be helpful for you to know the answer. (Criterion 2) Does something make you think I might not be from New York City? (Criterion 3)
Example Response to Beginner Client Statement 2
Great question! (Criterion 1) I *have* seen *Harry Potter*. (Criterion 2) I'm curious, what made you wonder about that today? What was on your mind? (Criterion 3)
Example Response to Beginner Client Statement 3
I am definitely a grown-up. (Criterion 2) You're pretty observant—you can tell we're not the same age. (Criterion 1) I wonder what made you feel curious about that today. (Criterion 3)
Example Response to Beginner Client Statement 4
You are trying so hard to make these tough shots—it's not easy. (Criterion 1) I didn't play basketball, but I did play other sports and remember that frustrated feeling when I couldn't make the shot I wanted. (Criterion 2) Maybe you're wondering if I can relate to how hard this is? (Criterion 3)
Example Response to Beginner Client Statement 5
It probably feels like a bit of a mystery where all these toys come from. (Criterion 1) They don't come from my house. (Criterion 2) Maybe you're also curious about whether I have kids? (Criteria 3)
Example Response to Beginner Client Statement 6
That's such an important question. (Criterion 1) I've been helping kids with their feelings for a few years now. (Criterion 2) I also feel myself wanting to know more about what prompted this question now. Can you tell me more? (Criterion 3)

EXAMPLE RESPONSES TO INTERMEDIATE-LEVEL CLIENT STATEMENTS FOR EXERCISE 8

Example Response to Intermediate Client Statement 1

What a great question. (Criterion 1) You know, I *have*. (Criterion 2) I suppose there's a lot behind that question, things you're wondering about? Maybe whether I know what it's like to talk about private stuff and feelings with another person? (Criterion 3)

Example Response to Intermediate Client Statement 2

I get that (Criterion 1), and I'm feeling torn right now. (Criterion 2) I'd like to make it feel more fair and comfortable for you (Criterion 1), but I am not sure what I could share about myself that would help with that. In fact, I am concerned (Criterion 2) it could backfire, and you might find it disappointing and wish you didn't know something I shared. What do you think? (Criterion 3)

Example Response to Intermediate Client Statement 3

It is so hard to feel like you're going to get in trouble or get yelled at if you make even the smallest mistake. (Criterion 1) I *have* had bosses in the past who got mad at me. (Criterion 2) What is it like for you to feel all that pressure? (Criterion 3)

Example Response to Intermediate Client Statement 4

That's a great question—we have some things in common. (Criterion 1) I am still in school but it's the kind of school you go to after college, where you learn how to be a feelings doctor. (Criterion 2) What do you think about that? (Criterion 3)

Example Response to Intermediate Client Statement 5

We communicate so many things about ourselves without even saying words. I'm really struck by how important your question is (Criteria 1 and 2), especially since we've been talking about how your parents are getting divorced. Before I answer your question, I'm wondering (Criterion 2) if we can talk about how you felt when your daddy said that. (Criterion 3)

Example Response to Intermediate Client Statement 6

Mmm . . . I'm feeling a little torn about how to respond. (Criterion 2) I imagine that it might be meaningful to you that you're asking this question now. (Criterion 1) You might feel relieved or disappointed or something else either way. (Criterion 1) Can we talk about that first? (Criterion 3)

Example Response to Intermediate Client Statement 7

You guys are so close. (Criterion 1) I don't have any pets right now. (Criterion 2) In sharing that, I am thinking about what it means to you. (Criterion 2) Perhaps you're wondering if I can understand the kind of friendship you have with your dog? (Criterion 3)

Example Response to Intermediate Client Statement 8

There are so many fun things we play, and I can understand not wanting to stop playing this game. (Criterion 1) I was really enjoying this round. (Criterion 2) I'm curious about why you want me to choose another game—especially since you said you don't want to stop playing this one. (Criterion 3)

Example Response to Intermediate Client Statement 9

That is something we have in common. We are both learners. (Criteria 1 and 2) I'm in a part of school that doesn't have grades. (Criterion 2) That probably sounds a little strange, huh? (Criterion 1) But you know who my best teachers are? People like you (Criterion 2)—you're the primo expert in second-graders and I'd love to know more about what second grade is like for you. (Criterion 3)

EXAMPLE RESPONSES TO ADVANCED-LEVEL CLIENT STATEMENTS FOR EXERCISE 8
Example Response to Advanced Client Statement 1
I can imagine there are some complex feelings behind that question. (Criterion 1) I do see other kids here. (Criterion 2) I'm curious what it is like to think about other kids coming and playing here with me. (Criterion 3)
Example Response to Advanced Client Statement 2
That's a hard question but also an important one. (Criterion 1) I feel a bit sad thinking about how, in some ways, you feel deserving of punishment. (Criterion 2) I want to pause and understand more about what you're asking before I answer. (Criterion 1) I guess you're wondering if I agree with how your parents discipline you? Or whether I would handle it differently? (Criterion 3)
Example Response to Advanced Client Statement 3
I can see why you say your daddy and I look a bit alike. (Criterion 1) I'm thinking about how to respond. (Criterion 2) I'm taking my time because I wonder if you would feel disappointed if I said I am not Korean . . . maybe you're hoping that we have that in common? (Criterion 3)
Example Response to Advanced Client Statement 4
It sounds like you're a little worried about whether what we talk about here is private, especially because there is a camera. (Criterion 1) Your parents cannot see or hear what we do (Criterion 2)—the camera is only for me so I can review what we've done and think about how to help you feel better. (Criterion 2) What are some of the things that feel important to hide from your parents? (Criterion 3)
Example Response to Advanced Client Statement 5
It will be hard to say goodbye in June. (Criterion 1) I've really enjoyed working together this past year. (Criterion 2) We've talked a lot about how thoughts, feelings, and behaviors are related to each other. Can you tell me more about the feeling behind your questions? (Criterion 3)

APPENDIX E8.1. Examples of Inappropriate Self-Disclosure

Difficulty	Client Statement	Example Therapist Responses
Beginner	Have you seen *Harry Potter*?	No. I'm too old for those kinds of movies. They're more for little kids like you.
Beginner	How long have you been a feelings doctor?	Oh, gosh. I just started my training here at this clinic. I feel a little nervous because you're my first patient ever.
Intermediate	[*Curious*] Do you have kids?	Definitely not. I've never wanted kids myself. I consider the kids I meet with here at the clinic to be "my kids." *or* I do have kids. But since I got divorced, they spend a lot of time with their dad.
Intermediate	Do you have a husband yet? My daddy said that your shiny ring means you're married.	That makes me a little uncomfortable that your daddy noticed my ring. Does he talk to you a lot about things like that?
Advanced	[*Sad*] Yeah, sometimes I get spanked. But I understand why. I mean if your kid stole something from the store like I did, wouldn't you have spanked them too?	I *definitely* would not spank my child if they stole something. That's a really bad thing to do, and you should know it wasn't your fault. I'm going to talk to your parents about this right after we're done meeting today.
Advanced	Why do we have to end in June? I don't want to meet with a different therapist. Why do you need to take a summer vacation?	It will be hard to say goodbye in June. This job is hard work though, and I definitely need a break!

Gathering Information About Safety Concerns

Preparations for Exercise 9

1. Read the instructions in Chapter 2.

2. Download the Deliberate Practice Reaction Form and the Deliberate Practice Diary Form at https://www.apa.org/pubs/books/deliberate-practice-child-adolescent-psychotherapy (see the "Clinician and Practitioner Resources" tab; also available in Appendixes A and B, respectively).

Skill Description

Skill Difficulty Level: Advanced

Addressing safety concerns is one of the most challenging tasks child therapists face. Sometimes children present safety issues as concerns or worries, but very often they share information that therapists will note is a safety concern, yet the child (or parent) does not realize this or may downplay the concern or risk, as is often the case with adolescents. Common safety concerns include self-harm, suicidal ideation, abuse or neglect, exposure to domestic violence, and caregiver or child substance use. Although not necessarily always thought of as a safety concern, bullying (either as the target or bully), use of technology or the internet (e.g., chat rooms), or other risk-taking behavior may also reflect a safety concern.

Safety concerns often arouse the therapist's anxiety, and many therapists begin to think about what they will need to do—call a supervisor, make a report, or tell a parent. A first step when a safety concern arises is to settle your own anxieties, perhaps with a deep breath, to be thoughtful about how to proceed. It is critical that we make sure that children are safe, but we are also not investigators. We must find out enough information to determine what the most appropriate next step is, but we must not become so anxious about finding out the "truth" that we lose sight of and contact with

https://doi.org/10.1037/0000288-011

our patients. To do this, we incorporate the earlier skill of empathic validation, showing the child or parent that we are attending to and understanding what they are saying. It is particularly important in situations like this to respond in a way that is not punitive or judgmental.

We then invite children and parents to tell us more. Our goal, as with anything patients tell us, is to see things through their eyes. We take a similar approach, being careful not to interrogate but rather to approach safety concerns with curiosity and a desire to understand the experience. The more we practice responding in moments like these, the more comfortable we will become, which is of critical importance. In difficult moments, we can provide both children and parents with a sense of safety and security. We communicate that we can tolerate hearing what they have shared and can maintain a level head, seek support, and be with them through this challenge. Maintaining a calm, steady, nonjudgmental presence will allow you to obtain critical information so you can decide (in consultation with your supervisor) how to proceed.

All child therapists should be aware of mandated reporting laws in their locality. In the United States, Canada, and Australia, therapists are mandated reporters of suspected abuse or neglect. Mandated reporting laws are also on the books in many other countries, including Brazil, Denmark, Finland, France, Hungary, Israel, Malaysia, Mexico, Norway, South Africa, Sweden, and the United Kingdom. Most localities require mandated reporter training for therapists. Mandated reporter laws outline when therapists are required to make reports to local authorities and the processes for doing so.

In this exercise, we focus on how to respond to the child or parent immediately after a safety concern is voiced. The client statements are split between child statements and parent statements. The goals of the skill criteria in this exercise are to help you (a) manage the inevitable anxiety therapists feel when a safety concern arises and (b) create a therapeutic and calm environment that will allow you to obtain more information from the child or parent. After this has been achieved, you will be able to do a full risk assessment and identify next steps. For trainees, it is essential that you talk to your supervisor about safety concerns. In some cases, this will mean pausing the session to contact your supervisor immediately; in others—where the risk is not imminent, and it is clear that there is no mandated reporting responsibility—you may be able to finish the session and speak to your supervisor immediately afterward. In all cases, you will need to do further assessment. If a child or adolescent is at risk of suicide, therapists should consider a formal suicide assessment and possible referral for a higher level of care (e.g., hospitalization or intensive outpatient programs). The Columbia Lighthouse Project uses the Columbia-Suicide Severity Rating Scale (C-SSRS) to assess risk across multiple domains in which children and adolescents engage with adults (e.g., pediatric care, schools, behavioral health). Similar protocols exist for assessing other forms of risk in children and adolescents, including nonsuicidal self-injury (https://www.selfinjury.bctr.cornell.edu/perch/resources/fnssi.pdf) and child abuse. For an overview of signs and symptoms of child abuse and neglect, you can review the guidelines provided by the Child Welfare Information Gateway (https://www.childwelfare.gov/pubpdfs/whatiscan.pdf). Your supervisor and the professional organization that oversees your specific mental health discipline (e.g., American Psychological Association, National Association of Social Workers, American Counseling Association) will also have valuable resources to assist you in the assessment of risk.

SKILL CRITERIA FOR EXERCISE 9
1. Response validates the child's or parent's concern or feelings.
2. Therapist invites the child or parent to elaborate on the safety concern with a calm, nonjudgmental tone.

Examples of Gathering Information About Safety Concerns

Note: Underlined text in brackets should be read aloud to provide context.

Example 1

TEN-YEAR-OLD CHILD CLIENT: [*Assertive*] You should just tie me up and shoot me. I am never going to learn.

THERAPIST: You're feeling really terrible about this. So terrible you think you should be killed! What makes you so sure it isn't going to get any better?

ALTERNATIVE THERAPIST RESPONSE: You're feeling really terrible about this. So terrible you think you should be killed! Do you feel like you don't want to be alive?

Example 2

ADOLESCENT CLIENT: [*matter-of-factly*] I mean, my mom definitely has a temper, you don't want to cross her. She's slapped me across the face, washed my mouth out with soap. One time she was really pissed while she was cooking dinner, and she came after me with the knife. I don't think she would have actually done anything, because I am bigger than she is, but she was waving it like a crazy person. So, yeah, I'm definitely not telling her much, just trying to get through the next couple of years.

THERAPIST: I can't quite tell how you experienced this by the way you describe it. It sounds like on one hand it's pretty scary, how out of control it can be, but also you say it like you don't feel scared. Has she ever hurt you, like left a mark?

ALTERNATIVE THERAPIST RESPONSE: I can't quite tell how you experienced this by the way you describe it. It sounds like on one hand it's pretty scary, how out of control it can be, but also you say it like you don't feel scared. With the knife, you said now you don't think she would have done anything, but were you scared she might hurt you in that moment?

Example 3

MOTHER: [*Concerned, after disclosing domestic violence by boyfriend toward her, witnessed by child*] I just don't know what to do, I feel so badly. You're here to help me, right? You won't tell anyone or anything? You're not like the police?

THERAPIST: I am here to help you, and I'm really glad you could tell me this. I imagine it has been really hard, and that it was difficult to tell me. There are things that I am required to report, when children are in situations where they might not be safe. But we will get to that, whether this is something I need to report. The priority is helping you and Jesse through this. What happened afterward? Have you and Jesse talked at all about what happened?

INSTRUCTIONS FOR EXERCISE 9

Step 1: Role-Play and Feedback

- The client says the first beginner client statement, also reading aloud any <u>underlined text</u> in brackets to provide context. The therapist improvises a response based on the skill criteria.

- The trainer (or if not available, the client) provides brief feedback based on the skill criteria.

- The client then repeats the same statement, and the therapist again improvises a response. The trainer (or client) again provides brief feedback.

Step 2: Repeat

- Repeat Step 1 for all the statements in the current difficulty level (beginner, intermediate, or advanced).

Step 3: Assess and Adjust Difficulty

- The therapist completes the Deliberate Practice Reaction Form (see Appendix A) and decides whether to make the exercise easier or harder or to repeat the same difficulty level.

Step 4: Repeat for Approximately 15 Minutes

- Repeat Steps 1 to 3 for at least 15 minutes.
- The trainees then switch therapist/client roles and start over.

Now it's your turn! Follow Steps 1 and 2 from the instructions.

Remember: The goal of the role-play is for trainees to practice improvising responses to the client statements in a manner that (a) uses the skill criteria and (b) feels authentic for the trainee. **Example therapist responses for each client statement are provided at the end of this exercise. Trainees should attempt to improvise their own responses before reading the example responses.**

BEGINNER-LEVEL CLIENT STATEMENTS FOR EXERCISE 9
Beginner Child Client Statement 1
[**Ten-year-old, assertive**] You should just tie me up and shoot me. I am never going to learn.
Beginner Child Client Statement 2
[**Fifteen-year-old, anxious, with divorced parents**] Please don't make me go to my dad's this weekend. I don't want to be alone with him without my sister or anyone else around.
Beginner Child Client Statement 3
[**Seven-year-old, angry, <u>playing with action figures</u>**] I'm going to beat you in your face! Just like Sammy does to me!
Beginner Child Client Statement 4
[**Fourteen-year-old female, dismissive**] So I sent one topless picture of myself to my boyfriend over Snapchat . . . what's the big deal?! Everyone does it . . . it's not like anyone else will see it.
Beginner Parent Client Statement 1
[**Anxious**] I looked in her phone and she's been watching a lot of videos about suicide and self-injury on TikTok. I'm not sure what to do.
Beginner Parent Client Statement 2
[**Mother, concerned, <u>after disclosing domestic violence by boyfriend toward her, witnessed by child</u>**] I just don't know what to do, I feel so badly. You're here to help me, right? You won't tell anyone or anything? You're not like the police, right?
Beginner Parent Client Statement 3
[**Matter-of-factly**] We've figured out a way to keep things under control. We put a little deadbolt on the outside of his bedroom door. So, when he's really losing it, we can just lock the door. When he calms down, we let him out and things are better.

🛑 **Assess and adjust the difficulty before moving to the next difficulty level (see Step 3 in the exercise instructions).**

INTERMEDIATE-LEVEL CLIENT STATEMENTS FOR EXERCISE 9
Intermediate Child Client Statement 1
[**Fourteen-year-old, anxious**] Totally out of the blue sometimes I think about what it would be like to stand in front of a moving truck or jump off a building or set myself on fire.
Intermediate Child Client Statement 2
[**Ten-year-old, sad**] Yeah, my parents fight basically every day . . . like this one time I heard my daddy yelling so loudly that he broke our glass window in the kitchen and then my mommy started crying.
Intermediate Child Client Statement 3
[**Fifteen-year-old, hopeless and depressed**] This is pointless to keep talking about. Obviously, things would be so much easier if I could somehow fall asleep and not wake up again.
Intermediate Child Client Statement 4
[**Adolescent, anxious**] I've never told anyone this, but I guess I should tell you. A few times, when I've felt really bad like this, I cut myself.
Intermediate Parent Client Statement 1
[**Parent of an 8-year-old, conflicted**] Well, I have to be honest with you . . . I hit him last night. I was just so tired of watching my son torment his younger sibling for hours on end . . . I know what I did was wrong but at least now he knows what it feels like.
Intermediate Parent Client Statement 2
[**Irritated**] My husband and I are not abusive! I've never laid a hand on my child. You're telling me that you believe my 7-year-old daughter over me?!
Intermediate Parent Client Statement 3
[**Calm**] I let the kids drink at our house so I can keep an eye on them. When someone passes out, I tell them it's time to call it quits.

Assess and adjust the difficulty before moving to the next difficulty level (see Step 3 in the exercise instructions).

ADVANCED-LEVEL CLIENT STATEMENTS FOR EXERCISE 9
Advanced Child Client Statement 1
[**Thirteen-year-old, anxious and enthusiastic**] I tricked my mom into thinking I was sick so I could get out of going to in-person school last week . . . all I had to do was take a lot of sleeping pills. So funny, right!?
Advanced Child Client Statement 2
[**Sixteen-year-old, depressed**] I think about killing myself a lot . . . like how easy it would be to climb up to my roof and jump off or even sneak more of my Prozac from my mom's medicine cabinet. I'm obviously not saying I would actually do it but like . . . how easy?
Advanced Child Client Statement 3
[**Fifteen-year-old, flat affect**] I genuinely just don't care anymore. Like cool, fine, go ahead and tell my parents that I'm high right now. Seriously. Whatever. It doesn't matter anyway.
Advanced Child Client Statement 4
[**Thirteen-year-old, matter-of-factly**] I mean, my mom definitely has a temper, you don't want to cross her. She's slapped me across the face, washed my mouth out with soap. One time she was really pissed while cooking dinner, and she came after me with the knife. I don't think she would have actually done anything, because I am bigger than she is, but she was waving it like a crazy person. So, yeah, I'm definitely not telling her much, just trying to get through the next couple of years.
Advanced Parent Client Statement 1
[**Parent of an adolescent, dismissive**] You must have misinterpreted what he said. We don't need to fill out this "safety plan." I'm his mother, so I would know if my child was actively suicidal.
Advanced Parent Client Statement 2
[**Parent of an adolescent, dismissive, <u>the therapist has just reported the teen's nonsuicidal self-injury to the parent</u>**] Isn't cutting yourself like a rite of passage or something? I don't want to make a big deal out of this. I think if we just leave it alone, she'll lose interest and stop doing it.
Advanced Parent Client Statement 3
[**Angry**] You're reporting me to Children's Services? You're calling me an abuser? When I get home that little tattletale is *really* going to get it!

🛑 **Assess and adjust the difficulty here (see Step 3 in the exercise instructions). If appropriate, follow the instructions to make the exercise even more challenging (see Appendix A).**

Example Therapist Responses: Gathering Information About Safety Concerns

Remember: Trainees should attempt to improvise their own responses before reading the example responses. **Do not read the following responses verbatim unless you are having trouble coming up with your own responses!**

EXAMPLE RESPONSES TO BEGINNER-LEVEL CLIENT STATEMENTS FOR EXERCISE 9
Example Response to Beginner Child Client Statement 1
You're feeling really terrible about this. So terrible you think you should be killed! (Criterion 1) What makes you so sure it isn't going to get any better? (Criterion 2)   or You're feeling really terrible about this. So terrible you think you should be killed! (Criterion 1) Do you feel like you don't want to be alive? (Criterion 2)
Example Response to Beginner Child Client Statement 2
I can really hear how scared you feel about being alone with your dad. I want to help you stay safe. (Criterion 1) What has been happening at his house that is making you feel so frightened? (Criterion 2)
Example Response to Beginner Child Client Statement 3
Things are getting really intense between these guys—there are a lot of angry feelings. (Criterion 1) Can we take a pause for a moment? Who is Sammy, and what's been going on with him? (Criterion 2)
Example Response to Beginner Child Client Statement 4
It's annoying that everyone is making such a big deal over this. (Criterion 1) Especially when you feel like this is a private thing between you and your boyfriend. (Criterion 1) It's good we can talk about it here. I'd like to know more about what led up to your sending the picture. (Criterion 2)
Example Response to Beginner Parent Client Statement 1
I'm so glad you shared this with me. That must have been really upsetting to see. (Criterion 1) What prompted you to look in her phone? Was there something you were concerned about before making this discovery? (Criterion 2)
Example Response to Beginner Parent Client Statement 2
I am here to help you, and I'm really glad you could tell me this. I imagine it has been really hard, and that it was difficult to tell me. (Criterion 1) There are things that I am required to report, when children are in situations where they might not be safe. But we will get to that, whether this is something I need to report. The priority is helping you and Jesse through this. What happened afterward? Have you and Jesse talked at all about what happened? (Criterion 2)
Example Response to Beginner Parent Client Statement 3
So, it sounds like you were really at your wits end and tried to find something that would keep things calmer in the house. (Criterion 1) We've talked a bit about time-outs and how that can sometimes help everyone cool off. I want to understand more about how you're using the lock and see if we can find some alternatives. (Criterion 2)

EXAMPLE RESPONSES TO INTERMEDIATE-LEVEL CLIENT STATEMENTS FOR EXERCISE 9

Example Response to Intermediate Child Client Statement 1

I'm really glad you shared this with me. I'd like to understand more about these thoughts you're having. (Criterion 1) When you notice those thoughts, what sort of feeling comes up for you? Maybe it is kind of scary or maybe it feels like a bit of a relief? Something else? (Criterion 2)

Example Response to Intermediate Child Client Statement 2

That is a lot of fighting, and it must be scary to have your mommy and daddy getting so mad that windows get broken and mommy cries. (Criterion 1) Can you tell me more about that fight when Daddy broke the window? (Criterion 2)

Example Response to Intermediate Child Client Statement 3

Everything feels so hopeless right now. I can understand why it might feel pointless to keep talking. (Criterion 1) You mentioned wanting to fall asleep and never wake up again. Have you been having thoughts about hurting yourself? (Criterion 2)

Example Response to Intermediate Child Client Statement 4

So, things get really overwhelming and intense sometimes. So bad that you've hurt yourself. Thank you for trusting me with this information. (Criterion 1) You said you've never told anyone about this before. How does it feel to be talking about it now, with me? (Criterion 2)

Example Response to Intermediate Parent Client Statement 1

It sounds like it was such a hard night, and this has been building for a long time. I'm glad you're able to talk about this with me. (Criterion 1) Has this happened before? (Criterion 2)

Example Response to Intermediate Parent Client Statement 2

I know this information is really hard to hear. (Criterion 1) I've seen over the past few months how committed you are to your children. (Criterion 1) I wonder if we can slow things down a little bit and go back to what happened at the park. I'd like to hear what you remember from that day. (Criterion 2)

Example Response to Intermediate Parent Client Statement 3

So, it sounds like this is a way for you to monitor what they're up to. (Criterion 1) I'd like to hear more about what led you to take on this role. (Criterion 2)

EXAMPLE RESPONSES TO ADVANCED-LEVEL CLIENT STATEMENTS FOR EXERCISE 9

Example Response to Advanced Child Client Statement 1

You must have really not wanted to go to school. And it sounds like you didn't feel you could say that directly and had to use sleeping pills instead. (Criterion 1) Can you tell me more about how you came up with this plan? (Criterion 2)

Example Response to Advanced Child Client Statement 2

Those are some pretty scary thoughts. I'm glad you told me that these specific ideas are coming to mind so often. (Criterion 1) How often have you been thinking about ways to kill yourself? (Criterion 2)

Example Response to Advanced Child Client Statement 3

There's such a sense of hopelessness for you right now. Like it wouldn't even matter if your parents knew you were getting high. (Criterion 1) You mentioned that you are high right now. Can you tell me more about what you used before coming to session today? (Criterion 2)

Example Response to Advanced Child Client Statement 4

I can't quite tell how you experienced this by the way you describe it. It sounds like on one hand it's pretty scary, how out of control it can be, but also you say it like you don't feel scared. (Criterion 1) Has she ever hurt you, like left a mark? (Criterion 2)

or

I can't quite tell how you experienced this by the way you describe it. It sounds like on one hand it's pretty scary, how out of control it can be, but also you say it like you don't feel scared. (Criterion 1) With the knife, you said now you don't think she would have done anything, but were you scared she might hurt you in that moment? (Criterion 2)

Example Response to Advanced Parent Client Statement 1

I can understand how this must feel like a real shock. It's a lot to digest as a parent. (Criterion 1) I'd like us to work together to help keep him safe. Can we go back a little bit? I realize I didn't check in with you to see how you were feeling as I described the suicidal thoughts your son shared during our last session. Before we talk about the safety plan, I'd like to understand how you're feeling right now. (Criterion 2)

Example Response to Advanced Parent Client Statement 2

It sounds like you're hoping this will go away on its own. And maybe a little worried that it will get worse if we address it directly? (Criterion 1) I can provide some information about the interventions we use to help kids who are hurting themselves. But, before I do that, I'd like to understand a bit more about your concerns. Can you tell me more? (Criterion 2)

Example Response to Advanced Parent Client Statement 3

I do know how much you love her. That is clear to me. (Criterion 1) You love her and also, when tempers flare, things can get really physical. You've been under so much stress lately. (Criterion 1) I will help you navigate the process with Children's Services. Often they are able to provide some really valuable resources to help support you in your parenting goals. Could we take some time to talk about what you hope could change in your relationship with your daughter? (Criterion 2)

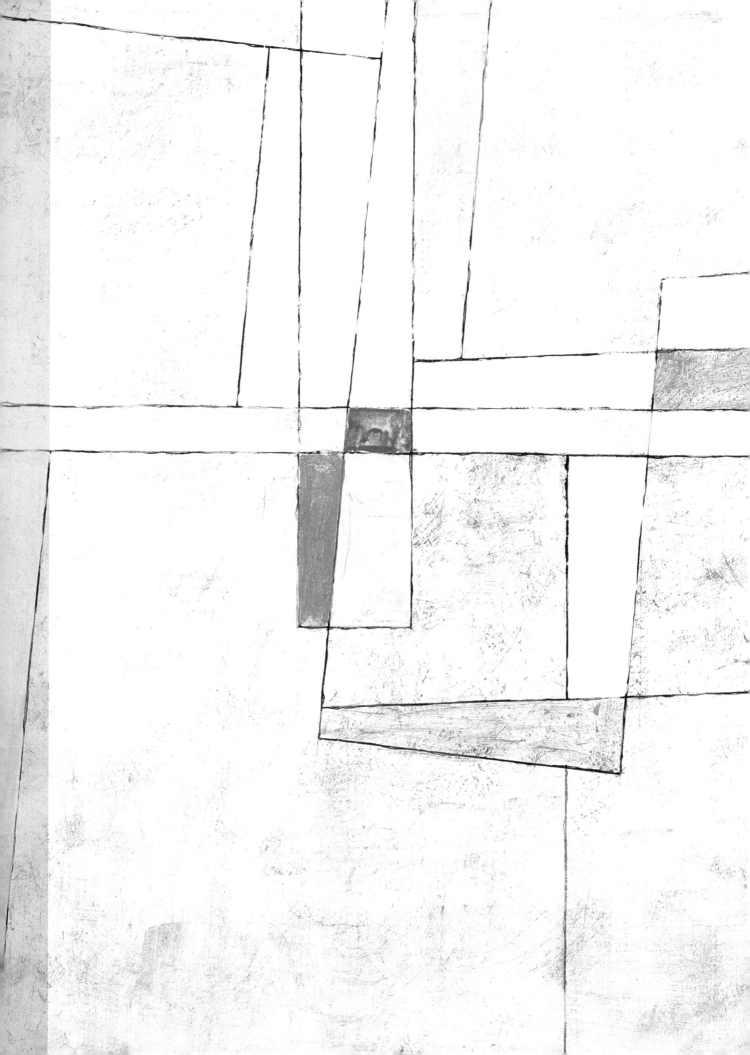

Setting Limits

Preparations for Exercise 10

1. Read the instructions in Chapter 2.

2. Download the Deliberate Practice Reaction Form and the Deliberate Practice Diary Form at https://www.apa.org/pubs/books/deliberate-practice-child-adolescent-psychotherapy (see the "Clinician and Practitioner Resources" tab; also available in Appendixes A and B, respectively).

Skill Description

Skill Difficulty Level: Advanced

Therapeutic limit-setting is an important component of any child treatment. It is difficult for children to feel safe and valued in a completely permissive environment. We recommend outlining some guiding principles of therapy at the very beginning of your therapeutic work with a child. For example, when the child comes into the playroom or therapy room for the first or second time, it can be worthwhile to say, "We can talk about anything you want here. The only rule is that we keep ourselves and the toys in this room safe." Even with those ground rules, sometimes things will occur in child therapy that require clear limits to be set.

Generally, there are several categories of limit-setting: in response to overt safety issues (e.g., hitting the therapist, breaking things in the playroom), in response to pro-social behaviors (e.g., cleaning up), and resetting of the frame of psychotherapy with children (e.g., staying in the room, participating, and maintaining a therapeutic relationship). This exercise focuses on all of those,[1] and it builds on the skills you practiced

---

1. This chapter does not address the kind of limit-setting that is an inherent part of behavioral treatments, such as parent–child interaction therapy or behavioral parent-training approaches.

https://doi.org/10.1037/0000288-012

Deliberate Practice in Child and Adolescent Psychotherapy, by J. Bate, T. A. Prout, T. Rousmaniere, and A. Vaz

in Exercise 9. In this exercise, we focus on how to address safety issues that arise inside the therapy room.

When children become intensely angry, throw things, or attempt to destroy property, it can provoke feelings of rejection, fear, and hopelessness in the therapist. These intense reactions can make it especially difficult for you to respond therapeutically. Practicing these skills will help you respond with a calm, appropriate, and child-centered way. It is often helpful to take a deep, quiet breath before you respond verbally. Setting appropriate limits around physical and emotional safety in the therapy room helps protect the child, the therapist, and the contents of the room (e.g., toys, electronics, other materials). For highly dysregulated children, limit-setting can help ground them back to reality and provide a scaffolding that allows them to build skills important for emotional development. Unsafe behaviors in the therapy room are also a form of communication. When children cannot find words to express themselves, they act. When children push back against the frame of therapy, it is important for therapists to reset the frame and emphasize the boundaries that help ensure the relationship and that the work of therapy provides safety and security.

There will be times in which limits are not called for. Child patients may ask to switch seats; sitting in the therapist's chair can, in some circumstances, be empowering and provide a sense of mastery. Also, they are likely to be louder and more boisterous than a typical adult patient; child sessions are often full of energy and unexpected events; such moments are often valuable and informative and do not require limit-setting.

In responding to challenging behaviors in child therapy, it is important to do several things. The therapist should acknowledge the child's feelings or wants—what is the child communicating through the behavior (e.g., "You're feeling so angry right now")? The therapist should also communicate the limit in a firm and supportive way (e.g., "Balls cannot be thrown at my face. We both need to stay safe"). Finally, the therapist may offer an acceptable alternative (e.g., "The wall is a great target for that ball"). If there is not an immediate or overt safety risk—for example, a child who is pushing the boundaries or frame of therapy—the limit-setting can be implicit and joined with the final step of offering a safe and acceptable alternative. For example, if a child is asking to sit on the therapist's lap, the limit-setting may be something like, "I can understand how sitting on my lap might seem like it would help you feel safer or closer to me. If we can both stay in our own seats, I'll be able to listen better, and we can use words to draw us closer."

SKILL CRITERIA FOR EXERCISE 10

1. Directly acknowledge the child's feelings, wants, and/or needs, without judgment.
2. Communicate the limit is with a firm but supportive tone. If there is not an overt safety risk, the limit can be implicit.
3. Offer a safe and acceptable alternative.

Examples of Setting Limits

Note: <u>Underlined text</u> in brackets should be read aloud to provide context.

Example 1

ELEVEN-YEAR-OLD CHILD CLIENT: [*Mischievous*] I want to cut the head off of this doll. Do you have scissors?

THERAPIST: I wonder if you're feeling angry right now. We need to keep the toys here in one piece. I do have some scissors and I have some pipe cleaners and paper that we can totally cut up as much as you want.

Example 2

SIX-YEAR-OLD CHILD CLIENT: [*Defiant*] No way! I am not cleaning up the toys! You have to do that after I leave! Byeee!

THERAPIST: Hmm, you don't want to help me clean up. Sounds like maybe you're not liking that we have to end our time together for today. It's tough to have to clean up after having fun. But it's an important part of what we do together, to take care of our stuff and put it away when we are done, even though it's not such a good feeling to end. And I will see you next week for more playing.

Example 3

NINE-YEAR-OLD CHILD CLIENT: [*Laughing, <u>playing with basketball</u>*] I'm gonna throw this ball as hard as I can at your head!

THERAPIST: Whoa, can we slow down? I guess you're feeling pretty frustrated. I am a little concerned that it could really hurt me if you throw it at my head. I'm thinking about where else you might be able to throw it hard, so it doesn't hurt me or break anything. Could we try again shooting it in the hoop?

INSTRUCTIONS FOR EXERCISE 10

Step 1: Role-Play and Feedback

- The client says the first beginner client statement, also reading aloud any <u>underlined text</u> in brackets to provide context.

- The trainer (or if not available, the client) provides brief feedback based on the skill criteria.

- The client then repeats the same statement, and the therapist again improvises a response. The trainer (or client) again provides brief feedback.

Step 2: Repeat

- Repeat Step 1 for all the statements in the current difficulty level (beginner, intermediate, or advanced).

Step 3: Assess and Adjust Difficulty

- The therapist completes the Deliberate Practice Reaction Form (see Appendix A) and decides whether to make the exercise easier or harder or to repeat the same difficulty level.

Step 4: Repeat for Approximately 15 Minutes

- Repeat Steps 1 to 3 for at least 15 minutes.
- The trainees then switch therapist and client roles and start over.

Now it's your turn! Follow Steps 1 and 2 from the instructions.

Remember: The goal of the role-play is for trainees to practice improvising responses to the client statements in a manner that (a) uses the skill criteria and (b) feels authentic for the trainee. **Example therapist responses for each client statement are provided at the end of this exercise. Trainees should attempt to improvise their own responses before reading the example responses.**

BEGINNER-LEVEL CLIENT STATEMENTS FOR EXERCISE 10
Beginner Client Statement 1
[Eleven-year-old, mischievous] I want to cut the head off of this doll. Do you have scissors?
Beginner Client Statement 2
[Seven-year-old, excited] I shook up this soda bottle the whole way here. Now I'm going to let it explode all over this place. Watch out!
Beginner Client Statement 3
[Nine-year-old, angry, <u>holding a marker up to a poster on the wall, about to draw all over it</u>] I can make way better art than *this*!
Beginner Client Statement 4
[Eight-year-old, animated, yelling] I'm going to yell as loud as I can this whole session! That way *everyone* in this place will know what I'm thinking and feeling.
Beginner Client Statement 5
[Adolescent, sad, <u>drawing a very detailed picture of a beautiful and inviting house</u>] I wish you and I could live here together. We would live happily ever after if I never had to go back to my actual home again.

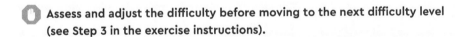 **Assess and adjust the difficulty before moving to the next difficulty level (see Step 3 in the exercise instructions).**

INTERMEDIATE-LEVEL CLIENT STATEMENTS FOR EXERCISE 10
Intermediate Client Statement 1
[**Fourteen-year-old, anxious**] I don't want to talk. All your toys are for little kids. I'm just gonna play games on my phone [<u>Begins to scroll on phone</u>].
Intermediate Client Statement 2
[**Six-year-old, defiant**] No way! I am not cleaning up the toys! You have to do that after I leave! Byeee!
Intermediate Client Statement 3
[**Ten-year-old, distracted, <u>the child has been leaving the room repeatedly during the session</u>**] I wanna go show this to my mom, I'll be right back.
Intermediate Client Statement 4
[**Nine-year-old, laughing, <u>playing with a basketball</u>**] I'm gonna throw this ball as hard as I can at your head!
Intermediate Client Statement 5
[**Adolescent, sad, <u>slowly breaking crayons in half one by one</u>**] I'm just broken and I want everything to look the way I feel.
Intermediate Client Statement 6
[**Eight-year-old, angry, <u>holding a small, plastic (not harmful) Play-Doh knife and rubbing it against the inside of their wrist in a cutting motion</u>**] It feels really good to do this. Can I do it to your wrist?

🛑 **Assess and adjust the difficulty before moving to the next difficulty level (see Step 3 in the exercise instructions).**

ADVANCED-LEVEL CLIENT STATEMENTS FOR EXERCISE 10
Advanced Client Statement 1
[**Seven-year-old, angry,** <u>plays with a soccer ball, pauses, then makes direct eye contact and kicks the ball as hard as possible at your face</u>]
Advanced Client Statement 2
[**Adolescent, pushy,** <u>arrives late to session</u>] Sorry, I forgot what time our sessions start again. I can never remember. But can we go 'til 6:30 p.m.? I have a lot to talk about.
Advanced Client Statement 3
[**Adolescent, happy,** <u>as they are walking out of the room at the end of session, you notice your cell phone sticking out of their back pocket</u>] See you next week!
Advanced Client Statement 4
[**Five-year-old, sad and withdrawn**] I don't like living at my house. Can I go home with you tonight?
Advanced Client Statement 5
[**Twelve-year-old, angry**] We can talk about all the horrible things my dad did to me for years. He used to turn off all the hot water in the house and then force me to stand in a freezing cold shower for hours. I want you to know what it's actually like. When you go home tonight, I want you to sit in the shower with the coldest water possible. Then tell me how long you last in there. Then you'll *really* know what I've been through.
Advanced Client Statement 6
[**Sixteen-year-old, flirtatious,** <u>the client looks the therapist up and down in a suggestive and provocative way</u>] Damn. You know . . . you're actually pretty hot.

🛑 **Assess and adjust the difficulty here (see Step 3 in the exercise instructions). If appropriate, follow the instructions to make the exercise even more challenging (see Appendix A).**

Example Therapist Responses: Setting Limits

Remember: Trainees should attempt to improvise their own responses before reading the example responses. **Do not read the following responses verbatim unless you are having trouble coming up with your own responses!**

EXAMPLE RESPONSES TO BEGINNER-LEVEL CLIENT STATEMENTS FOR EXERCISE 10
Example Response to Beginner Client Statement 1
I wonder if you're feeling angry right now. (Criterion 1) We need to keep the toys here in one piece. (Criterion 2) I do have some scissors and I have some pipe cleaners and paper that we can totally cut up as much as you want. (Criterion 3)
Example Response to Beginner Client Statement 2
Wow! It's ready to explode and maybe you are too, with a lot of big feelings inside of you. (Criterion 1) I want to make sure we don't get soda all over everything in here because then it would be super sticky and probably hard for us to clean up. (Criterion 2) Can we take a look at that bottle and all of the bubbles that are fighting to get out while we talk about what's gotten shaken up inside of you? (Criterion 3)
Example Response to Beginner Client Statement 3
Let's pause on that for a moment. (Criterion 2) You totally can make better art—I've seen it! Sounds like you're wanting to be creative, and maybe a part of you also wants to destroy that poster. (Criterion 1) How about I draw something on our art paper and then you can make something even better over it? (Criterion 3)
Example Response to Beginner Client Statement 4
It's not enough for me to hear about it. You want to be sure everyone knows your thoughts and feelings. (Criterion 1) It's important for us to make sure other people can talk to their therapists without too much disruption. (Criterion 2) Could we test out some different volumes and find one that feels loud enough for you, but not so loud that it makes it hard for the other people in the building? (Criterion 3)
Example Response to Beginner Client Statement 5
That is such a beautiful house, and I can hear the longing in your voice for a happily ever after. (Criterion 1) Even though we can't actually live together (Criterion 2), we can definitely imagine together what would be different for you if you never had to go back to your actual home again. (Criterion 3)

EXAMPLE RESPONSES TO INTERMEDIATE-LEVEL CLIENT STATEMENTS FOR EXERCISE 10

Example Response to Intermediate Client Statement 1

You don't want to do baby stuff—you're almost an adult. But it also sounds like you want to withdraw and be alone with your thoughts. (Criterion 1) I am always interested in what's on your mind and hope we'll be able to talk at least some of the time today. (Criterion 2) Could you tell me a little bit about the games you like to play on your phone? (Criterion 3)

Example Response to Intermediate Client Statement 2

Hmm, you don't want to help me clean up. Sounds like maybe you're not liking that we have to end our time together for today. (Criterion 1) It's tough to have to clean up after having fun. But it's an important part of what we do together, to take care of our stuff and put it away when we are done, even though it's not such a good feeling to end. (Criteria 2 and 3) And I will see you next week for more playing. (Criterion 3)

Example Response to Intermediate Client Statement 3

It's so hard to stay in the room today. You're really wanting to see your mom and check in with her. (Criterion 1) Instead of going to show her that, can we sit down together for a moment? (Criterion 2) It would be good for me to understand a bit more about what you're feeling when you get that urge to leave. Can you tell me about it? (Criterion 3)

Example Response to Intermediate Client Statement 4

Whoa, can we slow down? (Criterion 2) I guess you're feeling pretty frustrated. (Criterion 1) I am a little concerned that it could really hurt me if you throw it at my head. I'm thinking about where else you might be able to throw it hard, so it doesn't hurt me or break anything. Could we try again shooting it in the hoop? (Criterion 3) I know it was getting tough, but I think we'll get there with making our shots in.

Example Response to Intermediate Client Statement 5

Gosh. I can see how defeated and broken you're feeling. (Criterion 1) Breaking the crayons is a really clear way to communicate the intensity of those feelings. I want to make sure I still have crayons for people to use. (Criterion 2) I have some paper over here that you can tear to shreds instead, and I'm wondering if you can tell me more about this broken feeling. (Criterion 3)

Example Response to Intermediate Client Statement 6

Even though it feels good to do that, it also seems like you want to show me how angry or sad you feel? Maybe it's another kind of feeling. (Criterion 1) I don't want you to do that to my wrist. (Criterion 2) But we can each use a knife to cut through this Play-Doh together, and hopefully you can say more about what you're feeling right now. (Criterion 3).

| **EXAMPLE RESPONSES TO ADVANCED-LEVEL** |
| **CLIENT STATEMENTS FOR EXERCISE 10** |

Example Response to Advanced Client Statement 1

Ouch! Wow—that really surprised me and hurt my cheek. I'm going to put the ball away for now. (Criterion 2) I'm not sure what happened there, but it looked like you felt really angry before kicking that ball. (Criterion 1) In this space, we both need to make sure the other person feels safe. (Criterion 2) Let's take a minute for us both to calm down and figure out what happened just now. (Criterion 3)

Example Response to Advanced Client Statement 2

I understand you have a lot on your mind today, and I want to hear about it. It makes sense you'd want to have more time at the end. (Criterion 1) We still need to end at the regular time. Our sessions start at 5:30 p.m. (Criterion 2) How about we figure out a way for you to make a clear reminder to yourself on your phone about when our sessions start? (Criterion 3)

or

I understand you have a lot on your mind today and I want to hear about it. It makes sense you'd want to have more time at the end. (Criterion 1) We still need to end at the regular time. Our sessions start at 5:30 p.m. (Criterion 2) There's a way in which arriving late to session kind of short-changes you—you don't have the full time you need and want here. Can you tell me more about what makes it hard to remember? (Criterion 3)

Example Response to Advanced Client Statement 3

Oh, hey! Before you head out, I just noticed you've put my phone in your pocket. I'm going to need that back. (Criterion 2) I am really curious about this and what it all means—maybe wanting to take something of mine with you? (Criterion 1) I'd really like to talk more about this next week. It's good to talk about these times when you feel compelled to act on your impulses. (Criterion 3)

Example Response to Advanced Client Statement 4

It is so hard living at your house right now. (Criterion 1) I can't take you home with me (Criterion 2), but I can appreciate that there's something about our time together that helps you feel safe and comfortable. (Criterion 1) I want to hear more about what is going on at home that's making you feel so sad. Can we talk about that? (Criterion 3)

Example Response to Advanced Client Statement 5

You've been through so much. And you're right that I can't fully understand the agony and terror of what you experienced. (Criterion 1) I can understand you wanting me to know exactly what it felt like. Even without doing it myself (Criterion 2), I can tell you that I probably would not be able to tolerate the hours you spent under that freezing cold water. Our work together is about processing those awful things and my entering into those memories alongside you—with words and what we process here in this room. Your words are powerful and your memories are so painful. Would it be possible for you to put into words how you felt in that shower? (Criterion 3) I can go there with you in my mind as we talk about it.

Example Response to Advanced Client Statement 6

Hmmm . . . I'm not quite sure how to respond to that. I'm wondering if you are expecting me to react with shock, discomfort, or to somehow reciprocate. (Criterion 1) You talk about a lot of intimate things with me, but it's important for me to say that our relationship is a professional, therapeutic one. (Criterion 2) Instead of commenting on my appearance, can you tell me more about the feelings you're having? (Criterion 3)

or

I feel a little caught off guard. I wonder if you imagined I might be shocked by this statement. Or maybe you're feeling close to me in a way that is unfamiliar to you. (Criterion 1) It's really important for us to maintain a professional relationship and to keep certain boundaries here. (Criterion 2) So, if you're feeling particularly close to me or if you're wanting to shock me in some way, you can put those things into words. Then we can make sense of it together. (Criterion 3)

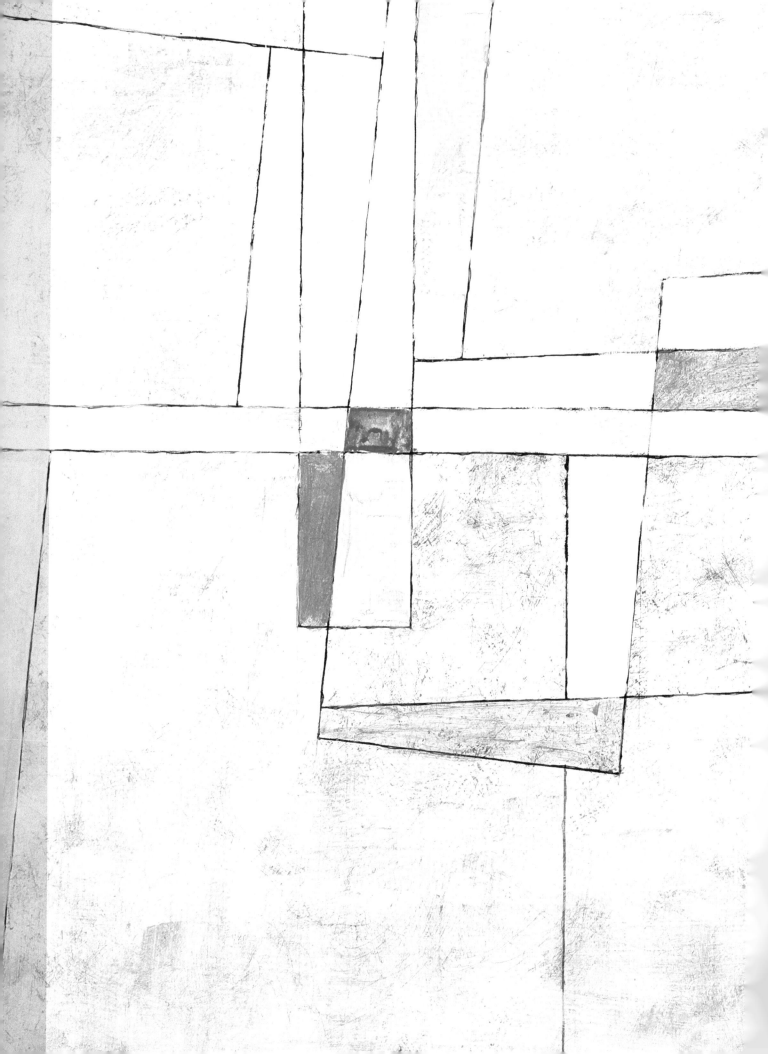

Talking About Sex

Preparations for Exercise 11

1. Read the instructions in Chapter 2.

2. Download the Deliberate Practice Reaction Form and the Deliberate Practice Diary Form at https://www.apa.org/pubs/books/deliberate-practice-child-adolescent-psychotherapy (see the "Clinician and Practitioner Resources" tab; also available in Appendixes A and B, respectively).

Skill Description

Skill Difficulty Level: Advanced

The purpose of this exercise is less about a specific skill or approach and more about getting comfortable talking with children, adolescents, and parents about sex. Given the focus on discomfort, before starting to practice this skill, we suggest taking a moment to notice what you are feeling and to consider the messages that you have gotten and that your social-cultural world communicates around sex and sexuality.

From birth, the body and our relationship to it is a central aspect of our experience, whether we are highly aware of and connected with our body or barely consider it and are largely disconnected. Sex and sexuality represent bodily experiences. In optimal circumstances, sex is about pleasure, although as we know, for many youth, sexual experiences may also be uncomfortable and too often occur in the context of abuse. Regardless of what a person's experiences have been, there is often a great deal of shame around sex, sexuality, and talking about sex, especially when it comes to talking about sex with grownups. As therapists, we strive to create a space where we can process topics that are difficult (or even forbidden) to think and speak about. Through this new experience with the therapist, shame is likely to be reduced.

https://doi.org/10.1037/0000288-013

In practicing this skill, it is important to try out responses that invite further discussion and exploration, rather than envisioning your response as a single intervention. Being able to think together in the context of therapy requires that the therapist to take an open, curious stance that is focused on gaining an understanding of the patient's experience and perspective. Exploration should be nonjudgmental of the patient, and in most cases a balance should be struck between the affective and the cognitive aspects of the experience. Your role as a therapist is very different from that of a parent. Talking about sex with children and adolescents often provokes an intense reaction in the therapist, which often lends itself to becoming more concrete and corrective. Although we each have our own values and preferences around sex and sexuality, we need to be careful that we do not take on the role of authority figure, teacher, or reprimander. And, as in the other skills, when children are talking about sex in the context of play, it is usually wise to stay within the play.

SKILL CRITERIA FOR EXERCISE 11

1. Monitor your own internal reaction (this is an internal skill—you do not need to disclose this reaction).
2. Respond to the sexual content of the child's statement directly (i.e., do not avoid the topic).
3. Invite the child to elaborate on their perspective and experience with a curious, nonjudgmental tone (avoid giving advice, taking a moral stance, preaching, or responding like a parent or teacher).

Examples of Talking About Sex

Note: <u>Underlined text</u> in brackets should be read aloud to provide context.

Example 1

SIX-YEAR-OLD CHILD CLIENT: [*Matter-of-factly, <u>playing with dolls, making them lie down</u>*] They are kissing, like grownups do.

THERAPIST: [<u>*Picking up another doll and speaking for her*</u>] Oh, they are kissing like grownups do! I'm not sure if they know I'm here and can see them. I wonder how they feel about each other. What should I do?

Example 2

ADOLESCENT CLIENT: [*Ambivalent*] It's weird to talk about this stuff, like sex and dating, with a grownup. I'd rather just talk to my friends.

THERAPIST: That makes a lot of sense. Talking about sex and dating with me might feel a little awkward. My role is different from a parent's or teacher's. I'm really just curious about your thoughts and experiences—no judgment here. How does it feel to talk about sex and dating with your friends?

Example 3

10-YEAR-OLD CHILD CLIENT: [*Silly, <u>cupping her breasts and dancing</u>*] Look at me, ha ha ha!

THERAPIST: Hmm, you are showing me some of your body parts. I wonder if they are parts that are starting to change?

INSTRUCTIONS FOR EXERCISE 11

Step 1: Role-Play and Feedback

- The client says the first beginner client statement, also reading aloud any <u>underlined text</u> in brackets to provide context. The therapist improvises a response based on the skill criteria.

- The trainer (or if not available, the client) provides brief feedback based on the skill criteria.

- The client then repeats the same statement, and the therapist again improvises a response. The trainer (or client) again provides brief feedback.

Step 2: Repeat

- Repeat Step 1 for all the statements in the current difficulty level (beginner, intermediate, or advanced).

Step 3: Assess and Adjust Difficulty

- The therapist completes the Deliberate Practice Reaction Form (see Appendix A) and decides whether to make the exercise easier or harder or to repeat the same difficulty level.

Step 4: Repeat for Approximately 15 Minutes

- Repeat Steps 1 to 3 for at least 15 minutes.
- The trainees then switch therapist and client roles and start over.

Now it's your turn! Follow Steps 1 and 2 from the instructions.

Remember: The goal of the role-play is for trainees to practice improvising responses to the client statements in a manner that (a) uses the skill criteria and (b) feels authentic for the trainee. **Example therapist responses for each client statement are provided at the end of this exercise. Trainees should attempt to improvise their own responses before reading the example responses.**

BEGINNER-LEVEL CLIENT STATEMENTS FOR EXERCISE 11
Beginner Client Statement 1
[**Six-year-old, matter-of-factly, <u>playing with dolls, making them lie down</u>**] They are kissing, like grownups do.
Beginner Client Statement 2
[**Adolescent, ambivalent**] It's weird to talk about this stuff, like sex and dating, with a grownup. I'd rather just talk to my friends.
Beginner Client Statement 3
[**Ten-year-old, silly, <u>cupping her breasts and dancing</u>**] Look at me, ha ha ha!
Beginner Client Statement 4
[**Twelve-year-old, anxious**] My parents haven't told me anything about puberty or sex at all. I think they don't really want me to know about it. Do you have any books you could recommend for someone my age?
Beginner Client Statement 5
[**Twelve-year-old, excited**] There are so many hot girls in middle school! I think I'm really going to like my new school.

 Assess and adjust the difficulty before moving to the next difficulty level (see Step 3 in the exercise instructions).

INTERMEDIATE-LEVEL CLIENT STATEMENTS FOR EXERCISE 11
Intermediate Client Statement 1
[**Adolescent, matter-of-factly**] I just love bad boys. I don't know why. I probably have daddy issues, I know.
Intermediate Client Statement 2
[**Adolescent, laughing**] Oh my gosh, today in health class, we had to watch this video. And none of us could take it seriously. It was about dating and sex, and we just like were cracking up the whole time.
Intermediate Client Statement 3
[**Twelve-year-old, disappointed**] Some people are starting to date. I have liked people, but they never like me back.
Intermediate Client Statement 4
[**Fourteen-year-old, unsure**] I don't know if I'm bisexual or pansexual or asexual or what. You know me pretty well. What do you think?
Intermediate Client Statement 5
[**Seven-year-old, inquisitive**] I had to stop seeing my last therapist because she had a baby and didn't come back to her office after. I never asked her, but I keep wondering . . . how exactly did the baby get into her tummy?
Intermediate Client Statement 6
[**Thirteen-year-old, self-assured; <u>therapist has just asked what the teen did over the weekend</u>**] Well, we went to Sam's house and watched some porn. We followed that up with some horror movies. It was pretty awesome.

🛑 **Assess and adjust the difficulty before moving to the next difficulty level (see Step 3 in the exercise instructions).**

ADVANCED-LEVEL CLIENT STATEMENTS FOR EXERCISE 11
Advanced Client Statement 1
[Adolescent, self-assured] I think I'm ready to lose my virginity.
Advanced Client Statement 2
[Six-year-old child, angry] I hate my penis. I want to chop it off.
Advanced Client Statement 3
[Adolescent, indifferent] Last weekend we got dressed up and did a photo shoot, and I posted some of the pictures on Snapchat. And there's this other group of girls, who apparently started like a private group and were calling us sluts and stuff. But whatever, I don't care.
Advanced Client Statement 4
[Fifteen-year-old, tearful] Remember that guy I was dating? I did some things with him last weekend and every time I think about it now, I just start crying.
Advanced Client Statement 5
[Eight-year-old, anxious] Mommy and Daddy say sex is only for people who are married and love each other a lot. It's not right to do it if you're not married, right?
Advanced Client Statement 6
[Fourteen-year-old, somewhat shyly] This is kind of awkward, but I feel like I should tell you. I've been watching porn since I was, like, 10 years old or something. Lately I've been watching some harder core stuff. I'm really worried my parents are going to find out. It's totally not a big deal, but they would think it is.
Advanced Client Statement 7
[Adolescent, unsure] My dad totally knows I'm gay. He's fine with it, but he's always had this rule about no porn on the internet. He just wants me to look at magazines like he did because he says the internet is a "cesspool." He got me some new magazines, but they're full of girls! He knows I'm not into women and he's just trying to be nice. But, it's weird, right?

🛑 **Assess and adjust the difficulty here (see Step 3 in the exercise instructions). If appropriate, follow the instructions to make the exercise even more challenging (see Appendix A).**

Example Therapist Responses: Talking About Sex

Remember: Trainees should attempt to improvise their own responses before reading the example responses. **Do not read the following responses verbatim unless you are having trouble coming up with your own responses!**

EXAMPLE RESPONSES TO BEGINNER-LEVEL CLIENT STATEMENTS FOR EXERCISE 11
Example Response to Beginner Client Statement 1
[<u>**Picking up another doll and speaking for her**</u>] Oh, they *are* kissing like grownups do! (Criterion 2) I'm not sure if they know I'm here and can see them. I wonder how they feel about each other. What should I do? (Criterion 3)
Example Response to Beginner Client Statement 2
That makes a lot of sense. Talking about sex and dating with me might feel a little awkward. My role is different than a parent's or teacher's. I'm really just curious about your thoughts and experiences—no judgment here. (Criterion 3) How does it feel to talk about sex and dating with your friends? (Criteria 2 and 3)
Example Response to Beginner Client Statement 3
Hmm, you are showing me some of your body parts. (Criterion 2) I wonder if they are parts that are starting to change? (Criterion 3)
Example Response to Beginner Client Statement 4
I do have some books I can recommend. It sounds like you have a lot of questions about puberty and sex, and like you wish your parents felt more comfortable talking about these things. (Criterion 2) What gives you the sense they don't want you to know more? (Criterion 3)
Example Response to Beginner Client Statement 5
That is a great thing about going to a new school. You're meeting all these new girls and you feel attracted to them. (Criterion 2) I'd love to hear more about some of the girls you're meeting. (Criterion 3)

EXAMPLE RESPONSES TO INTERMEDIATE-LEVEL CLIENT STATEMENTS FOR EXERCISE 11
Example Response to Intermediate Client Statement 1
I don't know about "daddy issues" [smiling], but I'm curious what you mean by "bad boys." (Criterion 2) Can you tell me more? (Criterion 3)
Example Response to Intermediate Client Statement 2
Yeah, that can be really uncomfortable when topics like sex and dating come up in a classroom setting. (Criterion 2) What was it like for you? Were there specific things that made you laugh? (Criterion 3)
Example Response to Intermediate Client Statement 3
I can imagine that not being liked back brings up some kind of painful feelings. Can you tell me more about one of the people you've liked? I'm also interested to know what gender or genders you are drawn to so I can be sure to use the right pronouns. (Criteria 2 and 3)
Example Response to Intermediate Client Statement 4
Sounds like you're really trying to figure out some important things about your sexuality. (Criterion 2) You have helped me get to know you pretty well, but when it comes to your sexual identity, that's something only you can determine. Often it takes time to figure this out—there's no rush. (Criterion 3) Can you tell me more about those identities and what your thoughts are about each one? (Criterion 3)
Example Response to Intermediate Client Statement 5
That must have been hard to say goodbye to your therapist. What a good question you're asking about how pregnancy begins. (Criteria 2 and 3) Can you tell me a little bit about what you do know about how babies are made? (Criterion 3)
Example Response to Intermediate Client Statement 6
Sounds like you had a great time with your friends. I'm curious about the porn—is that something you've done before at Sam's or on your own? (Criteria 2 and 3)
[Additional follow-up questions]
Are you watching things online or on television? Is there a particular type of porn you tend to watch? When you are watching with your friends, do you all masturbate? Is there any sexual contact between you and your friends when you're watching porn together?

EXAMPLE RESPONSES TO ADVANCED-LEVEL
CLIENT STATEMENTS FOR EXERCISE 11

Example Response to Advanced Client Statement 1

For some teenagers, having sex for the first time is an important and significant decision. (Criterion 2) And it sounds like you've really put some thought into it. Can you tell me more about how you made this decision? (Criterion 3)

Example Response to Advanced Client Statement 2

That is a difficult feeling, to hate a part of your body. I'm glad you're able to tell me about this. It sounds like the hate you have for your penis is really strong. (Criterion 2) I'd like us to talk more about it so that you don't have to hurt yourself. When did these feelings start? (Criterion 3)

Example Response to Advanced Client Statement 3

Gosh, I know you said you don't care but, to me, being called a "slut" by your peers sounds pretty awful. (Criterion 2) Dressing up and taking photos sounds like a lot of fun—I'm curious how that turned into this bullying situation. Can you tell me more about the photo shoot? (Criterion 3)

Example Response to Advanced Client Statement 4

Yes, I remember him. I'm so sorry you're going through this. It sounds like you're having some really intense feelings, and I'd like to know more about what happened between the two of you. (Criterion 2) Can we talk more about what happened last weekend with him? (Criterion 3)

Example Response to Advanced Client Statement 5

What an important question you're asking. Sex is an interesting thing because different people have really different ideas and values about it. It sounds like in your family, there is a strong value around sex being only for married people. (Criterion 2) There are other people in the world who think differently about that. I'm really curious what you think about sex and who should do it. (Criterion 3)

Example Response to Advanced Client Statement 6

I'm glad you feel comfortable sharing this with me—especially because it sounds like you're pretty worried about getting in trouble. So, you've been watching porn for a few years now. (Criterion 2) I'm curious what changed lately. What led you to watch harder core stuff and what exactly do you mean by "harder core"? (Criterion 3)

Example Response to Advanced Client Statement 7

Hmmm . . . so, on the one hand, your dad is pretty supportive of you being gay. And he wants to try and protect you from some of the uglier parts of the internet, so he buys you porn magazines. (Criterion 2) But there's this real mismatch. Even though he says he's fine with you being gay, the magazines he's giving you are all about girls. What's your take on it? (Criterion 3)

Responding to Resistance and Ruptures

Preparations for Exercise 12

1. Read the instructions in Chapter 2.

2. Download the Deliberate Practice Reaction Form and the Deliberate Practice Diary Form at https://www.apa.org/pubs/books/deliberate-practice-child-adolescent-psychotherapy (see the "Clinician and Practitioner Resources" tab; also available in Appendixes A and B, respectively).

Skill Description

Skill Difficulty Level: Advanced

One of the unique features of child therapy is that the impetus for seeking treatment often comes from an adult—a parent, caregiver, or teacher. Although some children and adolescents will ask their parents to find a therapist for them, the majority come to treatment at someone else's urging. Typically, an adult physically brings the child to the clinic or therapist's office, even when the child is disinterested or actively refusing therapy. With children, resistance (and even ruptures) can begin in the waiting room, or even on the way to the appointment. Unlike adults—whose resistance may be subtle or even polite—children are often more comfortable expressing their feelings overtly and directly. Resistance may take the form of crying, screaming at the therapist, running out of the room, hiding behind toys in a playroom, or simply refusing to speak at all. Of course, children and adolescents can also demonstrate more subdued forms of resistance, such as questioning the tasks and goals of therapy, withdrawing, "forgetting" to do homework assignments, or changing the subject. Sometimes resistance takes the form of an actual therapeutic rupture, a moment or period in therapy when there is a strain or breakdown in the therapeutic alliance. Research shows that in child therapy, the alliance with both the child and the parent is predictive of outcomes (Halfon, 2021;

https://doi.org/10.1037/0000288-014

Shirk et al., 2011). Although less research has been done on how the alliance unfolds in child and adolescent treatment, studies on adults have shown that a strong therapeutic alliance is associated not with a lack of ruptures, but with repair of ruptures in the relationship (Eubanks et al., 2018; Kramer et al., 2014; Muran et al., 2021). There is reason to theorize that the same may be true for children (Halfon, 2021; Karver et al., 2005).

Whether resistance to or ruptures within the therapeutic process include active refusal, disengagement, or passivity and silence, it can be challenging for child therapists to know how to respond. Resistance is common across all types of psychotherapy. Responding to resistance and ruptures requires therapist empathy, patience, curiosity, and, sometimes, a departure from the immediate therapeutic focus. Repairing ruptures in psychotherapy involves explicitly recognizing the rupture, and bringing attention to it, rather than continuing without acknowledging that something has happened (Nof et al., 2019). This is followed by validating the child's assertion of their own needs, communicating an understanding of the rupture that helps the child feel seen and known, and collaborating with the child to move forward (Nof et al., 2019). This process often involves the renegotiation of the tasks and goals of the therapeutic moment or even the broader therapeutic agenda. It may also involve renegotiation of the bond between client and therapist.

Motivational interviewing is one approach that prioritizes exploring resistance and resolving client ambivalence to change. One of the key phrases in motivational interviewing is to "roll with" the resistance; that is, the therapist seeks to understand the resistance and avoids confrontation, attempts at persuasion, and arguing. Although not originally designed for use with children, some of the components of motivational interviewing—namely, collaboration, supporting client autonomy, and integrating empathy and nurturance—offer an empathic and effective way of responding to resistance and ruptures in any child psychotherapy modality.

In this exercise, we focus on how to respond to children's unique forms of resistance in therapy and how to address these even when they present a rupture in the therapeutic alliance—including overt refusal to engage and more passive or dismissive forms of resistance. The goals of the skill criteria in this exercise are to help you effectively engage with the child's resistance and learn more about the resistance (or rupture), in the service of moving the therapy forward and strengthening the therapeutic relationship.

SKILL CRITERIA FOR EXERCISE 12

1. Acknowledge the resistance or rupture.
2. Empathically communicate understanding of the resistance/rupture and "roll with" the resistance (vs. challenging or arguing with the child).
3. Provide support for the child's autonomy.

Examples of Responding to Resistance and Ruptures

Note: Underlined text in brackets should be read aloud to provide context.

Example 1

FIFTEEN-YEAR-OLD CLIENT: [*Dismissive*] Yeah, I don't know why I'm here. I have nothing to talk about.

THERAPIST: You're not sure why your mom wanted you to come talk with me and it sounds like there's nothing you feel comfortable sharing. That's got to make it really tough to be here. Maybe it even seems a little unfair. It's really up to you how we use our time together—we can even talk about how annoying it is to have to come to therapy at all.

Example 2

FOUR-YEAR-OLD CLIENT: [*Withdrawn, <u>the child has turned their back to the therapist and is hunched over on the playroom floor, playing silently and refusing to talk</u>*]

THERAPIST: [<u>*Sits on the floor at a slight distance from the child, on their level, but giving them personal space*</u>] I can see you are wanting some space . . . to play and maybe even for your own thoughts. It's really hard to talk today. I can sit quietly until you feel more comfortable. We can also play together without talking. We can do whatever feels best to you.

Example 3

13-YEAR-OLD CLIENT: [*Anxious and depressed*] Honestly, you have no idea what it's like to be a teenager today. I don't see how you think you can help me.

THERAPIST: That's a good point. I know a little bit about being a teenager today only from other teens I've worked with, but I really don't know what it's like to be you. I can understand why it's hard to think I could help at all. I would like to get to know you and to understand more about what's been making you feel so down lately. Could we start there?

INSTRUCTIONS FOR EXERCISE 12

Step 1: Role-Play and Feedback

- The client says the first beginner client statement, also reading aloud any <u>underlined text</u> in brackets to provide context. The therapist improvises a response based on the skill criteria.

- The trainer (or if not available, the client) provides brief feedback based on the skill criteria.

- The client then repeats the same statement, and the therapist again improvises a response. The trainer (or client) again provides brief feedback.

Step 2: Repeat

- Repeat Step 1 for all the statements in the current difficulty level (beginner, intermediate, or advanced).

Step 3: Assess and Adjust Difficulty

- The therapist completes the Deliberate Practice Reaction Form (see Appendix A) and decides whether to make the exercise easier or harder or to repeat the same difficulty level.

Step 4: Repeat for Approximately 15 Minutes

- Repeat Steps 1 to 3 for at least 15 minutes.
- The trainees then switch therapist and client roles and start over.

Now it's your turn! Follow Steps 1 and 2 from the instructions.

Remember: The goal of the role-play is for trainees to practice improvising responses to the client statements in a manner that (a) uses the skill criteria and (b) feels authentic for the trainee. **Example therapist responses for each client statement are provided at the end of this exercise. Trainees should attempt to improvise their own responses before reading the example responses.**

BEGINNER-LEVEL CLIENT STATEMENTS FOR EXERCISE 12
Beginner Client Statement 1
[**Fifteen-year-old, dismissive**] Yeah, I don't know why I'm here. I have nothing to talk about.
Beginner Client Statement 2
[**Eight-year-old, annoyed**] It's so *boring* here!
Beginner Client Statement 3
[**Thirteen-year-old, calm and subdued,** <u>the client has been talking about the movies they watched over the weekend for 10 minutes straight, leaving no room for the therapist to get a word in</u>] Oh! And there's another movie too. So, on Saturday I watched the *third* one in the series. The plot was amazing. Like, the characters were so relatable, too.
Beginner Client Statement 4
[**Four-year-old, withdrawn,** <u>the child has turned their back to the therapist and is hunched over on the playroom floor, playing silently and refusing to talk</u>]
Beginner Client Statement 5
[**Ten-year-old, irritable**] How did I *feel*? Come on. Feelings, feelings, feelings. There's not really any point to talking about that.

🛑 **Assess and adjust the difficulty before moving to the next difficulty level (see Step 3 in the exercise instructions).**

INTERMEDIATE-LEVEL CLIENT STATEMENTS FOR EXERCISE 12
Intermediate Client Statement 1
[Five-year-old, fearful, <u>the child is in the waiting room for a first appointment with the therapist, clinging to mother, refusing to look at or speak to the therapist</u>]
Intermediate Client Statement 2
[Fifteen-year-old, assertive] I've been watching these awesome self-help videos on social media and joined a few online groups for depressed teens. They've made me realize that I don't really need therapy. I can sort it out on my own.
Intermediate Client Statement 3
[Eight-year-old, withdrawn, <u>the therapist has just asked if the child knows why their parents brought them to therapy</u>] I don't know. [Long silence]
Intermediate Client Statement 4
[Fifteen-year-old, defeated] This is pointless to keep talking about. Obviously, things would be so much easier if I didn't have to come here every week.
Intermediate Client Statement 5
[Six-year-old, silly, closes eyes and covers ears with hands] I can't heeeear you! Nah-nah-nah-nah. I can't hear you!

🛑 **Assess and adjust the difficulty before moving to the next difficulty level (see Step 3 in the exercise instructions).**

ADVANCED-LEVEL CLIENT STATEMENTS FOR EXERCISE 12
Advanced Client Statement 1
[Thirteen-year-old, anxious and depressed] Honestly, you have no idea what it's like to be a teenager today. I don't see how you think you can help me.
Advanced Client Statement 2
[Ten-year-old, angry] This is a waste of time. You want me to talk about myself when the actual problem is my parents, my school, the kids in my neighborhood. You should be talking to all of *them*!
Advanced Client Statement 3
[Eight-year-old, dismissive] Yeah, my parents tried that stupid chart you gave them, trying to get me to "shape up"?! I guess all the grown-ups just think I'm like a dog that needs to be trained, huh?
Advanced Client Statement 4
[Seven-year-old, angry] I hate you! I hate you! You hear me? I hate you! Ugh, I'm so sick of this place and *really* sick of you.
Advanced Client Statement 5
[Nine-year-old, silly, <u>the child has agreed to do breathing exercises in session and the therapist has just begun instructions for belly breathing</u>] Sponge Bob Poopy Pants! Porta potty! Stupid dummy face! Why did the chicken cross the road? Knock, knock! Come on . . . you know you wanna laugh!

Assess and adjust the difficulty here (see Step 3 in the exercise instructions). If appropriate, follow the instructions to make the exercise even more challenging (see Appendix A).

Example Therapist Responses: Responding to Resistance and Ruptures

Remember: Trainees should attempt to improvise their own responses before reading the example responses. **Do not read the following responses verbatim unless you are having trouble coming up with your own responses!**

EXAMPLE RESPONSES TO BEGINNER-LEVEL CLIENT STATEMENTS FOR EXERCISE 12
Example Response to Beginner Client Statement 1
You're not sure why your mom wanted you to come talk with me and it sounds like there's nothing you feel comfortable sharing. (Criterion 1) That's got to make it really tough to be here. Maybe it even seems a little unfair. (Criterion 2) It's really up to you how we use our time together—we can even talk about how annoying it is to have to come to therapy at all. (Criterion 3)
Example Response to Beginner Client Statement 2
Ugh. I hear that—it's hard to even know what to do or what to talk about today. (Criteria 1 and 2) Would you like to choose what we play or would it be better for me to offer some choices? (Criterion 3)
Example Response to Beginner Client Statement 3
I'm sorry to interrupt. I can tell how much you like these movies. You've been telling me about them, and I'm wondering if there is anything you're avoiding talking about (Criterion 1) or if there's something I should be listening for as you tell me about the characters and the plot that would help me understand the difficult feelings you've been having lately. (Criteria 2 and 3)
Example Response to Beginner Client Statement 4
[**Sits on the floor at a slight distance from the child, on their level, but giving them personal space**] I can see you are wanting some space . . . to play and maybe even for your own thoughts. (Criterion 2) It's really hard to talk today. (Criterion 1) I can sit quietly until you feel more comfortable. We can also play together without talking. We can do whatever feels best to you. (Criterion 3)
Example Response to Beginner Client Statement 5
You really don't want to talk about feelings. (Criterion 1) It feels pretty pointless. (Criterion 2) What would feel more meaningful or valuable for us to focus on? (Criterion 3)

EXAMPLE RESPONSES TO INTERMEDIATE-LEVEL CLIENT STATEMENTS FOR EXERCISE 12

Example Response to Intermediate Client Statement 1

[**Speaking calmly and softly**] Oh, I can see it is really hard for you to come into the playroom right now. (Criterion 1) I'm a new person and you've never been here before. (Criterion 2) What if Mommy came with us and we could all look at the toys together? (Criterion 3)

Example Response to Intermediate Client Statement 2

Sounds like you've found some really great resources! (Criterion 2) And they have been so helpful that you're not sure if therapy can add much to that. (Criterion 1) I'd love to hear more about the videos and what you've been learning about within those online groups. Would you be willing to tell me about them? (Criterion 3)

Example Response to Intermediate Client Statement 3

So, it might feel like a bit of a mystery. You're not sure why we're meeting or even maybe what therapy is all about. (Criterion 2) And it feels hard to talk much or even ask questions. (Criterion 1) Would it be helpful for me to share what your parents shared with me? Or should we start with something else? (Criterion 3)

Example Response to Intermediate Client Statement 4

You're really not wanting to talk today. (Criterion 1) I can understand that. And it sounds like coming to therapy feels like it's actually making things harder for you in some ways. (Criterion 2) Do you want to tell me more about that? I am very interested in understanding what is making things feel so pointless and frustrating. (Criterion 3)

Example Response to Intermediate Client Statement 5

You really don't want to hear what I'm saying. (Criterion 1) I guess what we were starting to talk about was really hard. (Criterion 2) Should we take a break from that for now and be silly together for a few minutes? (Criterion 3)

EXAMPLE RESPONSES TO ADVANCED-LEVEL CLIENT STATEMENTS FOR EXERCISE 12

Example Response to Advanced Client Statement 1

That's a good point. I know a little bit about being a teenager today only from other teens I've worked with, but I really don't know what it's like to be you. (Criterion 2) I can understand why it's hard to think I could help at all. (Criterion 1) I would like to get to know you and to understand more about what's been making you feel so down lately. Could we start there? (Criterion 3)

Example Response to Advanced Client Statement 2

I have been focusing a lot on you and how we can work together to help you change—and that is frustrating! (Criterion 1) It must seem like I've overlooked a big piece of the puzzle—how everyone else around you is contributing to the difficulties you've been having. (Criterion 2) I can set up a meeting with your parents, for sure. Would it be helpful to tell me what all of these folks have been doing to cause problems? (Criterion 3)

Example Response to Advanced Client Statement 3

That cannot feel good—like you're just an animal in need of training. (Criterion 2) I'm glad you're telling me about how stupid the chart seemed and how annoyed you are. (Criterion 1) I'm thinking about how you've been telling me about how often you're getting in trouble and people are getting on your case all the time. Sometimes behavior charts like this can help kids and parents get along better, but it sounds like, in this case, it didn't work out that way. I'm curious what your ideas are for how to make things better between you and your parents. (Criterion 3)

Example Response to Advanced Client Statement 4

I do hear you. You're really fed up—with me, with therapy, with this place. (Criterion 1) I've been asking you a lot of questions, and maybe I haven't given you enough space to vent and really let me know how angry you feel. (Criterion 2) Would it be helpful to let some of that out? (Criterion 3)

Example Response to Advanced Client Statement 5

We're in a tough spot here. We have different ideas about whether we should do these exercises or not. (Criterion 1) Sounds like you want to be silly and tell some jokes, maybe because you don't want to do the breathing or maybe because you're a little nervous about it. (Criterion 2) Is there some way we could try the belly breathing? Maybe we could have some silly time first and then try it out? Or we could do some breathing first and then be super silly? What works for you? (Criterion 3)

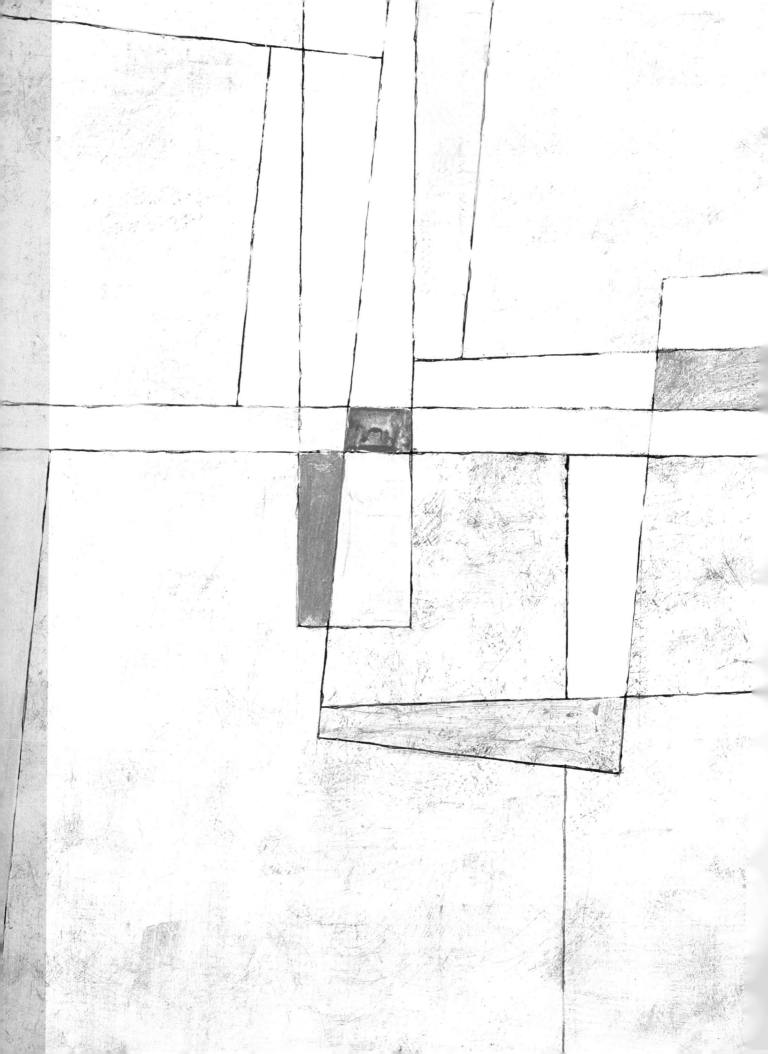

Annotated Child Psychotherapy Practice Session Transcripts

It is now time to put all the skills you have learned together! This exercise presents two transcripts from typical child therapy sessions. The first transcript is from a play therapy session, and the second is from a more structured cognitive behavioral approach, both with a 9-year-old child. Each therapist statement is annotated to indicate which therapeutic skill from Exercises 1 to 12 is used. The transcript provides an example of how therapists can interweave many skills in response to child clients.

Instructions

As in the previous exercises, one trainee can play the client while the other plays the therapist. Each transcript begins with a brief introduction that provides background information. Additional information about the client's nonverbal behavior, including the child's play and the therapist's actions, are presented in brackets. Underlined text in brackets should be read out loud to make sure the nonverbal actions are clear. However, both client and therapist should try to incorporate the nonverbal actions into the session to make the experience as realistic as possible. As much as possible, the trainee who plays the client should try to adopt an authentic emotional tone and nonverbal behavior as if they were a real child client.

The first time through, both partners can read verbatim from the transcript. After one complete run-through, try it again.

This time, the client can read from the script, while the therapist can improvise to the degree that they feel comfortable. At this point, you may also want to reflect on it with a supervisor and go through it again.

Before you start, it is recommended that both the therapist and the client read the entire transcript through, on their own, to the end. The purpose of the sample transcript is to give trainees the opportunity to try out what it is like to use the child therapy skills in a sequence that mimics live therapy sessions.

https://doi.org/10.1037/0000288-015
Deliberate Practice in Child and Adolescent Psychotherapy, by J. Bate, T. A. Prout, T. Rousmaniere, and A. Vaz

Note to Therapists

Remember to be playful; this does not necessarily mean being happy or positive. You can be playful by imagining, reflecting back emotions with marked mirroring (i.e., emphasizing the emotion in your face that you imagine the child is feeling), or using humor. Match the way you speak to the child's developmental level. Consider that although young children can think and talk about emotions, they may still describe relationships superficially. Children 8 years and older may be able to talk about their own personalities or qualities of others with more richness and depth. Finally, pay attention to how you use your face and your body because nonverbal communication is as important as verbal content in therapy with children.

Transcript 1: Play Therapy Session

The following session is with a child client who is 9 years old—can be any gender—whose parents recently divorced and who presents with symptoms of generalized anxiety disorder. This is the fifth session of therapy.

CLIENT 1: [The child enters the room slowly and quietly, scanning eyes around the room]

THERAPIST 1: Hi there, it's nice to see you. You're having a look around the room? I have some toys here, and we can play or talk however you want. In this playroom, we have just one rule—we cannot hurt anyone or anything, but besides that, this is a place where you can be free to say, think, feel, or play anything. (Skill 10: Setting Limits)

CLIENT 2: [The child walks around the room, looking at a box of LEGOs]

THERAPIST 2: Looks like you're eyeing the LEGOs, shall we take them out? (Skill 1: Interest and Curiosity)

CLIENT 3: [nods] I have this same set at home, but bigger.

THERAPIST 3: Bigger!? You must be able to build a lot of things then. What do you like to build? (Skill 1: Interest and Curiosity)

CLIENT 4: I mostly build cars, or sometimes airplanes.

THERAPIST 4: Oh, so you have fun building vehicles? (Skill 2: Naming Feelings) Things that can move and go places? (Skill 1: Interest and Curiosity)

CLIENT 5: [The child digs around through the LEGO box, a bit fast and flustered]

THERAPIST 5: Looks like you are searching for something you have in mind. (Skill 3: Observing and Describing Play)

CLIENT 6: Yeah, I am trying to find all of the wheels that are this size [holds up a wheel]. I am going to build a race car.

THERAPIST 6: [While digging slowly and carefully] Hmm, this is tough to find. (Skill 3: Praise and Encouragement) They are small, we have to go slowly and look very carefully. (Skill 4: Observing and Describing Play)

CLIENT 7: It's fine, I have four of the bigger ones, I guess I can build a truck instead.

THERAPIST 7: You're pretty resourceful, huh? Changing your plan. (Skill 3: Praise and Encouragement) Is that how you usually are when you run into a problem? Or do you ever get frustrated? (Skill 2: Naming Feelings)

CLIENT 8: Umm, I get frustrated sometimes, I guess.

THERAPIST 8: But this kind of situation doesn't get you too frustrated?

CLIENT 9: [Continuing to build] No, it's fine, I like building trucks too.

THERAPIST 9: You had sounded excited about building the race car, so that's why I had wondered if it was disappointing or frustrating. Makes me curious, though . . . what kinds of situations do make you frustrated? (Skill 1: Interest and Curiosity)

CLIENT 10: Mostly things my brother does. Like, when he cheats at games or when he tries to beat me up.

THERAPIST 10: When he tries to beat you up! What does he do? (Skill 9: Gathering Information About Safety Concerns)

CLIENT 11: Like punches me and stuff.

THERAPIST 11: Punches you and stuff, like really hard? (Skill 9: Gathering Information About Safety Concerns)

CLIENT 12: Kinda hard. One time, when I was little, like, maybe like 5, he hit me with a book and it gave me a black eye.

THERAPIST 12: Ouch! That sounds like it hurt! No wonder you feel frustrated with him sometimes. I might even feel angry. (Skill 5: Empathic Validation)

CLIENT 13: Yeah, it did hurt.

THERAPIST 13: What do you do when he beats you up like that? Do you go to your parents? (Skill 9: Gathering Information About Safety Concerns)

CLIENT 14: Yeah, but they always take his side. He's like the prince of the house.

THERAPIST 14: So if he's the prince, who are you in the house? (Skill 6: Elaborating Play)

CLIENT 15: I don't know.

THERAPIST 15: Hmm, you don't know what your role is, but he is the prince. Like he is treated special and everybody loves him?

CLIENT 16: Yeah.

THERAPIST 16: That can be hard to have a brother who is a prince, especially when you feel like they listen to him all the time and don't listen to you. I can imagine it would be frustrating, and maybe sometimes make you angry or sad? (Skill 2: Naming Feelings; Skill 5: Empathic Validation)

CLIENT 17: Yeah, I dunno. The truck is ready! [Starts rolling the truck on the ground]

THERAPIST 17: Ah, it's ready to go! I wonder where it wants to go or what it wants to do? (Skill 1: Interest and Curiosity; Skill 4: Observing and Describing Play)

CLIENT 18: It is going to carry these LEGOs over here to build a house. [Starts carrying LEGOs over to another spot]

THERAPIST 18: The truck is working hard to get all of the materials to build the house. (Skill 4: Observing and Describing Play)

CLIENT 19: Yeah, it can't carry too much at once, it's not very big.

THERAPIST 19: So it has to take many trips, and it looks like it has to be careful so that the blocks don't fall. (Skill 5: Observing and Describing Play)

CLIENT 20: Yeah, it has to be really careful. [Block falls from the truck]

THERAPIST 20: Uh-oh, we've had a spill. What's the truck driver going to do? Is there a cleanup crew? (Skill 6: Elaborating Play)

CLIENT 21: We can put it back in.

THERAPIST 21: Oh phew, that seemed like a relatively easy fix. And now the truck driver is back on the road. (Skill 5: Observing and Describing Play)

CLIENT 22: Yeah, he has to hurry up, though. He needs to get all of the blocks to build the house by nightfall.

THERAPIST 22: By nightfall? What will happen at nightfall? (Skill 1: Communicating Interest and Curiosity)

CLIENT 23: Well, they're in the woods, so when it gets dark, the animals will come out hunting.

THERAPIST 23: That sounds scary—he must be afraid! (Skill 2: Naming Feelings) Could some other people come help so that it gets built in time for him to feel safe? [The therapist reaches for a toy to join the play] (Skill 6: Elaborating Play)

CLIENT 24: [Becoming dysregulated] No! No! No one can help! Stop!

THERAPIST 24: Oh, okay, I can tell by your voice that you really don't want that. I'm sorry. (Skill 12: Responding to Resistance) So, he has to do this all alone, huh? That's hard work. And he's under a lot of pressure, with the threat of the scary animals coming at nightfall. (Skill 4: Observing and Describing Play)

CLIENT 25: [continues building, very focused]

THERAPIST 25: He is very determined to make a safe place for himself. It looks like with those thick walls the animals won't be able to get through and he'll be safe for the night. Is that right? (Skill 4: Observing and Describing Play)

CLIENT 26: Yeah.

THERAPIST 26: I want to give you a heads up that we have just about 5 more minutes.

CLIENT 27: Okay, I just need to finish this part of the structure.

THERAPIST 27: Okay, so he works for one more minute, and then we will take a pause and we can continue next week.

[One minute later]

THERAPIST 28: All right. I know there is so much more to do, but it's time to stop and clean up for today. (Skill 10: Setting Limits)

CLIENT 28: [Continuing to build] No, hold on, I just need to do this last thing.

THERAPIST 29: It's really tough to end and say goodbye, especially when we are right in the middle of things. I know it's not the best time. But we do have to stop and clean up for today. [Starting to move in and help move the pieces] So, I am going to help you put this away—safe—right here. [Helps move the structure to a cabinet] And we will say goodbye for today, but I will see you next week. (Skill 10: Setting Limits)

Transcript 2: Cognitive Behavioral Therapy Session

The following session is with a different child client who is also 9 years old and can be any gender, whose parents also recently divorced and who presents with symptoms of generalized anxiety disorder. This is the fifth session of therapy.

THERAPIST 1: Hi, good to see you. How are you today?

CLIENT 1: [smiling pleasantly] I'm good.

THERAPIST 2: So, you know how our sessions go by now, so let's go over the agenda for today. Of course I want to check in about how the week went, and how your practice at home went. And I have some ideas about what we might do today, but I'm curious if there is anything that came up this week that you want help with. (Skill 1: Interest and Curiosity) So let's start with how the week went. How was it overall?

CLIENT 2: It was good.

THERAPIST 3: So, you're good today, and the week was good. Tell me, what were the sunshines and raindrops of this week? Like the highlights and the not so good parts. (Skill 1: Interest and Curiosity)

CLIENT 3: Umm, well I had my friend Isa's birthday party over the weekend, so that was fun. It was at this cool indoor trampoline park thing. So I guess that's the sunshine.

THERAPIST 4: An indoor trampoline park, that sounds exciting. (Skill 2: Naming Feelings) What was it like? (Skill 1: Interest and Curiosity)

CLIENT 4: Yeah, it was cool. We could do flips and stuff.

THERAPIST 5: Had you done something like that before, or was it the first time? (Skill 1: Interest and Curiosity)

CLIENT 5: Umm, I had done it before.

THERAPIST 6: So there was some fun with friends this week. And what raindrops were there this week? (Skill 1: Interest and Curiosity)

CLIENT 6: I dunno . . . [long pause]

THERAPIST 7: Yeah, I know sometimes you find these a bit harder to think about. Let's see if you can come up with one though . . . take your time. (Skill 3: Praise and Encouragement)

CLIENT 7: I guess the raindrop was that my mom yelled at me about doing my homework the other night.

THERAPIST 8: Mom yelled at you, huh? That never feels good. (Skill 5: Empathic Validation) What was the situation? (Skill 1: Interest and Curiosity)

CLIENT 8: Well, she got home from work and I wasn't done with my math, and I was supposed to be done by the time she got home. But I didn't feel like doing it earlier. And I did it when she got home.

THERAPIST 9: So, it sounds like you and mom had different ideas about how things should go in the evening. But you did it, so that's always a good thing, when you do your homework. (Skill 3: Praise and Encouragement) And you did it on your own?

CLIENT 9: Yeah.

THERAPIST 10: Nice. I know math can be tough, so it's pretty impressive that you did eventually do it. (Skill 3: Praise and Encouragement) And how was your anxiety about throwing up this week?

CLIENT 10: It was okay.

THERAPIST 11: "Okay" means different things for everyone. How much did it bother you this week? (Skill 1: Interest and Curiosity)

CLIENT 11: Maybe a 5?

THERAPIST 12: Okay, a 5, like somewhere in the middle. How much did it get in the way of you doing things, like how much did you avoid? (Skill 1: Interest and Curiosity)

CLIENT 12: Well, I didn't ride to the trampoline place with my friends, because I was afraid I would throw up in the car. Because it was Isa actually who threw up that time when I started to be afraid of throwing up.

THERAPIST 13: So, you made a link there, between Isa and throwing up and then the fear of throwing up. So I just want to make sure I understand, did you not ride in the car because you were afraid of Isa throwing up or because you were afraid you would throw up? (Skill 1: Interest and Curiosity)

CLIENT 13: Umm, both.

THERAPIST 14: Okay, both. So maybe we can work today on some of those thoughts. Do you remember why we work on these thoughts?

CLIENT 14: Umm, not really.

THERAPIST 15: So, I can remind you, which I'll do in just a second, but before we go over that. I want to check about your homework for the week. You had agreed to get rid of the Tums and not use them at all. Were you able to do that?

CLIENT 15: Yeah, I didn't have them at all.

THERAPIST 16: Wow, awesome job! How'd it feel to accomplish that? (Skill 3: Praise and Encouragement)

CLIENT 16: Well, I like the taste of them, so I kinda wished I could have them.

THERAPIST 17: I think hopefully as we work on these things, you'll be able to eat tastier things than Tums! But that brings us to why we are doing this. And it's super important that you and I are on the same page. Even though I'm the adult and the one with the office, this is your therapy, and this is to help you to live your best life. What's that saying, YOLO? You only live once?

CLIENT 17: [Giggles]

THERAPIST 18: We want you to be able to live a bit more like that, free to do things you enjoy. So here's the thing, I know you are really worried about throwing up, and so you are really careful about what you eat and when you eat. And, of course, we don't want you to throw up, but right now, who would you say has more control in your life, you or the throw-up fear—shall we give it a name? Like the vomit monster? (Skill 6: Elaborating Play)

CLIENT 18: It should rhyme I think, like the "vomit-grommit."

THERAPIST 19: Ooh, I like that, the vomit-grommit, I can picture it I think, it's really gross and ugly. Can you picture it? (Skill 6: Elaborating Play)

CLIENT 19: Yeah.

THERAPIST 20: I have some paper here, maybe you want to draw a picture of it. (Skill 6: Elaborating Play)

CLIENT 20: Ha ha, okay. [Starts drawing picture]

THERAPIST 21: So the thing about this vomit-grommit is that it controls you, and we want you to be free to make your own choices and this vomit-grommit to beat it. Because it gets in the way of your being able to eat what you want, when you want, and from riding in the car with your friends. (Skill 5: Empathy) But here's the catch, if you avoid the vomit-grommit, what happens? (Skill 1: Interest and Curiosity)

CLIENT 21: It doesn't bother me.

THERAPIST 22: Well, yeah, it doesn't bother you by giving you anxiety, but does it go away and actually leave you alone? (Skill 1: Interest and Curiosity)

CLIENT 22: No.

THERAPIST 23: Right, it sticks around. And when it sticks around, it stops you from doing things and being free to live your life. So, let me ask you, did you ever have other worries when you were younger? (Skill 1: Interest and Curiosity)

CLIENT 23: Yeah, I used to cry a lot when my mom went to work.

THERAPIST 24: And what about now, do you cry when she goes to work? (Skill 1: Interest and Curiosity)

CLIENT 24: Ha ha, no. That would be weird.

THERAPIST 25: And when you cried, did she stay home from work until you were not upset anymore? (Skill 1: Interest and Curiosity)

CLIENT 25: No, she had to go to work.

THERAPIST 26: But you said you don't cry anymore, how did that happen then? (Skill 1: Interest and Curiosity)

CLIENT 26: Well, I got used to it.

THERAPIST 27: Right, you got used to it. I imagine that you cried, but you got through it once, and then maybe the next time it was a little easier. And maybe you even started to feel okay and have fun with your babysitter. (Skill 5: Empathy)

CLIENT 27: Yeah, Rosie, my nanny. She's still my nanny after school. She's the best.

THERAPIST 28: So, facing the vomit-grommit is going to be a bit like facing the fears of your mom leaving when you were younger. So, I don't want you to feel caught off guard. It can be hard at first, but the idea is that I'm here to help you get through it. And then it will get easier with time. (Skill 3: Praise and Encouragement)

CLIENT 28: But I don't care if the vomit-grommit is in control. I don't care if I ride in a different car. It's not that big a deal.

THERAPIST 29: Oh, I see. So, this is important, because you and I are a bit like you and Mom this week. We have different ideas. So, I'm glad that you told me you don't think it's a problem. But now I'm curious. Does anyone have a problem with the vomit-grommit, or was this just in my head that I thought it was a problem? (Skill 12: Responding to Resistance)

CLIENT 29: My mom and dad do.

THERAPIST 30: Oooh, Mom and Dad have a problem. Tell me, what's their problem with the vomit-grommit? (Skill 1: Interest and Curiosity)

CLIENT 30: They don't like driving me places, and my dad gets really annoyed with how I eat my food, especially when we are at restaurants. But, I don't really care.

THERAPIST 31: You don't really care that they get annoyed or mad? (Skill 1: Interest and Curiosity)

CLIENT 31: No.

THERAPIST 32: It doesn't bother you. You don't want them to chill out and relax so you can all have a good time together? (Skill 5: Empathic Validation)

CLIENT 32: I don't really care. It doesn't bother me that much. Besides, they need to get their own lives and stop worrying about mine. I don't know why they care what I eat or how I eat.

THERAPIST 33: That's an interesting question actually, maybe we can come back to it, because I wonder why they do care. But first, I want to make sure I really understand what matters to you. (Skill 1: Interest and Curiosity)

CLIENT 33: What matters to me is that they stop bothering me about everything.

THERAPIST 34: Like things like your homework, like the example you gave earlier? (Skill 1: Interest and Curiosity)

CLIENT 34: Yeah, like they just let me be.

THERAPIST 35: I can understand that. Sounds like you want more independence? And you think they're having some trouble with that? (Skill 5: Empathic Validation)

CLIENT 35: Not necessarily more independence, but yeah, I don't need them to be all over me about everything.

THERAPIST 36: You know, as I'm listening to how you describe it, like they're all over you, they bother you, they need to get their own lives, you haven't said this, but I wonder if you feel angry toward them? (Skill 2: Naming Feelings; Skill 5: Empathic Validation)

CLIENT 36: I wouldn't say angry, but maybe annoyed.

THERAPIST 37: Yeah, they do things that annoy you. And I just imagine that when you are annoyed you could feel angry. (Skill 2: Naming Feelings)

CLIENT 37: I guess.

THERAPIST 38: The reason I'm asking, let me tell you because you might be thinking, "Where is this going?" is that this stage of life that you're at is a tricky one in just the way you're describing. (Skill 8: Self-Disclosure) You are not a little kid anymore; you can do more things on your own, but you also still need your parents and maybe even want them sometimes, but not as much or in the same way as you did when you were younger. Does that sound like how you're feeling? (Skill 5: Empathic Validation)

CLIENT 38: Yeah, pretty much.

THERAPIST 39: Pretty much . . . anything that you would add so it's more specific to you? (Skill 1: Interest and Curiosity)

CLIENT 39: Yeah, I don't need them for my homework and stuff. I will get it done.

THERAPIST 40: But maybe there is stuff you do need them for . . . (Skill 1: Interest and Curiosity)

CLIENT 40: Yeah, and like, I love them, especially my mom.

THERAPIST 41: Of course, and I imagine you wouldn't want them to think that just because you don't need them in the same ways, you don't love them. (Skill 5: Empathy)

CLIENT 41: Yea.

THERAPIST 42: Or even that if you are annoyed or mad at them that you don't love them. You can be annoyed and angry and still love them. (Skill 5: Empathy)

CLIENT 42: I guess.

THERAPIST 43: You don't seem so sure about that one! So maybe that's something for us to look at a bit more. But we don't have much more time for today, so I'll tell you what I'm thinking. I'm thinking that it might be helpful for us to have another family session with your parents and reset our goals together, so we are all on the same page. Because I think what you're bringing up today is that it's not just all about you here—everyone in the family has an effect on each other, and maybe we can try working together in a different way so that we tackle your goals. (Skill 8: Self-Disclosure; Skill 12: Responding to Resistance and Rupture) And maybe in the process we can deal with that vomit-grommit, what do you think?

CLIENT 43: Yeah, okay.

THERAPIST 44: So, before we end, we should spend some time thinking together about what you can do this week on your own to move toward your goals. I wonder if you could do some writing on your own about the things that you wish your parents did more of, and the things you wish they did less of. I'm not necessarily suggesting that we can work this out so you can get your wishes—that's not always realistic. But then we can look at them together and maybe see if they make sense or where we might be able to work on changing things. How does that sound to you? (Skill 1: Interest and Curiosity)

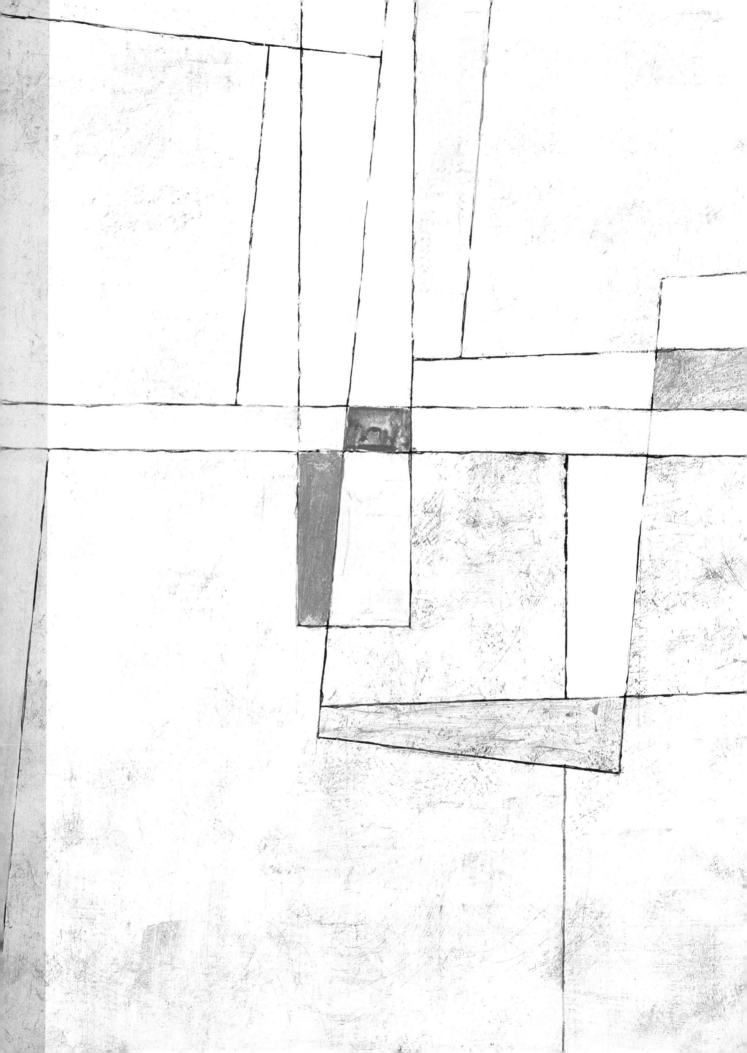

Mock Child and Adolescent Psychotherapy Sessions

In contrast to highly structured and repetitive deliberate practice exercises, a mock child therapy session is an unstructured and improvised role-play therapy session. Like a jazz rehearsal, mock sessions let you practice the art and science of *appropriate responsiveness* (Hatcher, 2015; Stiles & Horvath, 2017), putting your psychotherapy skills together in a way that is helpful to your mock client.

This exercise outlines the procedure for conducting a mock child therapy session. It offers different client profiles you may choose to adopt when enacting a client. The last recommendation gives you the option to play yourself (as a child), a choice we have found to be highly rewarding. Mock sessions are also an opportunity for trainees to practice the following:

- using psychotherapy skills responsively
- navigating challenging choice-points in therapy
- choosing which responses to use
- tracking the arc of a therapy session and the overall big-picture therapy treatment
- guiding treatment in the context of the client's preferences
- knowing how to proceed when the therapist is unsure, lost, or confused
- recognizing and recovering from therapeutic errors
- discovering your personal therapeutic style
- building endurance for working with real clients

Mock Child Session Overview

For the mock session, **you will perform a role-play of an initial therapy session.** As is true with the exercises to build individual skills, the role-play involves three people: One trainee role-plays the therapist, another trainee role-plays the client, and a third person serves as a trainer (a professor, supervisor, or peer observer) to observe and provide feedback.

https://doi.org/10.1037/0000288-016

Deliberate Practice in Child and Adolescent Psychotherapy, by J. Bate, T. A. Prout, T. Rousmaniere, and A. Vaz

This is an open-ended role-play, as is commonly done in training. However, this differs in two important ways from the role-plays used in more traditional training:

1. The therapist will use their hand to indicate how difficult the role-play feels.
2. The client will attempt to make the role-play easier or harder to ensure the therapist is practicing at the right difficulty level.

Preparation

1. Read the instructions in Chapter 2.

2. Download the Deliberate Practice Reaction Form and the Deliberate Practice Diary Form at https://www.apa.org/pubs/books/deliberate-practice-child-adolescent-psychotherapy (see the "Clinician and Practitioner Resources" tab; also available in Appendixes A and B, respectively).

3. Designate one person to role-play the therapist and one person to role-play the client. The trainer will observe and provide corrective feedback.

4. Each person will need their own copy of the Deliberate Practice Reaction Form on a separate piece of paper so they can access it quickly.

Mock Child Therapy Session Procedure

1. The trainees will role-play an initial (first) therapy session. The trainee role-playing the client selects a client profile from the end of this exercise.

2. Before beginning the role-play, the therapist raises a hand to their side, at the level of their chair seat (see Figure E14.1). They will use this hand throughout the role-play to indicate how challenging it feels to them to help the client. The therapist's starting hand level (chair seat) indicates that the role-play feels easy. By raising a hand, the therapist indicates that the difficulty is rising. If the therapist's hand rises above neck level, it indicates that the role-play is too difficult.

3. The therapist begins the role-play. The therapist and client should engage in the role-play in an improvised manner, as they would engage in a real therapy session. The therapist keeps their hand out at their side throughout this process. (This may feel strange at first!)

4. Whenever the therapist feels that the difficulty of the role-play has changed significantly, they should move their hand up if it feels more difficult and down if it feels easier. If the therapist's hand drops below the seat of the chair, the client should make the role-play more challenging; if the therapist's hand rises above neck level, the client should make the role-play easier. Instructions for adjusting the difficulty of the role-play are described in the Varying the Level of Challenge section.

5. The role-play continues for at least 15 minutes. The trainer may provide corrective feedback during this process if the therapist gets significantly off track. However, trainers should exercise restraint and keep feedback as short and tight as possible because this will reduce the therapist's opportunity for experiential training.

6. After the role-play is finished, the therapist and client switch roles and begin a new mock session.

FIGURE E14.1. Ongoing Difficulty Assessment Through Hand Level

Note. Left: Start of role-play. Right: Role-play is too difficult. From *Deliberate Practice in Emotion-Focused Therapy* (p. 156), by R. N. Goldman, A. Vaz, and T. Rousmaniere, 2021, American Psychological Association (https://doi.org/10.1037/0000227–000). Copyright 2021 by the American Psychological Association.

Varying The Level of Challenge

If the therapist indicates that the mock session is too easy, the person enacting the role of the client can use the following modifications to make it more challenging (see also Appendix A):

- The client can improvise with topics that are more evocative or make the therapist uncomfortable, such as expressing currently held strong feelings (see Figure A.2).

- The client can use a distressed voice (e.g., angry, sad, sarcastic) or unpleasant facial expression. This increases the emotional tone.

- Blend complex mixtures of opposing feelings (e.g., love and rage).

- Become confrontational, questioning the purpose of therapy or the therapist's fitness for the role.

  If the therapist indicates that the mock session is too hard:

- The client can be guided by Figure A.2 to
  - present topics that are less evocative,
  - present material on any topic but without expressing feelings, or
  - present material concerning the future or the past or events outside therapy.

- The client can ask the questions in a soft voice or with a smile. This softens the emotional stimulus.

- The therapist can take short breaks during the role-play.

- The trainer can expand the "feedback phase" by discussing child therapy theories.

Mock Session Client Profiles

Following are six client profiles for trainees to use during mock sessions, presented in order of difficulty. The choice of client profile may be determined by the trainee playing the therapist, the trainee playing the client, or assigned by the trainer.

The most important aspect of role-plays is for trainees to be playful, use their bodies similarly to how they would in an actual therapy session, and convey the emotional tone indicated by the client profile (e.g., "angry," "sad"). The demographics of the client (e.g., age, gender) and specific content of the client profiles are not important. Thus, trainees should adjust the client profile to be most comfortable and easy for the trainee to role-play. For example, a trainee may change the client profile from female to male or from 8 to 14 years old.

Beginner Profile: Talking About Parents' Divorce With a Receptive Client Who Is Able to Play

Luke is an 11-year-old, Black boy whose parents divorced last year and are in the middle of a contentious custody case in court. Luke has been showing signs of inattention and anxiety, raising questions about whether he meets criteria for attention-deficit/hyperactivity disorder or whether his presentation is related to his emotions and the family situation. Luke has an older sister, Sarah, who is considered the "golden child." Luke presents to therapy eager to play and interested in talking to the therapist about his life and his thoughts and feelings.

- **Symptoms:** Inattention, hyperactivity, and generalized worries.
- **Goals for therapy:** Process and express a range of emotions, including those centered around the parents' divorce.
- **Attitude toward therapy:** Luke is open to coming to therapy and eager to talk to someone other than his parents about his experiences.
- **Strengths:** Luke has the capacity for symbolic play and relationships and to think about feelings and cognitions.

Beginner Profile: Addressing Perfectionism With an Adolescent Client Who Is Eager for Help

Jennifer is a 15-year-old, Latinx young woman who is in her sophomore year of high school and generally does very well academically, has a group of close friends, and is competitive in gymnastics. She experiences significant stress, however, surrounding her academic and athletic performance, feeling she needs to be perfect to get into a top college. These pressures cause her to experience what she refers to as anxiety attacks—moments when she becomes overwhelmed with emotion and paralyzed, unable to do anything.

- **Symptoms:** Stress, perfectionism, and panic.
- **Goals for therapy:** Be able to better manage her emotions when she is overwhelmed.
- **Attitude toward therapy:** Jennifer asked her parents if she could see a therapist but is slightly nervous because it is her first time seeing someone.
- **Strengths:** Jennifer is highly intelligent, curious about herself, and highly engaged in her therapy, taking notes in between sessions to guide the focus.

Intermediate Profile: Establishing Trust With an Angry Adolescent Client

Cat is a 15-year-old, Latinx gender-fluid teen (they/them pronouns) who is in their junior year of high school. They are diagnosed with depression and recently disclosed for the first time that they have been using pins to scratch their forearms. They are the oldest of three children, and their two siblings are significantly younger and are half-siblings. Cat is in therapy at their mother's insistence, although Cat does not think there is a point to it. They think, "My mom just wants someone else to deal with me." They are guarded about giving more details about their self-harm and prefer to spend the sessions playing simple games like checkers or Jenga. They occasionally talk about their relationships with friends, as well as their frustration with their mother, whom they perceive as overwhelmed with their younger siblings and not understanding of them.

- **Symptoms:** Self-harm, lack of motivation, insomnia, angry outbursts, and impulsivity.
- **Goals for therapy:** Be able to voice their negative emotions instead of acting them out through self-harm.
- **Attitude toward therapy:** Cat is guarded, mistrustful, and withholding.
- **Strengths:** Cat has a sharp sense of humor, close friendships, consistent attendance, and is confident and comfortable with their gender identity.

Intermediate Profile: Fostering Interpersonal Interaction With a Young Girl on the Autism Spectrum

Shira is a 6-year-old, White girl who has a diagnosis of autism spectrum disorder and was referred to therapy to address social and emotional skills. She is high-functioning and verbal, but she has difficulty with imaginative play and tends to stick to rigid interests in computer games, like Pokémon and Roblox. However, she also loves music. Her parents are particularly concerned about her lack of social connections and that her rigidity, makes it difficult for her to make friends. Additionally, she has some anxious behaviors like picking her skin, which bothers her mother, who is concerned about her lack of self-awareness.

- **Symptoms:** Fixed interests, repetitive play, skin picking, and lack of reciprocal social engagement.

- **Goals for therapy:** Increase capacity for emotion recognition and reciprocal interpersonal relationships.

- **Attitude toward therapy:** Shira has engaged in therapy readily after the first few sessions, but she often wants to play computer games or show the therapist the latest games that she is playing on her tablet.

- **Strengths:** Shira has a strong memory and an ability to engage and interact within her areas of interest.

Advanced Profile: Improving Emotion Regulation in a Young Boy

Bo is a 7-year-old, White boy who was adopted 3 years ago, after having been removed and then reunited with his birth brother twice before. It is known that he experienced physical abuse at the hands of his birth mother's boyfriend, although he never talks about his birth mother or his experiences before adoption. He presents with symptoms of inattention, hyperactivity, and increasing oppositional behavior including meltdowns when he has to do something that he does not want to do in school or at home. Although he has never been seriously aggressive, when he tantrums, he swings his arms and has accidentally hit his mother in the face. In sessions, he plays readily, but at the smallest misunderstanding or frustration, he loses interest.

- **Symptoms:** Impulsivity, emotional reactivity and dysregulation, irritability, and inattention.
- **Goals for therapy:** Improved attention, emotion regulation, and distress tolerance.

- **Attitude toward therapy:** Bo is playful and engaging but at times emotionally labile or unpredictable.
- **Strengths:** Bo has the capacity to build an alliance with a therapist and to play symbolically.

Advanced Profile: Identifying Sources of Motivation for Teenage Male

Carl is a 15-year-old, Asian American boy who is the older of two siblings and was referred to therapy by his teachers because he has been skipping class, failing courses in school, and, according to his mother, spending all of his time on video games. His mother is worried that he is using marijuana, although she does not have confirmation, and she puts pressure on the therapist to find out what is going on with her son. Carl's father is strict and, according to his mother, was physically abused by his own parents; he does not have tolerance for Carl's behavior. She notes that he "does not believe in therapy."

- **Symptoms:** Lack of interest or pleasure, lack of motivation, and possible substance use.
- **Goals for therapy:** Build a therapeutic alliance and engage the patient in identifying goals for himself.
- **Attitude toward therapy:** Carl is ambivalent about attending therapy and is withdrawn and quiet but agrees to attend.
- **Strengths:** Carl's strengths are unknown at this time, although his parents described him as previously being a typically developing boy who worked hard in school.

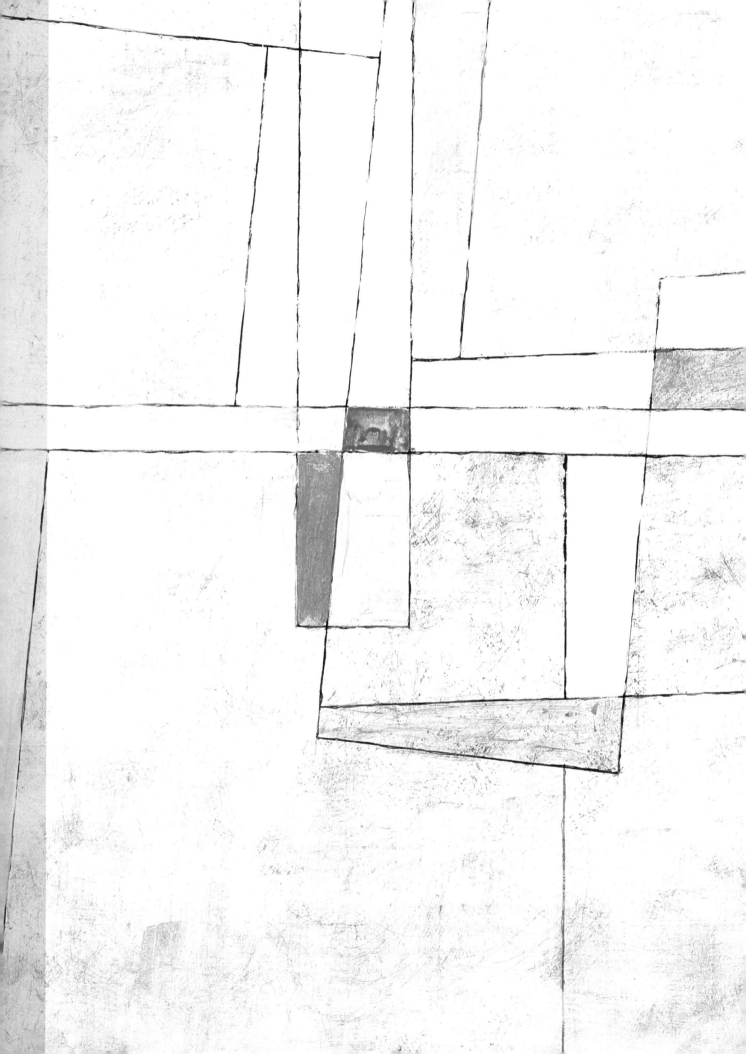

Strategies for Enhancing the Deliberate Practice Exercises

Part III consists of one chapter, Chapter 3, that provides additional advice and instructions for trainers and trainees so that they can reap more benefits from the deliberate practice exercises in Part II. Chapter 3 offers six key points for getting the most out of deliberate practice, guidelines for practicing appropriately responsive treatment, evaluation strategies, methods for ensuring trainee well-being and respecting their privacy, and advice for monitoring the trainer–trainee relationship.

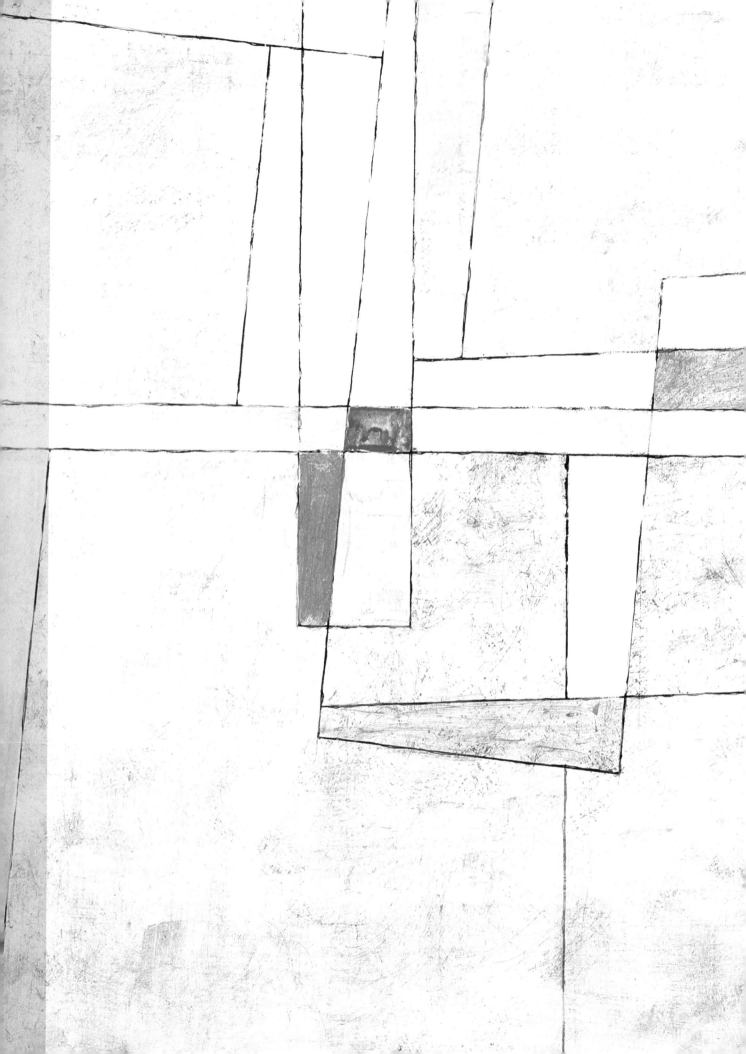

How to Get the Most Out of Deliberate Practice: Additional Guidance for Trainers and Trainees

In Chapter 2 and in the exercises themselves, we provide instructions for completing these deliberate practice exercises. This chapter provides guidance on big-picture topics that trainers will need to successfully integrate deliberate practice into their training program. This guidance is based on relevant research and the experiences and feedback from trainers at more than a dozen psychotherapy training programs who volunteered to test the deliberate practice exercises in this book. We cover topics including evaluation, getting the most from deliberate practice, trainee well-being, respecting trainee privacy, trainer self-evaluation, responsive treatment, and the trainee–trainer alliance.

Six Key Points for Getting the Most From Deliberate Practice

Following are six key points of advice for trainers and trainees to get the greatest benefit from the child therapy deliberate practice exercises. The following advice is gleaned from experiences vetting and practicing the exercises, sometimes in different languages, with many trainees across many countries, on different occasions.

Key Point 1: Create Realistic Emotional Stimuli

A key component of deliberate practice is using stimuli that provoke similar reactions to challenging real-life work settings. For example, pilots train with flight simulators that present mechanical failures and dangerous weather conditions; surgeons practice with surgical simulators that present medical complications with only seconds to respond. Training with challenging stimuli will increase trainees' capacity to perform therapy effectively under stress, for example, with clients they find challenging. The stimuli used for child therapy deliberate practice exercises are role-plays of challenging client statements in therapy. **It is important that the trainee who is role-playing the client perform the script with appropriate emotional expression and maintain eye**

https://doi.org/10.1037/0000288-017
Deliberate Practice in Child and Adolescent Psychotherapy, by J. Bate, T. A. Prout, T. Rousmaniere, and A. Vaz

contact with the therapist. For example, if the client statement calls for sad emotion, the trainee should try to express sadness eye-to-eye with the therapist. We offer the following suggestions regarding emotional expressiveness:

- The emotional tone of the role-play matters more than the exact words of each script. Trainees role-playing the client should feel free to improvise and change the words if it will help them be more emotionally expressive. Trainees do not need to stick 100% exactly to the script. In fact, to read off the script during the exercise can sound flat and prohibit eye contact. Rather, trainees in the client role should first read the client statement silently to themselves, then, when ready, say it in an emotional manner while looking directly at the trainee playing the therapist. This will help the experience feel more real and engaging for the therapist.

- Trainees whose first language isn't English may particularly benefit from reviewing and changing the words in the client statement script before each role-play so they can find words that feel congruent and facilitate emotional expression.

- Trainees role-playing the client should try to use tonal and nonverbal expressions of feelings. For example, if a script calls for anger, the trainee can speak with an angry voice and make fists with their hands; if a script calls for shame or guilt, the trainee could hunch over and wince; if a script calls for sadness, the trainee could speak in a soft or deflated voice.

- If trainees are having persistent difficulties acting believably when following a particular script in the role of client, it may help to first do a "demo round" by reading directly from paper, and then, immediately after, dropping the paper to make eye contact and repeating the same client statement from memory. Some trainees reported this helped them "become available as real clients" and made the role-play feel less artificial. Some trainees did three or four demo rounds to get fully into their role as a client.

Key Point 2: Customize the Exercises to Fit Your Unique Training Circumstances

Deliberate practice is less about adhering to specific rules than it is about using training principles. Every trainer has their own individual teaching style and every trainee their own learning process. Thus, the exercises in this book are designed to be flexibly customized by trainers across different training contexts within different cultures. Trainees and trainers are encouraged to continually adjust exercises to optimize their practice. The most effective training will occur when deliberate practice exercises are customized to fit the learning needs of each trainee and culture of each training site. In our experience with more than a dozen child therapy trainers and trainees across many countries, we found that everyone spontaneously customized the exercises for their unique training circumstances. No two trainers followed the exact same procedure. Following are a few examples.

- One supervisor used the exercises with a trainee who found all the client statements to be too hard, including the "beginner" stimuli. This trainee had multiple reactions in the "too hard" category, including nausea and severe shame and self-doubt. The trainee disclosed to the supervisor that she had experienced extremely harsh learning environments earlier in her life and found the role-plays to be highly evocative. To help, the supervisor followed the suggestions offered earlier to make the stimuli progressively easier until the trainee reported feeling "good challenge" on the Deliberate Practice Reaction Form. Over many weeks of practice, the trainee developed a sense of safety and was able to practice with more difficult client statements. (Note that if the supervisor had proceeded at the too hard difficulty level, the trainee might have complied while hiding her negative reactions, become emotionally flooded and overwhelmed leading to withdrawal and thus prohibiting her skill development and risking dropout from training.)

- Supervisors of trainees for whom English was not their first language adjusted the client statements to their own primary language.

- One supervisor used the exercises with a trainee who found all the stimuli to be too easy, including the advanced client statements. This supervisor quickly moved to improvising more challenging client statements from scratch by following the instructions on how to make client statements more challenging.

Key Point 3: Discover Your Own Unique Personal Therapeutic Style

Deliberate practice in psychotherapy can be likened to the process of learning to play jazz music. Jazz musicians pride themselves on their skillful improvisations, and the process of "finding your own voice" is a prerequisite for expertise in jazz musicianship. Yet improvisations are not a collection of random notes but the culmination of extensive deliberate practice over time. Indeed, the ability to improvise is built on many hours of dedicated practice of scales, melodies, harmonies, and so on. Much in the same way, psychotherapy trainees are encouraged to experience the scripted interventions in this book not as ends in themselves but as a means to promote skill in a systematic fashion. Over time, effective therapeutic creativity can be aided, instead of constrained, by dedicated practice in these therapeutic "melodies."

Key Point 4: Engage in a Sufficient Amount of Rehearsal

Deliberate practice uses rehearsal to move skills into procedural memory, which helps trainees maintain access to skills even when working with challenging clients. This only works if trainees engage in many repetitions of the exercises. Think of a challenging sport or musical instrument you learned: How many rehearsals would a professional need to feel confident performing a new skill? Psychotherapy is no easier than those other fields!

Key Point 5: Continually Adjust Difficulty

A crucial element of deliberate practice is training at an optimal difficulty level: neither too easy nor too hard. To achieve this, do difficulty assessments and adjustments with the Deliberate Practice Reaction Form in Appendix A. **Do not skip this step!** If trainees don't feel any of the "good challenge" reactions at the bottom of the Deliberate Practice Reaction Form, then the exercise is probably too easy; if they feel any of the "too hard" reactions, then the exercise could be too difficult for the trainee to benefit. Advanced child therapy trainees and therapists may find all the client statements too easy. If so, they should follow the instructions in Appendix A on making client statements harder to make the role-plays sufficiently challenging.

Key Point 6: Put It All Together With the Practice Transcript and Mock Therapy Sessions

Some trainees may feel a further need for greater contextualization of the individual therapy responses associated with each skill, feeling the need to integrate the disparate pieces of their training in a more coherent manner, with a simulation that mimics a real therapy session. The practice therapy transcript is offered after the skill exercises as it culminates all skills together. To provide trainees with the possibility of practicing different responses together in a sequence that mimics an actual therapy session. The mock therapy sessions outlined in Exercise 14 serve the same function, allowing therapists to put their skill training into practice.

Responsive Treatment

Appropriate Responsiveness

The exercises in this book are designed to help trainees to not only acquire specific skills of child therapy but also to use them in ways that are responsive to each individual client (Chorpita et al., 2015; Chu & Kendall, 2009; Halfon et al., 2017). Across the psychotherapy literature, this stance has been referred to as *appropriate responsiveness*, wherein the therapists exercise flexible judgment, based in their perception of the client's emotional state, needs, and goals, and integrates techniques and other interpersonal skills in pursuit of optimal client outcomes (Hatcher, 2015; Stiles et al., 1998). The effective therapist is responsive to the emerging context. As Stiles and Horvath (2017) argued, therapists are effective because they are appropriately responsive. Doing the "right thing" may be different each time and means providing each client with an individually tailored response.

Appropriate responsiveness counters a misconception that deliberate practice rehearsal is designed to promote robotic repetition of therapy techniques. Psychotherapy researchers have shown that overadherence to a particular model while neglecting client preferences reduces therapy effectiveness (e.g., Castonguay et al., 1996; Hudson et al., 2014; Owen & Hilsenroth, 2014). Therapist flexibility, on the other hand, has been shown to improve outcomes (e.g., Bugatti & Boswell, 2016; Hudson et al., 2014; Kendall & Frank, 2018). It is important, therefore, that trainees practice their newly learned skills in a manner that is flexible and responsive to the unique needs of a diverse range of clients (Hatcher, 2015; Hill & Knox, 2013). It is thus of paramount importance for trainees to develop the necessary perceptual skills to be able to attune to what the client is experiencing in the moment and form their response based on the client moment-by-moment context (Greenberg & Goldman, 1988).

It is also important that deliberate practice occurs within a context of wider child therapy learning. As noted in Chapter 1, training should be combined with supervision of actual therapy recordings, theoretical learning, observation of competent child psychotherapists, as well as personal therapeutic work. When the trainer or trainee determine that the trainee is having difficulty acquiring child therapy skills, it is important to carefully assess what is missing or needed. Assessment should then lead to the appropriate remedy, as the trainer and trainee collaboratively determine what is needed.

Responsiveness and Cultural Diversity

It is important to highlight that cultural misattunement can also mark the need for therapist responsiveness. Like the previous examples, responsive maneuvers toward greater attunement can be nested within manualized treatments or may need to replace them. Regarding the former, it is possible that clients will see a particular treatment as well-matched to their understanding of their mental health issues and how they conceive of change. However, that treatment, although likely helpful, might also be incomplete. For example, it may be that a client also hopes, needs, or expects spirituality to be a part of the clinical change process. A failure to accommodate spirituality into the treatment plan could result in any number of maladaptive processes (e.g., a reduced sense of trust in the therapist) or outcomes (e.g., premature termination).

In other cases, the client may expect something more than a simple addition or tweak to the therapeutic approach. They may, for example, seek a traditional healing practice within their culture. Whereas this may precipitate a complex decision-making chain, for the purposes of the current book, the skilled child therapist can put their own plans on the shelf to explore cultural needs and meanings. Although not explicitly addressed in this book, we find the theory and research on multicultural orientation to be a compelling means to guiding cultural responsiveness in a theory-neutral manner (see Park-Taylor et al., 2010). Namely, therapists can apply the evidence-informed multicultural orientation pillars of cultural humility (e.g., relinquishing one's sense of superiority by being open and curious about the client's identities), cultural opportunity (e.g., attending to negative process or cultural missteps with a willingness to learn from the client), and cultural comfort (e.g., exhibiting a sense of ease working with diverse people).

Our hope is that this section demonstrates our interest in teaching the skills of both child therapy and contextual responsiveness. We believe that both sets of skills are evidence informed and can be facilitated through deliberate practice training methods. Finally, in addition to the individual skills presented in Exercises 1 through 12, there are examples of developmentally appropriate responsiveness in the annotated psychotherapy sessions that we provide in Exercise 13. We hope these examples of therapist pliability will help you practice child therapy in a way that embraces psychotherapy's inherent complexities and meets children and adolescents at their most personally salient needs at a given time.

Being Mindful of Trainee Well-Being

Although negative effects that some clients experience in psychotherapy have been well documented (Barlow, 2010), negative effects of training and supervision on trainees has received less attention. To support strong self-efficacy, trainers must ensure that trainees are practicing at a correct difficulty level. The exercises in this book feature guidance for frequently assessing and adjusting the difficulty level, so trainees can rehearse at a level that precisely targets their personal skill threshold. Trainers and supervisors must be mindful to provide an appropriate challenge. One risk to trainees that is particularly pertinent to this book occurs when using role-plays that are too difficult. The Reaction Form in Appendix A is provided to help trainers ensure that role-plays are done at an appropriate challenge level. Trainers or trainees may be tempted to skip the difficulty assessments and adjustments, out of their motivation to focus on rehearsal to make fast progress and quickly acquire skills. But across all our test sites, we found that skipping the difficulty assessments and adjustments caused more problems and hindered skill acquisition more than any other error. Thus, trainers are advised to remember that **one of their most important responsibilities is to remind trainees to do the difficulty assessments and adjustments.**

As in child therapy itself, a spirit of playfulness and warmth is encouraged in deliberate practice supervision of child therapy trainees. The parallel process between supervision and clinical work allows for experiential learning that translates into the therapist–client dyad (Mullen et al., 2007). Additionally, the Reaction Form serves a dual purpose of helping trainees develop the important skills of self-monitoring and self-awareness (Bennett-Levy, 2019). This will help trainees adopt a positive and empowered stance regarding their own self-care and should facilitate career-long professional development.

Respecting Trainee Privacy

The deliberate practice exercises in this book may stir up complex or uncomfortable personal reactions within trainees, including, for example, memories of past traumas. Exploring psychological and emotional reactions may make some trainees feel vulnerable. Therapists of every career stage, from trainees to seasoned therapists with decades of experience, commonly experience shame, embarrassment, and self-doubt in this process. Although these experiences can be valuable for building trainees' self-awareness, it is important that training remain focused on professional skill development and not blur into personal therapy (e.g., Ellis et al., 2014). Therefore, one trainer role is to remind trainees to maintain appropriate boundaries.

Trainees must have the final say about what to disclose or not disclose to their trainer. Trainees should keep in mind that the goal is for the trainee to expand their own self-awareness and psychological capacity to stay active and helpful while experiencing uncomfortable reactions. The trainer does not need to know the specific details about the trainee's inner world for this to happen.

Trainees should be instructed to share only personal information that they feel comfortable sharing. The Reaction Form and difficulty assessment process are designed to help trainees build their self-awareness while retaining control over their privacy. Trainees can be reminded that the goal is for them to learn about their own inner world. They do not necessarily have to share that information with trainers or peers (Bennett-Levy & Finlay-Jones, 2018). Likewise, trainees should be instructed to respect the confidentiality of their peers.

Trainer Self-Evaluation

The exercises in this book were tested at a wide range of training sites around the world, including graduate courses, practicum sites, and private practice offices. Although trainers reported that the exercises were highly effective for training, some also said that they felt disoriented by how different deliberate practice feels compared with their traditional methods of clinical education. Many felt comfortable evaluating their trainees' performance but were less sure about their own performance as trainers.

The most common concern we heard from trainers was: "My trainees are doing great, but I'm not sure if I am doing this correctly!" To address this concern, we recommend trainers perform periodic self-evaluations along the following five criteria:

1. Observe trainees' work performance.
2. Provide continual corrective feedback.
3. Ensure rehearsal of specific skills is just beyond the trainees' current ability.
4. Ensure that the trainee is practicing at the right difficulty level (neither too easy nor too challenging).
5. Continuously assess trainee performance with real clients.

Criterion 1: Observe Trainees' Work Performance

Determining how well we are doing as trainers means first having valid information about how well trainees are responding to training. This requires that we directly observe trainees practicing skills to provide corrective feedback and evaluation. One risk of deliberate practice is that trainees gain competence in performing therapy skills in role-plays, but those skills do not transfer to trainees' work with real clients. Thus, trainers will ideally also have the opportunity to observe samples of trainees' work with real clients, either live or via recorded video. Supervisors and consultants rely heavily—and, too often, exclusively—on supervisees' and consultees' narrative accounts of their work with clients (Goodyear & Nelson, 1997). Haggerty and Hilsenroth (2011) described this challenge as follows:

> Suppose a loved one has to undergo surgery and you need to choose between two surgeons, one of whom has never been directly observed by an experienced surgeon while performing any surgery. He or she would perform the surgery and return to his or her attending physician and try to recall, sometimes incompletely or inaccurately, the intricate steps of the surgery they just performed. It is hard to imagine that anyone, given a choice, would prefer this over a professional who has been routinely observed in the practice of their craft. (p. 193)

Criterion 2: Provide Continual Corrective Feedback

Trainees need corrective feedback to learn what they are doing well, what they are doing less successfully, and how to improve their skills. Feedback should be as specific and incremental as possible. Examples of specific feedback are: "Your voice sounds rushed. Try slowing down by pausing for a few seconds between your statements to the client" and "That's excellent how you're making eye contact with the client." Examples of vague and nonspecific feedback are: "Try to build better rapport with the client" and "Try to be more open to the client's feelings."

Criterion 3: Rehearse Specific Skills Just Beyond the Trainees' Current Ability (Zone of Proximal Development)

Deliberate practice emphasizes skill acquisition via behavioral rehearsal. Trainers should endeavor to not get caught up in client conceptualization at the expense of focusing on skills. For many trainers, this requires significant discipline and self-restraint. It is simply more enjoyable to talk about psychotherapy theory (e.g., case conceptualization, treatment planning, nuances of psychotherapy models, similar cases the supervisor has had) than watch trainees rehearse skills. Trainees have many questions, and supervisors have an abundance of experience; the allotted supervision time can easily be filled sharing knowledge. The supervisor gets to sound smart, while the trainee doesn't have to struggle with acquiring skills at their learning edge. While answering questions is important, trainees' intellectual knowledge about psychotherapy can quickly surpass their procedural ability to perform it, particularly with clients they find challenging. Here's a simple rule of thumb: The trainer provides the knowledge, but the behavioral rehearsal provides the skill (Rousmaniere, 2019).

Criterion 4: Practice at the Right Difficulty Level (Neither Too Easy nor Too Challenging)

Deliberate practice involves *optimal strain*: practicing skills just beyond the trainee's current skill threshold so he or she can learn incrementally without becoming overwhelmed (K. A. Ericsson, 2006).

Trainers should use difficulty assessments and adjustments throughout deliberate practice to ensure that trainees are practicing at the right difficulty level. Note that some trainees are surprised by their unpleasant reactions to exercises (e.g., disassociation, nausea, blanking out), and may be tempted to "push through" exercises that are too hard. This can happen out of fear of failing a course, fear of being judged as incompetent, or negative self-impressions by the trainee (e.g., "This shouldn't be so hard"). Trainers should normalize the fact that there will be wide variation in perceived difficulty of the exercises and encourage trainees to respect their own personal training process.

Criterion 5: Continuously Assess Trainee Performance With Real Clients

The goal of deliberately practicing psychotherapy skills is to improve trainees' effectiveness at helping real clients. One of the risks in deliberate practice training is that the benefits will not generalize: Trainees' acquired competence in specific skills may not translate into work with real clients. Thus, it is important that trainers assess the impact of deliberate practice on trainees' work with real clients. Ideally, this is done through triangulation of multiple data points:

1. Client data (verbal self-report and routine outcome monitoring data)
2. Supervisor's report
3. Trainee's self-report

If the trainee's effectiveness with real clients is not improving after deliberate practice, the trainer should do a careful assessment of the difficulty. If the supervisor or trainer feels it is a skill acquisition issues, they may want to consider adjusting the deliberate practice routine to better suit the trainee's learning needs or style.

Therapists are held to *process accountability* (Markman & Tetlock, 2000; see also Goodyear, 2015): being responsible for demonstrating particular target behaviors (e.g., fidelity to a particular treatment model) regardless of the impacts of those behaviors on clients. Achieving clinical effectiveness means moving beyond competence to more reliably improve client outcomes. Learning objectives shift at this point from normative ones that others have declared to be desirable for all therapists to achieve (i.e., competence) to highly individualized goals informed by the learner's objectives and performance feedback. *Outcome accountability* (Goodyear, 2015) becomes especially salient. Outcome accountability concerns the extent to which the therapist is able to achieve intended client changes, independent of how the therapist might be performing expected tasks. Of course, the reasonable question in any discussion of accountability concerns "accountability to whom?" In this case, it is ultimately to clients.

Guidance for Trainees

The central theme of this book has been that skill rehearsal is not automatically helpful. Deliberate practice must be done well for trainees to benefit (A. Ericsson & Pool, 2016). In this chapter and in the exercises, we offer guidance for effective deliberate practice. We would also like to provide additional advice specifically for trainees. That advice is drawn from what we have learned at our volunteer deliberate practice test sites around the world. We cover how to discover your own training process, active effort, playfulness and taking breaks during deliberate practice, your right to control your self-disclosure to trainers, monitoring training results, monitoring complex reactions toward the trainer, and your own personal therapy.

Individualized Child Therapy Training: Finding Your Zone of Proximal Development

Deliberate practice works best when training targets each trainee's personal skill thresholds. Also termed the *zone of proximal development*, a term first coined by Vygotsky in reference to developmental learning theory (Zaretskii, 2009), this is the area just beyond the trainee's current ability but which is possible to reach with the assistance of a teacher or coach (Wass & Golding, 2014). **If a deliberate practice exercise is either too easy or too hard, the trainee will not benefit.** To maximize training productivity, elite performers follow a "challenging but not overwhelming" principle: Tasks that are too far beyond their capacity will prove ineffective and even harmful, but it is equally true that mindlessly repeating what they can already do confidently will prove fruitless. Because of this, deliberate practice requires ongoing assessment of the trainee's current skill and concurrent difficulty adjustment to consistently target a "good enough" challenge. Thus, if you are practicing "Exercise 8: Self-Disclosure" and it just feels too difficult, consider moving back to a more comfortable skill, such as communicating interest and curiosity (Exercise 1) or empathic validation (Exercise 5), that they may feel they have already mastered.

Active Effort

It is important for trainees to maintain an active and sustained effort, while doing the deliberate practice exercises in this book. Deliberate practice really helps when trainees push themselves up to and past their current ability. This is best achieved when trainees take ownership of their own practice by guiding their training partners to adjust role-plays to be as high on the difficulty scale as possible without hurting themselves. This will look different for every trainee. Although it can feel uncomfortable or even frightening, this is the zone of proximal development where the most gains can be made. Simply reading and repeating the written scripts will provide little or no benefit. Trainees are advised to remember that their effort from training should lead to more confidence and comfort in session with real clients.

Stay the Course: Effort Versus Flow

Deliberate practice only works if trainees push themselves hard enough to break out of their old patterns of performance, which then permits growth of new skills (A. Ericsson & Pool, 2016). Because deliberate practice constantly focuses on the current edge of one's performance capacity, it is inevitably a straining endeavor. Indeed, professionals are unlikely to make lasting performance improvements unless there is sufficient engagement in tasks that are just at the edge of one's current capacity (K. A. Ericsson, 2003, 2006). From athletics or fitness training, many of us are familiar with this process of being pushed out of our comfort zones followed by adaptation. The same process applies to our mental and emotional abilities.

Many trainees might feel surprised to discover that deliberate practice for child therapy feels harder than psychotherapy with a real client. This may be because when working with a real client a therapist can get into a state of *flow* (Csikszentmihalyi, 1997), in which work feels effortless. In such cases, therapists may want to move back to offering response formats with which they are more familiar and feel more proficient and try those for a short time, in part to increase a sense of confidence and mastery.

Discover Your Own Training Process

The effectiveness of deliberate practice is directly related to the effort and ownership trainees exert while doing the exercises. Trainers can provide guidance, but it is important for trainees to learn about their own idiosyncratic training processes over time. This will let them become masters of their own training and prepare for a career-long process of professional development. The following are a few examples of personal training processes trainees discovered while engaging in deliberate practice:

- One trainee noticed that she is good at persisting while an exercise is challenging but also that she requires more rehearsal than other trainees to feel comfortable with a new skill. This trainee focused on developing patience with her own pace of progress.

- One trainee noticed that he was surprised by which prompts felt challenging to him. He noticed that his internal reactions to seemingly "beginner" stimuli felt overwhelming at times. Using the Reaction Form and checking in with his partner about adjusting the difficulty level helped a great deal.

- One trainee described feeling "stilted" and "awkward" doing exercises closely linked to play. She described feeling like she was "just playing" and didn't feel like a "real therapist" in these moments. The trainee sought support from peers who had more experience with play therapy and also focused on practicing self-compassion as she flexed her "playfulness muscles" in these new and uncomfortable scenarios, all while checking in to adjust the difficulty level as she progressed.

Trainees are encouraged to reflect deeply on their own experiences using the exercises to learn the most about themselves and their personal learning processes.

Playfulness and Taking Breaks

Psychotherapy is serious work that often involves painful feelings. However, just like child therapy itself, practicing psychotherapy can be playful and fun (Mullen et al., 2007). Trainees should remember that one of the main goals of deliberate practice is to experiment with different approaches and styles of therapy. If deliberate practice ever feels rote, boring, or routine, it probably isn't going to help advance trainees' skill. In this case, trainees should try to liven it up. A good way to do this is to introduce an atmosphere of playfulness. For example, trainees can try the following:

- Use different vocal tones, speech pacing, body gestures, or other languages. This can expand trainees' communication range.
- Practice while simulating being blind (with a cloth) or deaf. This can increase sensitivity in the other senses.
- Practice while standing up or walking around outside. This can help trainees get new perspectives on the process of therapy.

The supervisor can also ask trainees if they would like to take a 5- to 10-minute break between questions, particularly if the trainees are dealing with difficult emotions and are feeling stressed out.

Additional Deliberate Practice Opportunities

This book focuses on deliberate practice methods that involve active, live engagement between trainees and a supervisor. Importantly, deliberate practice can extend beyond these focused training sessions. For example, a trainee might read the client stimuli quietly or aloud and practice their responses independently between sessions with a supervisor. In such cases, it is important for the trainee to say their therapist responses aloud, rather than rehearse silently in one's head. Alternatively, two trainees can practice as a pair, without the supervisor. Although the absence of a supervisor limits one source of feedback, the peer trainee who is playing the client can serve this role, as they can when a supervisor is present. Importantly, these additional deliberate practice opportunities are intended to take place between focused training sessions with a supervisor. To optimize the quality of the deliberate practice when conducted independently or without a supervisor, we have developed a Deliberate Practice Therapist Diary Form that can be found in Appendix B and can also be downloaded from https://www.apa.org/pubs/books/deliberate-practice-child-adolescent-psychotherapy (see the "Clinician and Practitioner Resources" tab). This form provides a template for the trainee to record their experience of the deliberate practice activity, and, ideally, it will aid in the consolidation of learning. This form can be used as part of the evaluation process with the supervisor but is not necessarily intended for that purpose; trainees are certainly welcome to bring their experience with the independent practice into the next meeting with the supervisor.

Monitoring Training Results

While trainers will evaluate trainees using a competency-focused model, trainees are also encouraged to take ownership of their own training process and look for results of deliberate practice themselves. Trainees should experience the results of deliberate practice within a few training sessions. A lack of results can be demoralizing for trainees and can result in trainees applying less effort and focus in deliberate practice. Trainees who are not seeing results should openly discuss this problem with their trainer and experiment with adjusting their deliberate practice process. Results can include client outcomes and improving the trainee's own work as a therapist, their personal development, and their overall training.

Client Outcomes

The most important result of deliberate practice is an improvement in trainees' client outcomes. This can be assessed via routine outcome measurement (Lambert, 2010; Prescott et al., 2018), qualitative data (McLeod, 2017), and informal discussions with clients. However, trainees should note that an improvement in client outcome due to deliberate practice can sometimes be challenging to achieve quickly, given that the largest amount of variance in client outcome is due to client variables (Bohart & Wade, 2013). For example, a client with severe chronic symptoms may not respond quickly to any treatment, regardless of how effectively a trainee practices. For some clients, an increase in patience and self-compassion regarding their symptoms may be a sign of progress, rather than an immediate decrease in symptoms. Thus, trainees are advised to keep their expectations for client change realistic in the context of their client's symptoms, history, and presentation. It is important that trainees do not try to force their clients to improve in therapy in order for the trainee to feel like they are making progress in their training (Rousmaniere, 2016).

Trainee's Work as a Therapist

One important result of deliberate practice is change within the trainee regarding their work with clients. For example, trainees at test sites reported feeling more comfortable sitting with evocative clients, more confident addressing uncomfortable topics in therapy, and more responsive to a broader range of clients.

Trainee's Personal Development

Another important result of deliberate practice is personal growth within the trainee. For example, trainees at test sites reported becoming more in touch with their own feelings, increased self-compassion, and enhanced motivation to work with a broader range of clients.

Trainee's Training Process

Another valuable result of deliberate practice is improvement in the trainees' training process. For example, trainees at test sites reported becoming more aware of their personal training style, preferences, strengths, and challenges. Over time, trainees should grow to feel more ownership of their training process. Training to be a psychotherapist is a complex process that occurs over many years. Experienced, expert therapists still report continuing to grow well beyond their graduate school years (Orlinsky et al., 2005). Furthermore, training is not a linear process. In our personal experience of learning to be psychotherapists, we can recall feeling, at times, that we were really "learning the ropes" and doing great work with our child clients, only to be confronted the next day with a huge feeling of disappointment and setback when confronted with a resistant or particularly unhappy or oppositional child. Remember, be easy on yourself. And trust the process!

The Trainee–Trainer Alliance: Monitoring Complex Reactions Toward the Trainer

Trainees who engage in hard deliberate practice often report experiencing complex feelings toward their trainer. For example, one trainee said, "I know this is helping, but I also don't look forward to it!" Another trainee reported feeling both appreciation and frustration simultaneously toward her trainer. Trainees are advised to remember intensive training they have done in other fields, such as athletics or music. When a coach pushes a trainee to the edge of their ability, it is common for trainees to have complex reactions toward the coach.

This does not necessarily mean that the trainer is doing anything wrong. In fact, intensive training inevitably stirs up reactions toward the trainer, such as frustration, annoyance, disappointment, or anger that coexist with the appreciation they feel. In fact, if trainees do not experience complex reactions, it is worth considering whether the deliberate practice is sufficiently challenging. But what we asserted earlier about rights to privacy applies here as well. Because professional mental health training is hierarchical and evaluative, trainers should not require or even expect trainees to share complex reactions they may be experiencing toward them. Trainers should stay open to their sharing, but the choice always remains with the trainee.

Trainee's Own Therapy

When engaging in deliberate practice, many trainees discover aspects of their inner world that may benefit from attending their own psychotherapy. For example, one trainee discovered that her clients' anger stirred up her own painful memories of abuse, another trainee found himself disassociating while practicing empathy skills, and another trainee experienced overwhelming shame and self-judgment when she couldn't master skills after just a few repetitions.

Although these discoveries were unnerving at first, they ultimately were beneficial, as they motivated the trainees to seek out their own therapy. Many therapists attend their own therapy. In fact, Norcross and Guy (2005) found in their review of 17 studies that about 75% of the more than 8,000 therapist participants have attended their own therapy (Norcross & Guy, 2005). Orlinsky et al. (2005) found that more than 90% of therapists who attended their own therapy reported it as helpful.

QUESTIONS FOR TRAINEES

1. Are you balancing the effort to improve your skills with patience and self-compassion for your learning process?
2. Are you attending to any shame or self-judgment that arising from training?
3. Are you being mindful of your personal boundaries and also respecting any complex feelings you may have toward your trainers?

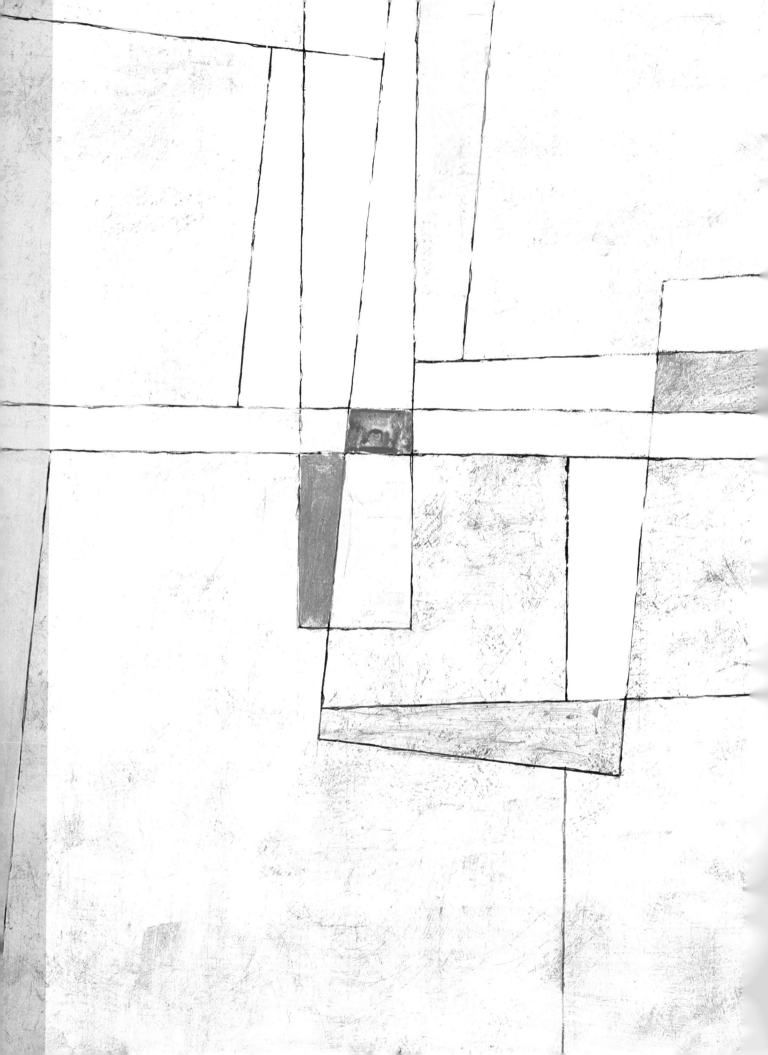

Difficulty Assessments and Adjustments

Deliberate practice works best if the exercises are performed at a challenge level that is neither too hard nor too easy. To ensure that they are practicing at the correct difficulty, trainees should do a *difficulty assessment and adjustment* after each level of client statement is completed (beginner, intermediate, and advanced). To do this, use the following instructions and the Deliberate Practice Reaction Form (Figure A.1), which is also available at https://www.apa.org/pubs/books/deliberate-practice-child-adolescent-psychotherapy (see the "Clinician and Practitioner Resources" tab). **Do not skip this process!**

How to Assess Difficulty

The *therapist* completes the Deliberate Practice Reaction Form (Figure A.1). If they

- rate the difficulty of the exercise higher than an 8 or had any of the reactions in the "Too Hard" column, follow the instructions to make the exercise easier;

- rate the difficulty of the exercise below a 4 or didn't have any of the reactions in the "Good Challenge" column, proceed to the next level of harder client statements or follow the instructions to make the exercise harder; or

- rate the difficulty of the exercise between 4 and 8 and have at least one reaction in the "Good Challenge" column, do not proceed to the harder client statements but rather repeat the same level.

Making Client Statements Easier

If the therapist ever rates the difficulty of the exercise above an 8 or has any of the reactions in the "Too Hard" column, use the next level easier client statements (e.g., if you were using Advanced client statements, switch to Intermediate). But if you already were using Beginner client statements, use the following methods to make the client statements even easier:

- The person playing the client can use the same beginner client statements but this time in a softer, calmer voice and with a smile. This softens the emotional tone.

191

FIGURE A.1. Deliberate Practice Reaction Form

Question 1: How challenging was it to fulfill the skill criteria for this exercise?

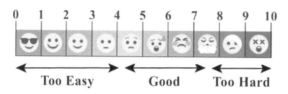

Question 2: Did you have any reactions in "good challenge" or "too hard" categories? (yes/no)					
Good Challenge			**Too Hard**		
Emotions and Thoughts	Body Reactions	Urges	Emotions and Thoughts	Body Reactions	Urges
Manageable shame, self-judgment, irritation, anger, sadness, etc.	Body tension, sighs, shallow breathing, increased heart rate, warmth, dry mouth	Looking away, withdrawing, changing focus	Severe or overwhelming shame, self-judgment, rage, grief, guilt, etc.	Migraines, dizziness, foggy thinking, diarrhea, disassociation, numbness, blanking out, nausea, etc.	Shutting down, giving up

Too Easy ⬇ Proceed to next difficulty level	Good Challenge ⬇ Repeat the same difficulty level	Too Hard ⬇ Go back to previous difficulty level

Note. From *Deliberate Practice in Emotion-Focused Therapy* (p. 180), by R. N. Goldman, A. Vaz, and T. Rousmaniere, 2021, American Psychological Association (https://doi.org/10.1037/0000227–000). Copyright 2021 by the American Psychological Association.

- The client can improvise with topics that are less evocative or make the therapist more comfortable, such as talking about topics without expressing feelings, the future or past (avoiding the here and now), or any topic outside therapy (see Figure A.2).

- The therapist can take a short break (5–10 minutes) between questions.

- The trainer can expand the "feedback phase" by discussing child therapy or psychotherapy theory and research. This should shift the trainees' focus toward more detached/intellectual topics and reduce the emotional intensity.

Making Client Statements Harder

If the therapist rates the difficulty of the exercise below a 4 or didn't have any of the reactions in the "Good Challenge" column, proceed to next level harder client statements. If you were already using the Advanced client statements, the client should make the exercise even harder, using the following guidelines:

FIGURE A.2. How to Make Client Statements Easier or Harder in Role-Plays

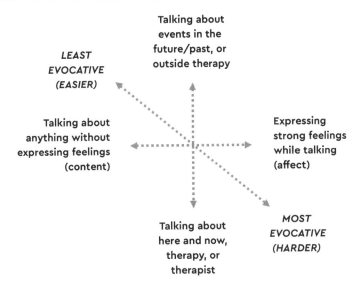

Note. Figure created by Jason Whipple, PhD.

- The person playing the client can use the Advanced client statements again with a more distressed voice (e.g., very angry, sad, sarcastic) or unpleasant facial expression. This should increase the emotional tone.

- The client can improvise new client statements with topics that are more evocative or make the therapist uncomfortable, such as expressing strong feelings or talking about the here and now, therapy, or the therapist (see Figure A.2).

Note. The purpose of a deliberate practice session is not to get through all the client statements and therapist responses but to spend as much time as possible practicing at the correct difficulty level. This may mean that trainees repeat the same statements and responses many times, which is okay as long as the difficulty remains in the "good challenge" level.

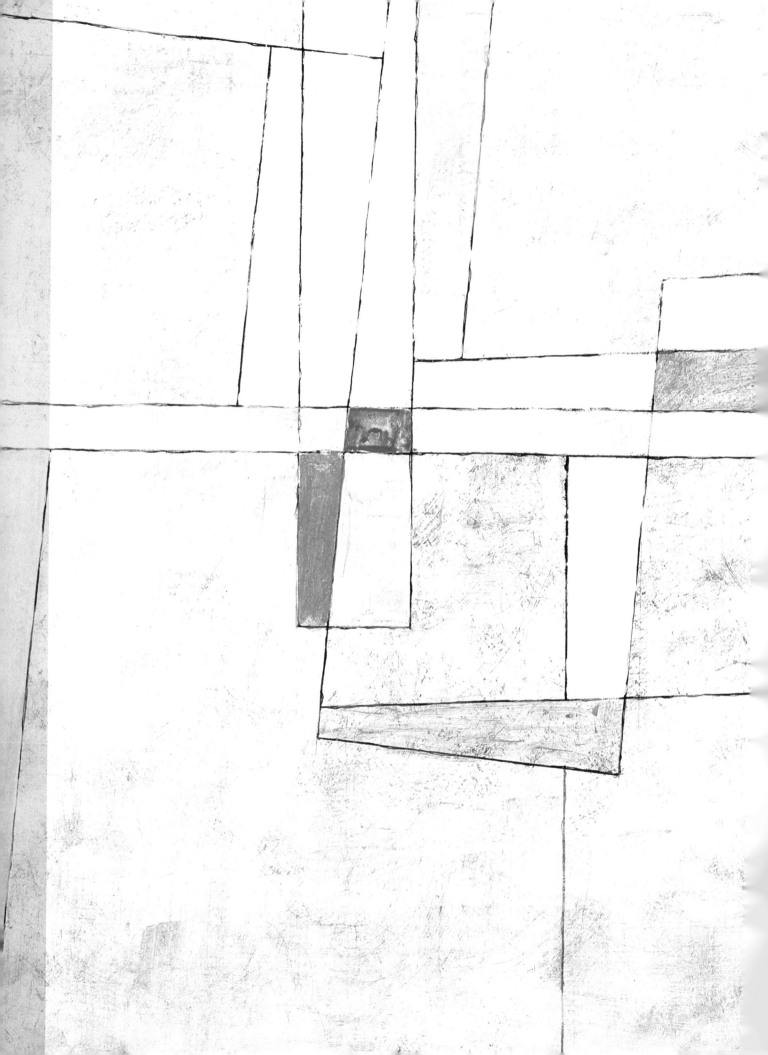

Deliberate Practice
Diary Form

To optimize the quality of the deliberate practice, we have developed a Deliberate Practice Diary Form that can also be downloaded from the "Clinician and Practitioner Resources" tab at https://www.apa.org/pubs/books/deliberate-practice-child-adolescent-psychotherapy. This form provides a template for the trainee to record their experience of the deliberate practice activity and, hopefully, will aid in the consolidation of learning. This form is not intended to be used as part of the evaluation process with the supervisor.

Deliberate Practice Diary Form

Use this form to consolidate learnings from the deliberate practice exercises. Please protect your personal boundaries by only sharing information that you are comfortable disclosing.

Name: _____ Date: _____
Exercise: _____

Question 1. What was helpful or worked well this deliberate practice session? In what way?

Question 2. What was unhelpful or didn't go well this deliberate practice session? In what way?

Question 3. What did you learn about yourself, your current skills, and skills you'd like to keep improving? Feel free to share any details, but only those you are comfortable disclosing.

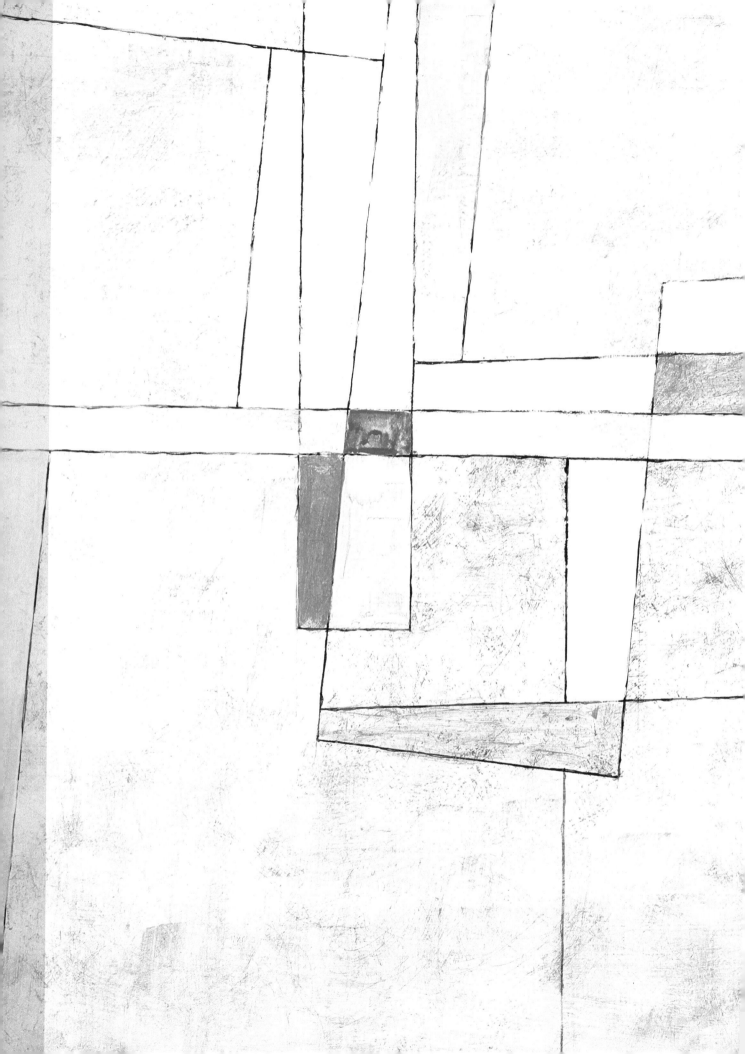

Sample Child and Adolescent Psychotherapy Syllabus With Embedded Deliberate Practice Exercises

This appendix provides a sample one-semester, three-unit course dedicated to teaching an introductory course on child therapy, from a pantheoretical lens. This course is appropriate for graduate students (master's and doctoral) at all levels of training, including first-year students who have not yet worked with clients. We present it as a model that can be adopted to a specific program's contexts and needs. For example, instructors may borrow portions of it to use in other courses, practica, didactic training events at externships and internships, workshops, and continuing education for post-graduate therapists.

Course Title: Beginning Work With Children, Parents, and Families: Theory and Deliberate Practice

Course Description

This course teaches theory, principles, and core skills of child psychotherapy. It is transtheoretical, in that it covers common factors across different types of child therapy, including psychodynamic, cognitive-behavioral, and family systems approaches to therapy. As a course with both didactic and practicum elements, it will review the theory and research on child therapy, psychotherapy change processes, and applications of transtheoretical approaches, and will foster the use of deliberate practice to enable students to acquire 12 key child therapy skills. Finally, we will explore specific issues that may be addressed in treatment, including mourning and loss, child abuse and neglect, foster care and adoption, substance use, gender and sexual identity, disordered eating, and marital conflicts.

Course Objectives

Students who complete this course will be able to

1. Describe the core theory, research, and skills of child therapy

2. Describe central principles of attachment, family systems, cognitive behavioral, and psychodynamic theories, and how these apply to understanding the meaning of behavior across the lifespan

3. Apply the principles of deliberate practice for career-long clinical skill development

4. Demonstrate key child therapy skills

5. Evaluate how they can fit these child therapy skills into their developing therapeutic framework

6. Employ child therapy with clients from diverse cultural backgrounds

7. Be playful and emotionally available for their clients as a result of the increased emotional self-awareness and experiential knowledge they gain in the course

8. Describe evidence-based practice approaches to child therapy

9. Demonstrate a curious and reflective stance

10. Maintain an effective balance of (a) emotional openness and authenticity and (b) appropriate personal boundaries

Date	Lecture and Discussion	Skills Lab	Homework (for next class)
Week 1	Introduction—bioecological models	Exercise 1: Communicating Interest and Curiosity	Bronfenbrenner and Evans (2000); Narvaez et al. (2013); Brown (2008)
Week 2	Attachment theory deliberate practice: naming feelings	Exercise 2: Naming Feelings	Bowlby (2012, Chapter 8); Slade (2005); Main et al. (2011); Granqvist et al. (2017)
Week 3	Family systems theories	Exercise 3: Praise and Encouragement	Minuchin et al. (2013, Chapters 1, 2, & 11); Wachtel (2004, Chapter 1); Diamond et al. (1999)
Week 4	Playing in therapy	Exercise 4: Observing and Describing Play	Winnicott (2012, Chapters 3 & 4); Royal (2015); Topel and Lachmann (2008)
Week 5	Working with parents and families	Exercise 5: Empathic Validation	Whitefield and Midgley (2015); Mayes et al. (2012); Kazdin et al. (1997); Novick and Novick (2013)
Week 6	Intergenerational trauma	Exercise 6: Elaborating Play	Fraiberg et al. (2003); Goodman (2013); Vaughans and Harris (2016); Lieberman et al. (2005)
Week 7	Culture and immigration	Exercise 7: Exploring Identity—Multicultural Orientation	**Helpful Handout 1—Intake Form Due** Sparrow (2016); Fleck and Fleck (2013); Tummala-Narra (2004)
Week 8	Psychodynamic approaches	Exercise 8: Self-Disclosure	Hurry (1998, Chapters 1, 2, & 4); Wachtel (2004, Chapters 6 & 7); Malberg (2015)
Week 9	Addressing risk part 1: abuse and neglect, domestic violence, and parental substance use	Exercise 9: Gathering Information About Safety Concerns	**Helpful Handout 2—Describing Therapy to Parents Due** Schilling and Christian (2014); Pietrantonio et al. (2013); Lieberman et al. (2015, pp. 7–44)
Week 10	Behavioral and cognitive behavioral treatment approaches	Exercise 10: Setting Limits	Wachtel (2004, Chapter 8); J. A. Cohen et al. (2010); Miller et al. (2002)
Week 11	Gender, sexuality, and the body	Exercise 11: Talking About Sex	Tishelman et al. (2015); Tasca and Balfour (2014); Silverstein et al. (2002) **Optional Readings:** Alvarez (2010); Riley et al. (2011); Eisler et al. (2007); Minuchin et al. (1978); Ordway et al. (2018)
Week 12	Addressing risk part 2: suicidal ideation, self-harm, and adolescent substance use	Exercise 12: Responding to Resistance and Ruptures	Sharp and Fonagy (2015); O'Connor et al. (2014); Deas (2008)
Week 13	Coping with grief and loss	Exercise 13: Annotated Transcript	**Helpful Handout 3—Risk Assessment Form Due** Markin and Zilcha-Mano (2018); Bowlby (1982); Lyons-Ruth et al. (2003)
Week 14	Foster care, adoption, and disruptions in caregiving deliberate practice: rupture repair responsiveness	Exercise 14: Improvised Session	Steele et al. (2003); Dozier and Bernard (2017); P. Cohen et al. (2016)
Week 15	Making treatment decisions—structuring treatment	Reflection on Experience	**Final Papers Due**

Format of Class

This course is a combination of lecture, class discussion, and small group skills labs (deliberate practice) sessions, and application of the topics and themes in the form of response papers, "helpful handouts," and literature review papers.

Skills Labs: Skills labs are for practicing child therapy skills using the exercises in this book. The exercises use therapy simulations (role-plays) with the following goals:

1. Build trainees' skill and confidence for using child therapy skills with real clients
2. Provide a safe space for experimenting with different therapeutic interventions, without fear of making mistakes
3. Provide plenty of opportunity to explore and "try on" different styles of therapy so that trainees can ultimately discover their own personal, unique therapy style

Course Requirements

Required Readings: Will be posted online and must be completed before class to engage in discussion about the material. The required readings are listed at the end of the syllables along with supplemental reading that we recommend adding to your personal library.

Assignments:

Assignment	Due date	Points
Helpful handouts	As scheduled	30 (10 each)
Canvas responses to weekly readings (seven total)	As desired	14 (2 each)
Final project	Week 14	30
Deliberate practice	Weekly	15
Participation in class discussion	Weekly	11

Small Group Deliberate Practice Exercises

Deliberate practice is a form of training that is similar to the way you would practice the skills involved in a sport or playing a musical instrument. For example, if you are a professional sports player, you do not just play in games on the weekend. Outside of when you are playing in games, you practice. That practice includes repetitive drills that help you strengthen specific skills that you will then use in the game.

Throughout this course, you will be required to complete weekly practice exercises in pairs (45 minutes) outside of class. You will receive a packet with an exercise for each week. The exercises include a description of the skill you will be working on, three criteria for evaluating yourself on the skill, and a set of client prompts that you will respond to to practice the skill. In each of these sessions, you will play the therapist and practice the skill for 15 minutes, and your partner will play the therapist and practice for 15 minutes.

Just like practice for a sport, the focus of these sessions is not on thinking or talking about the skill, it's on doing it! The repeated rehearsal does the training here. If you are having a hard time, figure out what's getting you stuck, get help from your partner, and give it another go. There are two components that will be submitted to obtain credit for deliberate practice exercises:

1. Video recording of group deliberate practice exercises
2. Weekly submission of the Diary Form postexercise

Review of the videos and Diary Forms is not evaluative. Videos will be reviewed by the professor or the TA to ensure that you are following the appropriate procedures for practicing—rehearsing repeatedly, without getting into lengthy discussions about theory (that's for class time) and evaluating the level of difficulty. Similarly, a check of Diary Cards is done to track your progress through your own self-assessment and is not evaluative of your therapy skills. One point will be received for each exercise you complete.

Toward the end of the semester (Week 14), trainees will participate in a deliberate practice in which they do a practice session using the annotated transcript in Exercise 13 or a mock practice session in which the "client" adopts one of the client profiles listed in Exercise 14 or plays themselves as the client. In contrast to highly structured and repetitive deliberate practice exercises, these are unstructured and improvised role-play therapy sessions.

Like a jazz rehearsal, mock sessions let trainees practice the art and science of putting psychotherapy skills together in a way that is helpful to clients. Practice sessions let trainees

1. Practice using psychotherapy skills responsively.
2. Experiment with clinical decision-making in an unscripted context.
3. Discover their personal therapeutic style.
4. Build endurance for working with real clients.

Reading Reflections

A short paragraph (less than one page) reflecting on your reactions and ideas about the readings for class that week, due by 8 p.m. on Wednesday before class. Reflections could be on passages that struck you, questions that came to mind, something the article helped you to understand better, or your own relevant experiences. You are responsible for submitting seven of these throughout the course of the semester. Your responses may involve one of the articles or make links between articles but must be directly grappling with issues raised in the readings.

Helpful Handouts

You will soon find yourself providing therapy with children, parents, and families. Very likely, the settings in which you work will have their own systems for intakes and risk assessment and safety planning. Depending on the treatments you are providing, you will discuss with supervisors how to orient families to psychotherapy.

The material in this course will cover clinical theories and techniques in a broad way. To connect these concepts with clinical practice, you will be asked to draw on the course materials, as well as other resources and your own experience, to develop "Helpful Handouts," similar to what you might receive from a supervisor.

You will submit three Helpful Handouts over the course of the semester.

- Helpful Handout 1—Clinical Intake Form: an outline of the questions you would ask in an initial assessment with a parent and child who present for therapy.

- Helpful Handout 2—Describing Therapy to Parents: a written description of how you would explain therapy to parents and their children, including your understanding of the tasks and how change occurs. Can be written from the orientation of your choice.

- Helpful Handout 3—Risk Assessment: a set of questions that you would use to guide you in asking about different categories of risk and probing further.

You are free to draw on any materials you wish for these, but the handout you submit must be your own original version, with an attached reference list indicating where you got ideas and content.

Final Paper

For this assignment, you will choose two child or family treatment approaches that are designed for the same presenting problem or patient population and write a 10-page paper (not including references) in American Psychological Association (APA) Style comparing and contrasting the interventions in terms of theoretical background and orientation, conceptualization of the symptom or patient, clinical approach, and empirical evidence base.

Class Participation

Active participation is essential to this learning environment. The quality and quantity of participation in discussion of assigned readings related material will contribute to the course grade.

A note on virtual class participation: All students are strongly urged to turn their cameras on and keep them on during course time to show engagement and to promote participation. However, it is understood that this is a time for flexibility and that each of us has different at-home responsibilities and restrictions. That being said, if you opt not to turn on your camera during a given class, verbal participation is highly encouraged for me to gain a sense of your engagement in weekly material and topics.

Please reach out to me if there are any issues with access to technology that will prohibit your participation in coursework this semester so that a solution can be found.

A note about respect for diversity: Much of what we consider science aims to be objective but is in many ways subjective. The field of psychology has been built on theories and ideas developed by people, often from a narrow set of cultural backgrounds and identities, who received support and funding from various institutions and systems.

I have attempted to include in this syllabus readings that will focus discussion on systemic oppression and social justice in the context of psychodynamic psychotherapy, including the application of psychodynamic theory and techniques with diverse populations. I have also made an effort to include voices of authors from diverse identities and backgrounds. However, I acknowledge that it is possible that there may be both overt and covert biases in the material due to the lens with which it was written. Integrating a diverse set of experiences is important for a more comprehensive understanding of science. Please contact me or submit anonymous feedback on course evaluations if you have any suggestions to improve the quality of the course materials.

Furthermore, I would like to create a learning environment for students that supports a diversity of perspectives and experiences and honors your identities. I believe trust and respect are central for creating spaces where there can be open discussion, mutual learning, and growth. It is expected that some of the material in this course may evoke strong emotions; please be respectful of others' emotions and mindful of your own.

I am always in the process of learning about diverse perspectives and identities. Please let me know if something said or done in the classroom, by either myself or other students, is particularly troubling or causes discomfort or offense. Although our intention may not be to cause discomfort or offense, the impact of what happens throughout the course is not to be ignored and is something that I consider to be very important and deserving of attention. If and when this occurs, please consider one of the following ways to address what you experienced and, I hope, somewhat alleviate distress:

- Discuss the situation privately with me. I am always open to listening to students' experiences and want to work with students to find acceptable ways to process and address the issue.

- Discuss the situation with the class. Chances are there is at least one other student in the class who had a similar response to the material or statements made. Discussion enhances the ability for all class participants to have a fuller understanding of context and impact of course material and class discussions.

- Notify me of the issue through another source, such as your academic advisor, a trusted faculty member, or a peer. If for any reason you do not feel comfortable discussing the issue directly with me, I encourage you to seek out another, more comfortable avenue to address the issue. If you are not sure of who to speak with, [insert names] are two faculty members who I will look to for feedback on my course.

Vulnerability, Privacy, Confidentiality, and Boundaries

This course is aimed at developing therapy skills, self-awareness, and interaction skills in an experiential framework and as relevant to clinical work. Doing child psychotherapy requires balancing emotional vulnerability and openness and simultaneously maintaining appropriate personal boundaries. We will explore and practice this balance as part of learning to deliver child therapy together.

Furthermore, working with children and parents can bring up memories of our own childhoods, our parents, and experiences with children and parents that we know. This course is not psychotherapy or a substitute for psychotherapy. Students should interact at a level of self-disclosure that is personally comfortable and helpful to their own learning. Although becoming aware of internal emotional and psychological processes is necessary for a therapist's development, it is not necessary to reveal all that information to the trainer. It is important for students to sense their own level of safety and privacy. Students are not evaluated on the level of material that they choose to reveal in the class.

Revealing Information About Self

In accordance with the *Ethical Principles of Psychologists and Code of Conduct* (APA, 2017), students are not required to disclose personal information. It is, however, recommended to disclose personal material, within comfortable limits, to learn the most from the exercises. Because this class is about developing both interpersonal and child psychotherapy competence, following are some important points so that students are fully informed as they make choices to self-disclose:

- Professional activities are affected by personal experiences, beliefs, and values, and these things have a bearing on students' professional functioning.

- Behaviors are influenced by personal experiences, beliefs, and values. Students may be asked to reflect on this in the specifically defined context of encouraging the growth of professional competence for the work environment only.

Student Evaluation

Final grades will be calculated based on the following grading scale:

A = 94.0–100.0	B+ = 87.0–89.9	C+ = 77.0–79.9
A– = 90.0–93.9	B = 83.0–86.9	C = 73.0–76.9
	B– = 80.0–82.9	C– = 70.0–72.9

Required Readings

Bowlby, J. (1982). Attachment and loss: Retrospect and prospect. *American Journal of Ortho-psychiatry, 52*(4), 664. https://doi.org/10.1111/j.1939-0025.1982.tb01456.x

Bowlby, J. (2012). *A secure base.* Routledge. https://doi.org/10.4324/9780203440841

Bronfenbrenner, U., & Evans, G. W. (2000). Developmental science in the 21st century: Emerging questions, theoretical models, research designs and empirical findings. *Social Development, 9*(1), 115–125. https://doi.org/10.1111/1467-9507.00114

Brown, L. S. (2008). Knowing difference or we're all diverse here. In L. S. Brown, *Cultural competence in trauma therapy: Beyond the flashback* (pp. 23–47). American Psychological Association. https://doi.org/10.1037/11752-001

Cohen, J. A., Berliner, L., & Mannarino, A. (2010). Trauma focused CBT for children with co-occurring trauma and behavior problems. *Child Abuse & Neglect, 34*(4), 215–224. https://doi.org/10.1016/j.chiabu.2009.12.003

Cohen, P., Remez, A., Edelman, R. C., Golub, A., Pacifici, A., Santillan, Y., & Wolfe, L. (2016). Promoting attachment and mentalization for parents and young children in the foster care system: Implementing a new training and treatment approach in an agency. *Journal of Infant, Child, and Adolescent Psychotherapy, 15*(2), 124–134. https://doi.org/10.1080/15289168.2016.1163992

Deas, D. (2008). Evidence-based treatments for alcohol use disorders in adolescents. *Pediatrics, 121*(Suppl. 4), S348–S354. https://doi.org/10.1542/peds.2007-2243G

Diamond, G. M., Liddle, H. A., Hogue, A., & Dakof, G. A. (1999). Alliance-building interventions with adolescents in family therapy: A process study. *Psychotherapy: Theory, Research, Practice, Training, 36*(4), 355–368. https://doi.org/10.1037/h0087729

Dozier, M., & Bernard, K. (2017). Attachment and biobehavioral catch-up: Addressing the needs of infants and toddlers exposed to inadequate or problematic caregiving. *Current Opinion in Psychology, 15*, 111–117. https://doi.org/10.1016/j.copsyc.2017.03.003

Fleck, J. R., & Fleck, D. T. (2013). The immigrant family: Parent–child dilemmas and therapy considerations. *American International Journal of Contemporary Research, 3*(8), 13–17. https://www.aijcrnet.com/journals/Vol_3_No_8_August_2013/2.pdf

Fraiberg, S., Adelson, E., & Shapiro, V. (2003). Ghosts in the nursery: A psychoanalytic approach to the problems of impaired infant–mother relationships. In J. Raphael-Leff (Ed.), *Parent–infant psychodynamics: Wild things, mirrors and ghosts* (pp. 87–117). Routledge.

Goodman, R. D. (2013). The transgenerational trauma and resilience genogram. *Counselling Psychology Quarterly, 26*(3–4), 386–405. https://doi.org/10.1080/09515070.2013.820172

Granqvist, P., Sroufe, L. A., Dozier, M., Hesse, E., Steele, M., van IJzendoorn, M., Solomon, J., Schuengel, C., Fearon, P., Bakermans-Kranenburg, M., Steele, H., Cassidy, J., Carlson, E., Madigan, S., Jacobvitz, D., Foster, S., Behrens, K., Rifkin-Graboi, A., Gribneau, N., . . . Duschinsky, R. (2017). Disorganized attachment in infancy: A review of the phenomenon and its implications for clinicians and policy-makers. *Attachment & Human Development, 19*(6), 534–558. https://doi.org/10.1080/14616734.2017.1354040

Hurry, A. (1998). *Psychoanalysis and developmental therapy* (Psychoanalytic Monographs; No. 3). Karnac Books.

Kazdin, A. E., Holland, L., & Crowley, M. (1997). Family experience of barriers to treatment and premature termination from child therapy. *Journal of Consulting and Clinical Psychology, 65*(3), 453–463. https://doi.org/10.1037/0022-006X.65.3.453

Lieberman, A. F., Ippen, C. G., & Van Horn, P. (2015). *Don't hit my mommy! A manual for child-parent psychotherapy with young children exposed to violence and other trauma* (pp. 7-44). Zero to Three.

Lieberman, A. F., Padrón, E., Van Horn, P., & Harris, W. W. (2005). Angels in the nursery: The intergenerational transmission of benevolent parental influences. *Infant Mental Health Journal, 26*(6), 504-520. https://doi.org/10.1002/imhj.20071

Lyons-Ruth, K., Yellin, C., Melnick, S., & Atwood, G. (2003). Childhood experiences of trauma and loss have different relations to maternal unresolved and hostile-helpless states of mind on the AAI. *Attachment & Human Development, 5*(4), 330-352. https://doi.org/10.1080/14616730310001633410

Main, M., Hesse, E., & Hesse, S. (2011). Attachment theory and research: Overview with suggested applications to child custody. *Family Court Review, 49*(3), 426-463. https://doi.org/10.1111/j.1744-1617.2011.01383.x

Malberg, N. T. (2015). Activating mentalization in parents: An integrative framework. *Journal of Infant, Child, and Adolescent Psychotherapy, 14*(3), 232-245. https://doi.org/10.1080/15289168.2015.1068002

Markin, R. D., & Zilcha-Mano, S. (2018). Cultural processes in psychotherapy for perinatal loss: Breaking the cultural taboo against perinatal grief. *Psychotherapy, 55*(1), 20-26. https://doi.org/10.1037/pst0000122

Mayes, L., Rutherford, H., Suchman, N., & Close, N. (2012). The neural and psychological dynamics of adults' transition to parenthood. *Zero to Three, 33*(2), 83-84.

Miller, A. L., Glinski, J., Woodberry, K. A., Mitchell, A. G., & Indik, J. (2002). Family therapy and dialectical behavior therapy with adolescents: Part I. Proposing a clinical synthesis. *American Journal of Psychotherapy, 56*(4), 568-584. https://doi.org/10.1176/appi.psychotherapy.2002.56.4.568

Minuchin, S., Reiter, M., & Borda, C. (2013) *The craft of family therapy: Challenging certainties.* Routledge. https://doi.org/10.4324/9781315886213

Narvaez, D., Panksepp, J., Schore, A. N., & Gleason, T. R. (2013). The value of using an evolutionary framework for gauging children's well-being. In D. Narvaez, J. Panksepp, A. N. Schore, & T. R. Gleason (Eds.), *Evolution, early experience and human development: From research to practice and policy* (pp. 3-30). Oxford University Press. https://doi.org/10.1093/acprof:oso/9780199755059.003.0001

Novick, K. K., & Novick, J. (2013). Concurrent work with parents of adolescent patients. *The Psychoanalytic Study of the Child, 67*(1), 103-136. https://doi.org/10.1080/00797308.2014.11785491

O'Connor, S. S., Brausch, A., Ridge Anderson, A., & Jobes, D. A. (2014). Applying the collaborative assessment and management of suicidality (CAMS) to suicidal adolescents. *International Journal of Behavioral Consultation and Therapy, 9*(3), 53-58. https://doi.org/10.1037/h0101641

Pietrantonio, A. M., Wright, E., Gibson, K. N., Alldred, T., Jacobson, D., & Niec, A. (2013). Mandatory reporting of child abuse and neglect: Crafting a positive process for health professionals and caregivers. *Child Abuse & Neglect, 37*(2-3), 102-109. https://doi.org/10.1016/j.chiabu.2012.12.007

Royal, J. (2015). "Following the affect": How my first child patient helped teach me to listen and see. In S. Tuber (Ed.), *Early encounters with children and adolescents: Beginning psychodynamic therapists' first cases* (pp. 105-124). Routledge. https://doi.org/10.4324/9781315746500

Schilling, S., & Christian, C. W. (2014). Child physical abuse and neglect. *Child and Adolescent Psychiatric Clinics, 23*(2), 309-319. https://doi.org/10.1016/j.chc.2014.01.001

Sharp, C., & Fonagy, P. (2015). Practitioner review: Borderline personality disorder in adolescence—Recent conceptualization, intervention, and implications for clinical practice. *Journal of Child Psychology and Psychiatry, 56*(12), 1266-1288. https://doi.org/10.1111/jcpp.12449

Silverstein, L. B., Auerbach, C. F., & Levant, R. F. (2002). Contemporary fathers reconstructing masculinity: Clinical implications of gender role strain. *Professional Psychology: Research and Practice, 33*(4), 361-369. https://doi.org/10.1037/0735-7028.33.4.361

Slade, A. (2005). Parental reflective functioning: An introduction. *Attachment & Human Development, 7*(3), 269–281. https://doi.org/10.1080/14616730500245906

Sparrow, J. (2016). Culture, community, and context in child development. In D. Navarez, J. M. Braungart-Rieker, L. E. Miller-Graff, L. T. Gettler, & P. D. Hastings (Eds.), *Contexts for young child flourishing: Evolution, family, and society* (pp. 333–346). Oxford University Press. https://doi.org/10.1093/acprof:oso/9780190237790.003.0017

Steele, M., Hodges, J., Kaniuk, J., Hillman, S., & Henderson, K. (2003). Attachment representations and adoption: Associations between maternal states of mind and emotion narratives in previously maltreated children. *Journal of Child Psychotherapy, 29*(2), 187–205. https://doi.org/10.1080/0075417031000138442

Tasca, G. A., & Balfour, L. (2014). Attachment and eating disorders: A review of current research. *International Journal of Eating Disorders, 47*(7), 710–717. https://doi.org/10.1002/eat.22302

Tishelman, A. C., Kaufman, R., Edwards-Leeper, L., Mandel, F. H., Shumer, D. E., & Spack, N. P. (2015). Serving transgender youth: Challenges, dilemmas, and clinical examples. *Professional Psychology: Research and Practice, 46*(1), 37–45. https://doi.org/10.1037/a0037490

Topel, E. M., & Lachmann, F. M. (2008). Life begins on an ant farm for two patients with Asperger's syndrome. *Psychoanalytic Psychology, 25*(4), 602–612. https://doi.org/10.1037/a0013890

Tummala-Narra, P. (2004). Mothering in a foreign land. *The American Journal of Psychoanalysis, 64*(2), 167–182. https://doi.org/10.1023/B:TAJP.0000027271.27008.60

Vaughans, K. C., & Harris, L. (2016). The police, Black and Hispanic boys: A dangerous inability to mentalize. *Journal of Infant, Child, and Adolescent Psychotherapy, 15*(3), 171–178. https://doi.org/10.1080/15289168.2016.1214454

Wachtel, E. F. (2004). *Treating troubled children and their families.* Guilford Press.

Whitefield, C., & Midgley, N. (2015). "And when you were a child?": How therapists working with parents alongside individual child psychotherapy bring the past into their work. *Journal of Child Psychotherapy, 41*(3), 272–292. https://doi.org/10.1080/0075417X.2015.1092678

Winnicott, D. W. (2012). *Playing and reality.* Routledge.

Supplemental Readings

Altman, N., Briggs, R., Frankel, J., Gensler, D., & Pantone, P. (2010). *Relational child psychotherapy.* Other Press.

Alvarez, A. (2010). Types of sexual transference and countertransference in psychotherapeutic work with children and adolescents. *Journal of Child Psychotherapy, 36*(3), 211–224. https://doi.org/10.1080/0075417X.2010.523815

Brown, L. S. (2008). *Cultural competence in trauma therapy: Beyond the flashback.* American Psychological Association. https://doi.org/10.1037/11752-000

Eisler, I., Simic, M., Russell, G. F. M., & Dare, C. (2007). A randomised controlled treatment trial of two forms of family therapy in adolescent anorexia nervosa: A five-year follow-up. *Journal of Child Psychology and Psychiatry, 48*(6), 552–560. https://doi.org/10.1111/j.1469-7610.2007.01726.x

Minuchin, S., Rosman, B. L., & Baker, L. (1978). *Psychosomatic families: Anorexia nervosa in context.* Harvard University Press. https://doi.org/10.4159/harvard.9780674418233

Novick, K. K., & Novick, J. (2011). *Working with parents makes therapy work.* Jason Aronson.

Ordway, M. R., Sadler, L. S., Holland, M. L., Slade, A., Close, N., & Mayes, L. C. (2018). A home visiting parenting program and child obesity: A randomized trial. *Pediatrics, 141*, e20171076. https://doi.org/10.1542/peds.2018-0770

Riley, E. A., Sitharthan, G., Clemson, L., & Diamond, M. (2011). The needs of gender-variant children and their parents according to health professionals. *International Journal of Transgenderism, 13*(2), 54–63. https://doi.org/10.1080/15532739.2011.622121

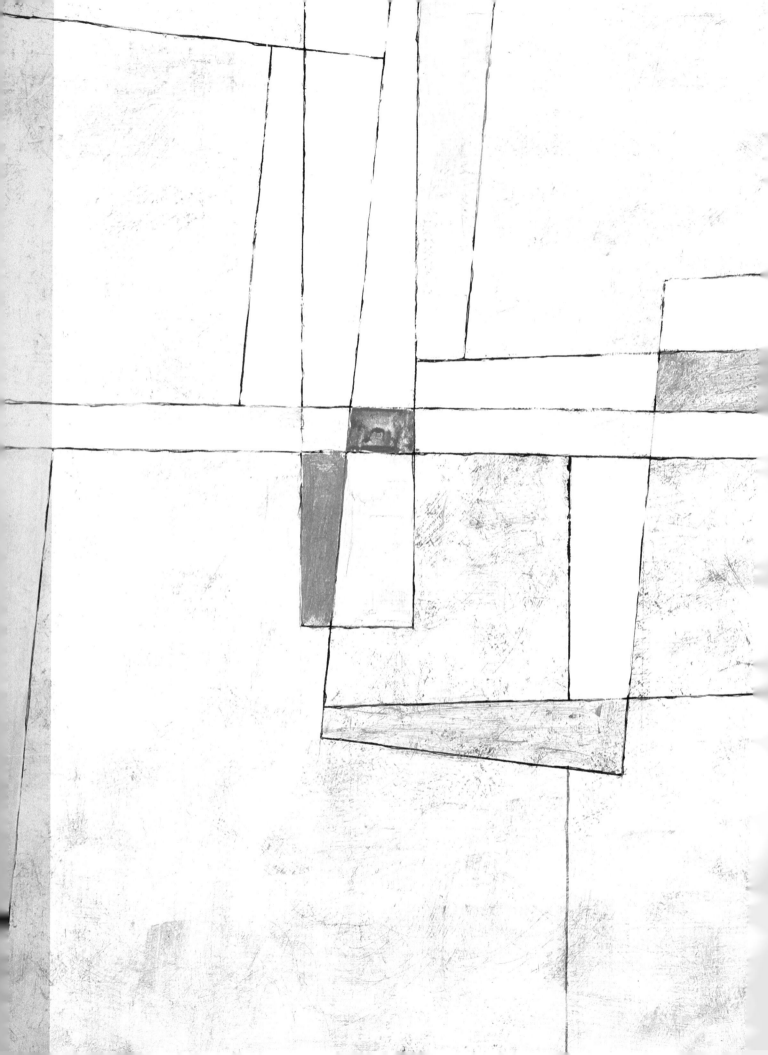

References

Abbass, A. A., Rabung, S., Leichsenring, F., Refseth, J. S., & Midgley, N. (2013). Psychodynamic psychotherapy for children and adolescents: A meta-analysis of short-term psychodynamic models. *Journal of the American Academy of Child & Adolescent Psychiatry*, *52*(8), 863–875. https://doi.org/10.1016/j.jaac.2013.05.014

American Psychological Association. (2017). *Ethical principles of psychologists and code of conduct* (2002, Amended June 1, 2010, and January 1, 2017). https://www.apa.org/ethics/code/

Anderson, T., Ogles, B. M., Patterson, C. L., Lambert, M. J., & Vermeersch, D. A. (2009). Therapist effects: Facilitative interpersonal skills as a predictor of therapist success. *Journal of Clinical Psychology*, *65*(7), 755–768. https://doi.org/10.1002/jclp.20583

Bailey, R. J., & Ogles, B. M. (2019). Common factors as a therapeutic approach: What is required? *Practice Innovations*, *4*(4), 241–254. https://doi.org/10.1037/pri0000100

Barish, K. (2018). Cycles of understanding and hope: Toward an integrative model of therapeutic change in child psychotherapy. *Journal of Infant, Child, and Adolescent Psychotherapy*, *17*(4), 232–242. https://doi.org/10.1080/15289168.2018.1526022

Barlow, D. H. (2010). Negative effects from psychological treatments: A perspective. *American Psychologist*, *65*(1), 13–20. https://doi.org/10.1037/a0015643

Bennett-Levy, J. (2019). Why therapists should walk the talk: The theoretical and empirical case for personal practice in therapist training and professional development. *Journal of Behavior Therapy and Experimental Psychiatry*, *62*, 133–145. https://doi.org/10.1016/j.jbtep.2018.08.004

Bennett-Levy, J., & Finlay-Jones, A. (2018). The role of personal practice in therapist skill development: A model to guide therapists, educators, supervisors and researchers. *Cognitive Behaviour Therapy*, *47*(3), 185–205. https://doi.org/10.1080/16506073.2018.1434678

Bohart, A. C., & Wade, A. G. (2013). The client in psychotherapy. In M. J. Lambert (Ed.), *Bergin and Garfield's handbook of psychotherapy and behavior change* (6th ed., pp. 219–257). John Wiley & Sons.

Bratton, S. C., Ray, D., Rhine, T., & Jones, L. (2005). The efficacy of play therapy with children: A meta-analytic review of treatment outcomes. *Professional Psychology, Research and Practice*, *36*(4), 376–390. https://doi.org/10.1037/0735-7028.36.4.376

Bugatti, M., & Boswell, J. F. (2016). Clinical errors as a lack of context responsiveness. *Psychotherapy: Theory, Research, & Practice*, *53*(3), 262–267. https://doi.org/10.1037/pst0000080

Carr, A. (2009). The effectiveness of family therapy and systemic interventions for child-focused problems. *Journal of Family Therapy*, *31*(1), 3–45. https://doi.org/10.1111/j.1467-6427.2008.00451.x

Castonguay, L. G., Goldfried, M. R., Wiser, S., Raue, P. J., & Hayes, A. M. (1996). Predicting the effect of cognitive therapy for depression: A study of unique and common factors. *Journal of*

Consulting and Clinical Psychology, 64(3), 497–504. https://doi.org/10.1037/0022-006X.64.3.497

Chorpita, B. F., Park, A., Tsai, K., Korathu-Larson, P., Higa-McMillan, C. K., Nakamura, B. J., Weisz, J. R., Krull, J., & the Research Network on Youth Mental Health. (2015). Balancing effectiveness with responsiveness: Therapist satisfaction across different treatment designs in the Child STEPs randomized effectiveness trial. *Journal of Consulting and Clinical Psychology, 83*(4), 709–718. https://doi.org/10.1037/a0039301

Chu, B. C., & Kendall, P. C. (2009). Therapist responsiveness to child engagement: Flexibility within manual-based CBT for anxious youth. *Journal of Clinical Psychology, 65*(7), 736–754. https://doi.org/10.1002/jclp.20582

Coker, J. (1990). *How to practice jazz.* Jamey Aebersold.

Cook, R. (2005). *It's about that time: Miles Davis on and off record.* Atlantic Books.

Crowe, K., & McKay, D. (2017). Efficacy of cognitive-behavioral therapy for childhood anxiety and depression. *Journal of Anxiety Disorders, 49*, 76–87. https://doi.org/10.1016/j.janxdis.2017.04.001

Csikszentmihalyi, M. (1997). *Finding flow: The psychology of engagement with everyday life.* Basic Books.

Curry, J. (2018). *Applying cognitive behavioral therapeutic strategies when working with adolescent depression* [Video]. American Psychological Association. https://doi.org/10.1037/v00619-001

Davis, D. E., DeBlaere, C., Owen, J., Hook, J. N., Rivera, D. P., Choe, E., Van Tongeren, D. R., Worthington, E. L., & Placeres, V. (2018). The multicultural orientation framework: A narrative review. *Psychotherapy: Theory, Research, & Practice, 55*(1), 89–100. https://doi.org/10.1037/pst0000160

Drewes, A. (2017). *Prescriptive integrative child play therapy with a young female client for emotional regulation issues* [Video]. American Psychological Association. https://doi.org/10.1037/v00580-001

Ellis, M. V., Berger, L., Hanus, A. E., Ayala, E. E., Swords, B. A., & Siembor, M. (2014). Inadequate and harmful clinical supervision: Testing a revised framework and assessing occurrence. *The Counseling Psychologist, 42*(4), 434–472. https://doi.org/10.1177/0011000013508656

Ericsson, A., & Pool, R. (2016). *Peak: Secrets from the new science of expertise.* Houghton Mifflin Harcourt.

Ericsson, K. A. (2003). The acquisition of expert performance as problem solving: Construction and modification of mediating mechanisms through deliberate practice. In J. E. Davidson & R. J. Sternberg (Eds.), *The psychology of problem solving* (pp. 31–83). Cambridge University Press. https://doi.org/10.1017/CBO9780511615771.003

Ericsson, K. A. (2004). Deliberate practice and the acquisition and maintenance of expert performance in medicine and related domains. *Academic Medicine, 79*(10, Suppl.), S70–S81. https://doi.org/10.1097/00001888-200410001-00022

Ericsson, K. A. (2006). The influence of experience and deliberate practice on the development of superior expert performance. In K. A. Ericsson, N. Charness, P. J. Feltovich, & R. R. Hoffman (Eds.), *The Cambridge handbook of expertise and expert performance* (pp. 683–703). Cambridge University Press. https://doi.org/10.1017/CBO9780511816796.038

Ericsson, K. A., Hoffman, R. R., Kozbelt, A., & Williams, A. M. (Eds.). (2018). *The Cambridge handbook of expertise and expert performance* (2nd ed.). Cambridge University Press. https://doi.org/10.1017/9781316480748

Ericsson, K. A., Krampe, R. T., & Tesch-Römer, C. (1993). The role of deliberate practice in the acquisition of expert performance. *Psychological Review, 100*(3), 363–406. https://doi.org/10.1037/0033-295X.100.3.363

Eubanks, C. F., Muran, J. C., & Safran, J. D. (2018). Alliance rupture repair: A meta-analysis. *Psychotherapy: Theory, Research, & Practice, 55*(4), 508–519. https://doi.org/10.1037/pst0000185

Eubanks-Carter, C., Muran, J. C., & Safran, J. D. (2015). Alliance-focused training. *Psychotherapy: Theory, Research, & Practice, 52*(2), 169–173. https://doi.org/10.1037/a0037596

Fisher, R. P., & Craik, F. I. M. (1977). Interaction between encoding and retrieval operations in cued recall. *Journal of Experimental Psychology: Human Learning and Memory, 3*(6), 701–711. https://doi.org/10.1037/0278-7393.3.6.701

Fonagy, P., & Allison, E. (2014). The role of mentalizing and epistemic trust in the therapeutic relationship. *Psychotherapy: Theory, Research, & Practice, 51*(3), 372–380. https://doi.org/10.1037/a0036505

Gitlin-Weiner, K., Sandgrund, A., & Schaefer, C. (Eds.). (2000). *Play diagnosis and assessment* (2nd ed.). John Wiley & Sons.

Gladwell, M. (2008). *Outliers: The story of success.* Little, Brown & Co.

Goldberg, S. B., Rousmaniere, T., Miller, S. D., Whipple, J., Nielsen, S. L., Hoyt, W. T., & Wampold, B. E. (2016). Do psychotherapists improve with time and experience? A longitudinal analysis of outcomes in a clinical setting. *Journal of Counseling Psychology, 63*(1), 1–11. https://doi.org/10.1037/cou0000131

Goodyear, R. K. (2015). Using accountability mechanisms more intentionally: A framework and its implications for training professional psychologists. *American Psychologist, 70*(8), 736–743. https://doi.org/10.1037/a0039828

Goodyear, R. K., & Nelson, M. L. (1997). The major formats of psychotherapy supervision. In C. E. Watkins, Jr. (Ed.), *Handbook of psychotherapy supervision* (pp. 328–344). John Wiley & Sons, Inc.

Goodyer, I. M., Reynolds, S., Barrett, B., Byford, S., Dubicka, B., Hill, J., Holland, F., Kelvin, R., Midgley, N., Roberts, C., Senior, R., Target, M., Widmer, B., Wilkinson, P., & Fonagy, P. (2017). Cognitive-behavioural therapy and short-term psychoanalytic psychotherapy versus brief psychosocial intervention in adolescents with unipolar major depression (IMPACT): A multicentre, pragmatic, observer-blind, randomised controlled trial. *Health Technology Assessment, 21*(12), 1–94. https://doi.org/10.3310/hta21120

Greenberg, L. S., & Goldman, R. L. (1988). Training in experiential therapy. *Journal of Consulting and Clinical Psychology, 56*(5), 696–702. https://doi.org/10.1037/0022-006X.56.5.696

Greenberg, L. S., Rice, L. N., & Elliott, R. (1996). *Facilitating emotional change: The moment-by-moment process.* Guilford Press.

Haggerty, G., & Hilsenroth, M. J. (2011). The use of video in psychotherapy supervision. *British Journal of Psychotherapy, 27*(2), 193–210. https://doi.org/10.1111/j.1752-0118.2011.01232.x

Halfon, S. (2021). Psychodynamic technique and therapeutic alliance in prediction of outcome in psychodynamic child psychotherapy. *Journal of Consulting and Clinical Psychology, 89*(2), 96–109. https://doi.org/10.1037/ccp0000620

Halfon, S., Bekar, O., & Gürleyen, B. (2017). An empirical analysis of mental state talk and affect regulation in two single-cases of psychodynamic child therapy. *Psychotherapy: Theory, Research, & Practice, 54*(2), 207–219. https://doi.org/10.1037/pst0000113

Harris, J., Jin, J., Hoffman, S., Prout, T. A., Rousmaniere, T., & Vaz, A. (2022). *Deliberate practice in multicultural counseling* [Manuscript in preparation].

Hatcher, R. L. (2015). Interpersonal competencies: Responsiveness, technique, and training in psychotherapy. *American Psychologist, 70*(8), 747–757. https://doi.org/10.1037/a0039803

Hayes, S. C., Follette, V. M., & Linehan, M. M. (Eds.). (2004). *Mindfulness and acceptance: Expanding the cognitive-behavioral tradition.* Guilford Press.

Hill, C. E. (2020). *Helping skills: Facilitating exploration, insight, and action* (5th ed.). American Psychological Association. https://doi.org/10.1037/0000147-000

Hill, C. E., Kivlighan, D. M., III, Rousmaniere, T., Kivlighan, D. M., Jr., Gerstenblith, J. A., & Hillman, J. W. (2020). Deliberate practice for the skill of immediacy: A multiple case study of doctoral student therapists and clients. *Psychotherapy, 57*(4), 587–597. https://doi.org/10.1037/pst0000247

Hill, C. E., & Knox, S. (2013). Training and supervision in psychotherapy: Evidence for effective practice. In M. J. Lambert (Ed.), *Handbook of psychotherapy and behavior change* (6th ed., pp. 775–811). John Wiley & Sons, Inc.

Hoffman, L., Rice, T., & Prout, T. (2016). *Manual of regulation-focused psychotherapy for children (RFP-C) with externalizing behaviors: A psychodynamic approach.* Routledge/Taylor & Francis Group.

Hudson, J. L., Kendall, P. C., Chu, B. C., Gosch, E., Martin, E., Taylor, A., & Knight, A. (2014). Child involvement, alliance, and therapist flexibility: Process variables in cognitive-behavioural therapy for anxiety disorders in childhood. *Behaviour Research and Therapy, 52*, 1–8. https://doi.org/10.1016/j.brat.2013.09.011

Karver, M. S., Handelsman, J. B., Fields, S., & Bickman, L. (2005). A theoretical model of common process factors in youth and family therapy. *Mental Health Services Research, 7*(1), 35–51. https://doi.org/10.1007/s11020-005-1964-4

Karver, M. S., Handelsman, J. B., Fields, S., & Bickman, L. (2006). Meta-analysis of therapeutic relationship variables in youth and family therapy: The evidence for different relationship variables in the child and adolescent treatment outcome literature. *Clinical Psychology Review, 26*(1), 50–65. https://doi.org/10.1016/j.cpr.2005.09.001

Kendall, P. C., & Frank, H. E. (2018). Implementing evidence-based treatment protocols: Flexibility within fidelity. *Clinical Psychology: Science and Practice, 25*(4), e12271. https://doi.org/10.1111/cpsp.12271

Koziol, L. F., & Budding, D. (2012). Requiem for a diagnosis: Attention-deficit hyperactivity disorder. *Applied Neuropsychology: Child, 1*(1), 2–5. https://doi.org/10.1080/21622965.2012.665774

Kramer, A. D. I., Guillory, J. E., & Hancock, J. T. (2014). Experimental evidence of massive-scale emotional contagion through social networks. *Proceedings of the National Academy of Sciences of the United States of America, 111*(24), 8788–8790. https://doi.org/10.1073/pnas.1320040111

Lambert, M. J. (2010). *Prevention of treatment failure: The use of measuring, monitoring, and feedback in clinical practice.* American Psychological Association. https://doi.org/10.1037/12141-000

Lieberman, A. F., & Van Horn, P. (2011). *Psychotherapy with infants and young children: Repairing the effects of stress and trauma on early attachment.* Guilford Press.

Malberg, N. (2018). *Mentalization-based treatment and play therapy with a young female client* [Video]. American Psychological Association. https://doi.org/10.1037/v00606-001

Markman, K. D., & Tetlock, P. E. (2000). Accountability and close-call counterfactuals: The loser who nearly won and the winner who nearly lost. *Personality and Social Psychology Bulletin, 26*(10), 1213–1224. https://doi.org/10.1177/0146167200262004

McGaghie, W. C., Issenberg, S. B., Barsuk, J. H., & Wayne, D. B. (2014). A critical review of simulation-based mastery learning with translational outcomes. *Medical Education, 48*(4), 375–385. https://doi.org/10.1111/medu.12391

McLeod, J. (2017). Qualitative methods for routine outcome measurement. In T. Rousmaniere, R. K. Goodyear, S. D. Miller, & B. E. Wampold (Eds.), *The cycle of excellence: Using deliberate practice to improve supervision and training* (pp. 97–122). Wiley-Blackwell. https://doi.org/10.1002/9781119165590.ch5

Midgley, N., Ensink, K., Lindqvist, K., Muller, N., & Malberg, N. T. (2017). *Mentalization-based treatment for children: A time-limited approach.* American Psychological Association. https://doi.org/10.1037/0000028-000

Midgley, N., Mortimer, R., Cirasola, A., Batra, P., & Kennedy, E. (2021). The evidence-base for psychodynamic psychotherapy with children and adolescents: A narrative synthesis. *Frontiers in Psychology, 12*, 662671. https://doi.org/10.3389/fpsyg.2021.662671

Midgley, N., O'Keeffe, S., French, L., & Kennedy, E. (2017). Psychodynamic psychotherapy for children and adolescents: An updated narrative review of the evidence base. *Journal of Child Psychotherapy, 43*(3), 307–329. https://doi.org/10.1080/0075417X.2017.1323945

Mullen, J. A., Luke, M., & Drewes, A. A. (2007). Supervision can be playful, too: Play therapy techniques that enhance supervision. *International Journal of Play Therapy, 16*(1), 69–85. https://doi.org/10.1037/1555-6824.16.1.69

Muran, J. C., Eubanks, C. F., & Samstag, L. W. (2021). One more time with less jargon: An introduction to "Rupture Repair in Practice." *Journal of Clinical Psychology, 77*(2), 361–368. https://doi.org/10.1002/jclp.23105

Nof, A., Dolev, T., Leibovich, L., Harel, J., & Zilcha-Mano, S. (2019). If you believe that breaking is possible, believe also that fixing is possible: A framework for ruptures and repairs in child psychotherapy. *Research in Psychotherapy, 22*(1), 45–57. https://doi.org/10.4081/ripppo.2019.364

Norcross, J. C., & Guy, J. D. (2005). The prevalence and parameters of personal therapy in the United States. In J. D. Geller, J. C. Norcross, & D. E. Orlinsky (Eds.), *The psychotherapist's own psychotherapy: Patient and clinician perspectives* (pp. 165–176). Oxford University Press.

Norcross, J. C., Lambert, M. J., & Wampold, B. E. (2019). *Psychotherapy relationships that work* (3rd ed.). Oxford University Press.

Normandin, L., Bate, J., Begin, M., Fonagy, P., & Ensink, K. (2021). *Fact or fiction 2: Play completion predicts internalizing and externalizing difficulties in children—A longitudinal study of mentalizing processes* [Unpublished manuscript].

Orlinsky, D. E., Rønnestad, M. H., & Collaborative Research Network of the Society for Psychotherapy Research. (2005). *How psychotherapists develop: A study of therapeutic work and professional growth.* American Psychological Association. https://doi.org/10.1037/11157-000

Owen, J., & Hilsenroth, M. J. (2014). Treatment adherence: The importance of therapist flexibility in relation to therapy outcomes. *Journal of Counseling Psychology, 61*(2), 280–288. https://doi.org/10.1037/a0035753

Park-Taylor, J., Ventura, A. B., & Ng, V. (2010). Multicultural counseling and assessment with children. In J. G. Ponterotto, J. M. Casas, L. A. Suzuki, & C. M. Alexander (Eds.), *Handbook of multicultural counseling* (pp. 621–631). Sage Publications.

Prescott, D. S., Maeschalck, C. L., & Miller, S. D. (2018). *Feedback-informed treatment in clinical practice.* American Psychological Association.

Preter, S. E., Shapiro, T., & Milrod, B. (2018). *Child and adolescent anxiety psychodynamic psychotherapy: A treatment manual.* Oxford University Press. https://doi.org/10.1093/med/9780190877712.001.0001

Ray, D. C. (2011). *Advanced play therapy: Essential conditions, knowledge, and skills for child practice.* Routledge. https://doi.org/10.4324/9780203837269

Rogers, C. R. (1980). *A way of being.* Houghton Mifflin.

Rossouw, T. (2021). *Mentalization-based teletherapy with an adolescent: Relationship anxiety and negative self-talk* [Video]. American Psychological Association. https://doi.org/10.1037/v00714-001

Rousmaniere, T. (2016). *Deliberate practice for psychotherapists: A guide to improving clinical effectiveness.* Routledge/Taylor & Francis Group. https://doi.org/10.4324/9781315472256

Rousmaniere, T. (2019). *Mastering the inner skills of psychotherapy: A deliberate practice manual.* Gold Lantern Books.

Rousmaniere, T., Goodyear, R. K., Miller, S. D., & Wampold, B. E. (Eds.). (2017). *The cycle of excellence: Using deliberate practice to improve supervision and training.* Wiley-Blackwell. https://doi.org/10.1002/9781119165590

Shirk, S. R., Karver, M. S., & Brown, R. (2011). The alliance in child and adolescent psychotherapy. *Psychotherapy, 48*(1), 17–24. https://doi.org/10.1037/a0022181

Smiler, A. (2019). *Reflecting strengths in an adolescent male client* [Video]. American Psychological Association. https://doi.org/10.1037/v00641-001

Smith, S. M. (1979). Remembering in and out of context. *Journal of Experimental Psychology: Human Learning and Memory, 5*(5), 460–471. https://doi.org/10.1037/0278-7393.5.5.460

Squire, L. R. (2004). Memory systems of the brain: A brief history and current perspective. *Neurobiology of Learning and Memory, 82*(3), 171–177. https://doi.org/10.1016/j.nlm.2004.06.005

Steele, W., & Malchiodi, C. A. (2012). *Trauma-informed practices with children and adolescents.* Routledge/Taylor & Francis Group. https://doi.org/10.4324/9780203829493

Stiles, W. B., Honos-Webb, L., & Surko, M. (1998). Responsiveness in psychotherapy. *Clinical Psychology: Science and Practice, 5*(4), 439–458. https://doi.org/10.1111/j.1468-2850.1998.tb00166.x

Stiles, W. B., & Horvath, A. O. (2017). Appropriate responsiveness as a contribution to therapist effects. In L. G. Castonguay & C. E. Hill (Eds.), *How and why are some therapists better than others? Understanding therapist effects* (pp. 71–84). American Psychological Association. https://doi.org/10.1037/0000034-005

Storch, E. (2020). *Cognitive behavioral therapy with a child who has obsessive compulsions* [Video]. American Psychological Association. https://doi.org/10.1037/v00659-001

Taylor, J. M., & Neimeyer, G. J. (2017). The ongoing evolution of continuing education: Past, present, and future. In T. Rousmaniere, R. K. Goodyear, S. D. Miller, & B. E. Wampold (Eds.), *The cycle of excellence: Using deliberate practice to improve supervision and training* (pp. 219–248). Wiley-Blackwell. https://doi.org/10.1002/9781119165590.ch11

Tracey, T. J. G., Wampold, B. E., Goodyear, R. K., & Lichtenberg, J. W. (2015). Improving expertise in psychotherapy. *Psychotherapy Bulletin, 50*(1), 7–13.

van der Pol, J., Vöö, S., Bucerius, J., & Mottaghy, F. M. (2017). Consequences of radiopharmaceutical extravasation and therapeutic interventions: A systematic review. *European Journal of Nuclear Medicine and Molecular Imaging, 44*(7), 1234–1243. https://doi.org/10.1007/s00259-017-3675-7

VanFleet, R., Sywulak, A. E., Sniscak, C. C., Guerney, L. F., & Butler, D. (2011). *Child-centered play therapy.* Guilford Press.

Wass, R., & Golding, C. (2014). Sharpening a tool for teaching: The zone of proximal development. *Teaching in Higher Education, 19*(6), 671–684. https://doi.org/10.1080/13562517.2014.901958

Weisz, J. R., & Kazdin, A. E. (Eds.). (2018). *Evidence-based psychotherapies for children and adolescents* (3rd ed.). Guilford Press.

Weisz, J. R., Kuppens, S., Ng, M. Y., Eckshtain, D., Ugueto, A. M., Vaughn-Coaxum, R., Jensen-Doss, A., Hawley, K. M., Krumholz Marchette, L. S., Chu, B. C., Weersing, V. R., & Fordwood, S. R. (2017). What five decades of research tells us about the effects of youth psychological therapy: A multilevel meta-analysis and implications for science and practice. *American Psychologist, 72*(2), 79–117. https://doi.org/10.1037/a0040360

Yasinski, C., Hayes, A. M., Alpert, E., McCauley, T., Ready, C. B., Webb, C., & Deblinger, E. (2018). Treatment processes and demographic variables as predictors of dropout from trauma-focused cognitive behavioral therapy (TF-CBT) for youth. *Behaviour Research and Therapy, 107*, 10–18. https://doi.org/10.1016/j.brat.2018.05.008

Zaretskii, V. (2009). The zone of proximal development: What Vygotsky did not have time to write. *Journal of Russian & East European Psychology, 47*(6), 70–93. https://doi.org/10.2753/RPO1061-0405470604

Zhou, X., Hetrick, S. E., Cuijpers, P., Qin, B., Barth, J., Whittington, C. J., Cohen, D., Del Giovane, C., Liu, Y., Michael, K. D., Zhang, Y., Weisz, J. R., & Xie, P. (2015). Comparative efficacy and acceptability of psychotherapies for depression in children and adolescents: A systematic review and network meta-analysis. *World Psychiatry, 14*(2), 207–222. https://doi.org/10.1002/wps.20217

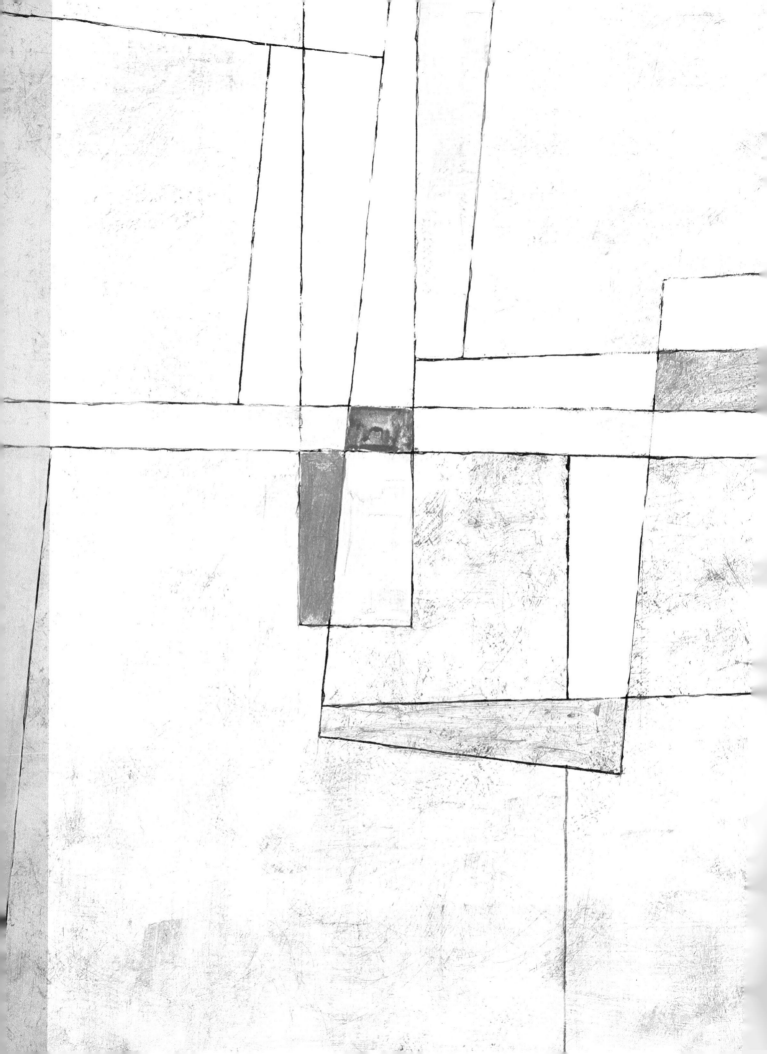

Index

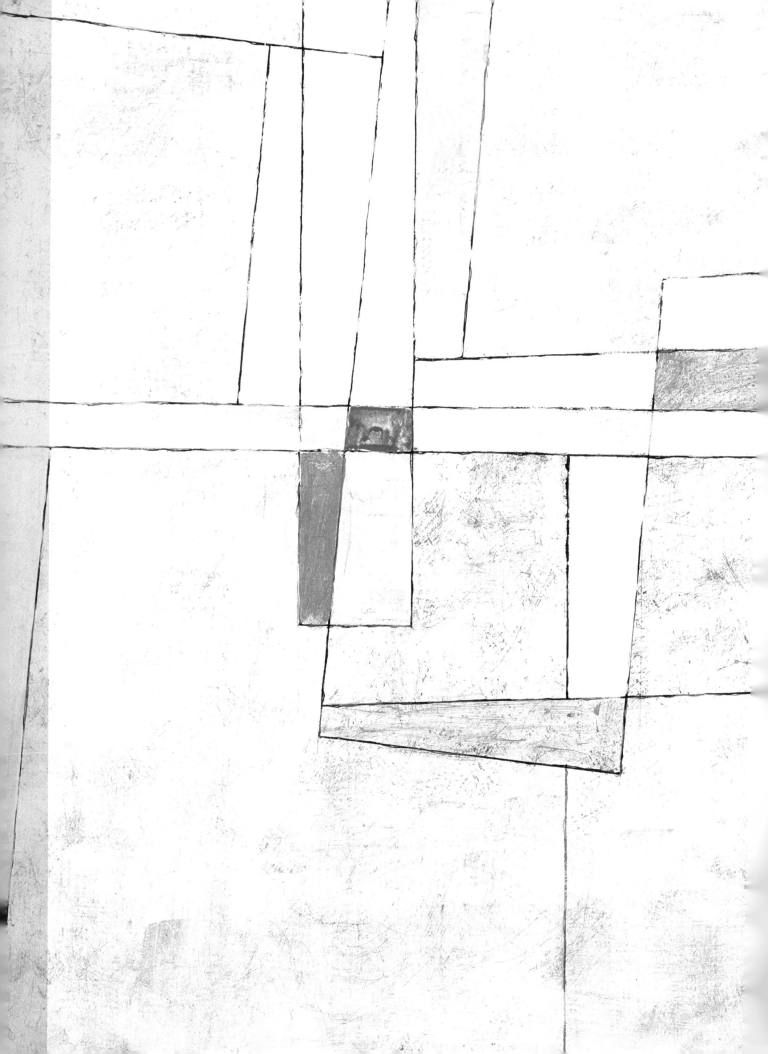

About the Authors

Jordan Bate, PhD, is an assistant professor of psychology at the Ferkauf Graduate School of Psychology at Yeshiva University. She teaches the courses Beginning Work With Children, Parents, and Families and Cognitive Assessment for Children; coleads the psychodynamic psychotherapy practicum; and runs the Attachment & Psychotherapy Process Research Lab. Dr. Bate's research centers on understanding therapeutic processes through the lens of attachment theory, including the effects of therapists' facilitative interpersonal skills and mentalization in child psychotherapy. She also specifically focuses on studying the effectiveness of clinical training for therapists across different orientations, including the utility of deliberate practice. She is a trainer and supervisor in mentalization-based treatment for children and a supervisor at Northwell Health, Lenox Hill Hospital, Department of Psychiatry in the Reproductive Mental Health program (New York, NY). Dr. Bate is also the current president of Section II (Childhood and Adolescence), Society for Psychoanalysis and Psychoanalytic Psychology (Division 39), of the American Psychological Association. She maintains a private practice in Manhattan, New York, where she works with patients across the lifespan, including children, adolescents, adults, families, and couples.

Tracy A. Prout, PhD, is an associate professor of psychology at the Ferkauf Graduate School of Psychology at Yeshiva University. She teaches evidence-based psychodynamic psychotherapy in the School-Clinical Child Combined Doctoral Program, supervises advanced graduate students in the psychodynamic psychotherapy practicum, and leads the psychodynamic psychotherapy lab at Ferkauf. Dr. Prout is principal investigator for several studies related to regulation-focused psychotherapy for children and supervises all graduate research assistants who work on these projects. She coleads IMPACT Psychological Services, an integrative, group private practice, with locations in Beacon and Mamaroneck, New York, serving children, teens, families, and adults.

Tony Rousmaniere, PsyD, is cofounder and program director of Sentio University, Los Angeles, California. He provides workshops, webinars, and advanced clinical training and supervision to clinicians around the world. Dr. Rousmaniere is the author and coeditor of six books on deliberate practice and psychotherapy training and two series of clinical training books: The Essentials of Deliberate Practice (American Psychological Association) and Advanced Therapeutics, Clinical and Interpersonal Skills (Elsevier). In 2017, he published the widely cited article in *The Atlantic Monthly*, "What Your Therapist Doesn't Know." Dr. Rousmaniere supports the open-data movement and publishes his aggregated clinical outcome data, in deidentified form, on his website at https://drtonyr.com/. A fellow of the American Psychological Association, Dr. Rousmaniere was awarded the Early Career Award by the Society for the Advancement of Psychotherapy (APA Division 29).

Alexandre Vaz, PhD, is cofounder and chief academic officer of Sentio University, Los Angeles, California. He provides deliberate practice workshops and advanced clinical training and supervision to clinicians around the world. Dr. Vaz is the author and coeditor of four books on deliberate practice and psychotherapy training and two series of clinical training books: The Essentials of Deliberate Practice (American Psychological Association) and Advanced Therapeutics, Clinical and Interpersonal Skills (Elsevier). He has held multiple committee roles for the Society for the Exploration of Psychotherapy Integration and the Society for Psychotherapy Research. Dr. Vaz is founder and host of *Psychotherapy Expert Talks*, an acclaimed interview series with distinguished psychotherapists and therapy researchers.